Queen of Clubs

Beezy Marsh is a top ten *Sunday Times* bestselling author, who has also held the coveted No.1 slot in Canada for three months. She puts family and relationships at the heart of her writing. She is an award-winning journalist who has spent more than 20 years making the headlines in newspapers including the *Daily Mail* and the *Sunday Times*. Beezy is married, with two young sons, and lives in Oxfordshire with a never-ending pile of laundry.

🐦 @beezymarsh
📘 @BeezyMarshAuthor
📷 @Beezy.Marsh

www.beezy-marsh.com

Also by Beezy Marsh

Queen of Thieves
Keeping My Sisters' Secrets
Mad Frank and Sons
Her Father's Daughter
All My Mother's Secrets

Queen of Clubs

Beezy Marsh

ORION

This edition first published in Great Britain in 2022 by Orion Dash,
an imprint of The Orion Publishing Group Ltd.,
Carmelite House, 50 Victoria Embankment
London EC4Y 0DZ

A CIP catalogue record for this book
is available from the British Library.

ISBN (eBook): 978 1 3987 0776 4
ISBN (Mass Market Paperback) 978 1 3987 1153 2

The Orion Publishing Group Ltd
Carmelite House
50 Victoria Embankment
London, EC4Y 0DZ

An Hachette UK company

www.orionbooks.co.uk

Above all, be the heroine of your life, not the victim
- Norah Ephron

PROLOGUE

NELL

Benidorm, Spain, 1960

Let's be frank.

Some people would give anything to escape the grey skies of London town for a carefree life in the sun.

But, looking back, we'd never had it so good.

They say crime doesn't pay; well, they'd certainly never spent time on my manor in the fifties.

I rarely went out without a grand in my handbag, and that was just fun money – the spoils of my days going shopping with my gang, the Forty Thieves.

Business was booming and hoisting, as we professionals like to call shoplifting, was in its heyday. Now, you might look down your nose at us, but we were more than common thieves, and any woman worth their salt in London knew she could earn a pretty penny from it. My girls out-earned most blokes doing mugs' jobs ten to one, but you had to learn the skill, like an apprentice, practising every day. There were risks, and the price you paid for getting caught was harsh, especially if you'd been up before the beak before.

As the leader, let's just say I was pretty choosy about who I let into the gang. I'd learned from the mistakes of the Queen who went before me.

So, I was very careful about who I trusted. If anyone

I

was going to be stabbing someone in the back, let's just say I'd be holding the knife, not getting it between my shoulder blades.

But mostly, we were all too happy in those days to worry about grasses and snitches, or having our collars felt by the long arm of the law, or ending up in Holloway for a stretch. Rationing was over, clothing coupons had been chucked in the dustbin, and there was so much stuff crammed on to the rails that store managers could barely keep tally of their stock. My light-fingered lot had a field day. Factory girls and secretaries, flush with cash on their lunch breaks, loved nothing more than to try on half a dozen outfits, and we joined them, blending in, liberating beautiful dresses to allow them to be bought for a fairer price in the pubs and back alleys of South London.

Some of the bigger stores got wise to us, and so I branched out into disguises to liven things up – prim little hats, horn-rimmed glasses, wigs. I could give the costume department at most theatres in Drury Lane a run for their money with the stuff I had stashed at my place in Queen's Buildings. I liked to keep the cozzers guessing, too. The wanted section of the *Police Gazette* was stuffed with like-nesses of notorious shoplifters: brunettes, blondes, sweet, sassy. Most of them were me.

When petrol rationing finally came to an end after the war, I got a bit more enterprising about our sprees. I learned to drive, and I insisted my girls did the same. Gone were the days when we had to rely on a fella to take us every-where and be our getaway driver, like they used to do. The shops beyond London became our playground. Teams of us took trips to other cities, as far afield as Birmingham or Manchester, or even down to the seaside, where the sleepy shop assistants weren't wise to our ruses.

They weren't expecting bag swaps or clouting, which is how we shoved the goods we wanted to nick down our shoplifter's bloomers. They had elastic at the knee, to stop things falling out on the floor and giving the game away. The world was changing around us, but some tried and tested methods were the very foundation of the gang, and our ridiculous bloomers were part of the uniform. Ditching my drawers would be like a cozzer going out without his hat.

Brighton was a place fit for a queen. I loved the fresh sea breezes and the blustery pier, and it gave me a taste not just for fish and chips but for antique jewellery – the kind you found in those little shops nestling up the Lanes. If it was small and sparkly it was so easy to pop into your pocket, shove up your sleeve, or even tuck under your hat when the assistant's back was turned. That made for a perfect day out.

I liked those trips most of all because it felt as if we were having an old-fashioned beano, like they had before the war. All that was missing was the charabanc and a crate of beer in the back.

At night, there was nowhere better to relax with a drink to toast our success than my Soho club, Rubies, where gangsters rubbed shoulders with would-be film stars, and aristos with fat wallets splurged on champagne with good-time girls. What a rum bunch we were. I should have known then that it was going to lead to trouble.

Back then, I saw running my club as a nice little earner, a bit of security for the future. I loved singing and I'd always dreamed of owning my own place, and everyone agreed I'd made a great job of it.

Maybe I was cocky, but I thought I could have it all.

I was riding high as Queen of the Forty Thieves and my fella, Jimmy the Razor, was King of Soho. We had a little princess safely tucked up at home while we did our villainy, so our family was complete.

It was the perfect life for thieves like us, but happy endings only happen in fairy tales, don't they?

These days, I wonder if things could have worked out differently.

But as the old saying goes: If if and ands were pots and pans, there'd be no work for tinker's hands.

I've had plenty of time to think about it, and I spend almost every afternoon at the seaside now, under the blazing Spanish sun. There are no cooling breezes, no seagulls and no fish and chips served up in old newspapers. The days roll into one another and I find myself gazing at the turquoise waves and dreaming about the life I left behind.

The late afternoon sunlight dapples the water and I watch the blond-haired little boy running along the beach towards me.

'Come on, Mum!' he yells. 'Play with me!'

I smile and walk towards him, catching him and spinning him in the air, as he squints at me. He plants a kiss on my cheek, laughing in a way that reminds me so much of his dad.

Spain is paradise, I suppose.

But I'm a long way from home.

And the way things are, I can never go back.

Chapter One

ZOE

Limehouse, London, January 1957

It's fair to say that I owe my life to a German bomb.

If it hadn't been for the Luftwaffe doing their worst in the East End, smashing all the houses in the next street to smithereens, my mother might not have been terrified enough to send me to the countryside with the other evacuee kids.

And then I might never have known that I wasn't born to be poor.

I was just a tiny scrap of a thing, with a cardboard label tied to my dirty coat and my threadbare teddy tucked under my arm, when my mother took me to Paddington Station after the shock of the first attack in the Blitz. My whole world had been shoved into a battered little case, which I clasped in my hand as I struggled to keep up with her. My few belongings – a hairbrush, a set of holey socks, a worn pinafore and an old toothbrush – rattled around inside it as she dragged me along beside her.

There were tearful hugs on the platform all around us, but Mum just shoved me up the steps into the waiting carriage. As the train drew away in a cloud of steam, there were howls of anguish from the other parents, but I only just caught sight of her departing back. She was off, sharpish, because the pub was opening soon and she didn't want to miss her slot at the bar, where a fella might buy her a drink.

My dad was away at sea and because of me, Mum didn't have to volunteer for war work, and so her days were spent gossiping on the front step rather than cleaning it – or scolding me for getting under her feet. My ears rang from being clobbered so often. Now, at last, she was free from the trouble of pretending to care for me, and I had half a chance of making it to adulthood without being deafened by her beatings.

Two little girls next to me in the carriage clung to each other and sobbed their hearts out. I sat and stared out of the window in wonder at the green fields filled with cows and sheep. Until then, the only greenery I'd seen was the cabbages stacked in boxes outside the corner shop. This beautiful countryside whizzing by me was a world away from the cobbled streets of Limehouse, and our basement rooms in a Victorian tenement, where the walls were paper-thin, and the damp seeped into every pore, coating everything in cold and misery.

The train journey went on for hours, but I was happy as a lark, with a jam sarnie handed out by a kindly woman in the smartest suit I had ever laid eyes on. Mum's clothes were all second-hand from the market, faded, or torn where she'd had a barney with Dad. They had that funny smell about them, too. Other people's clothes were musty and the disappointment of their lives hung around Mum's shoulders, making her even more miserable and difficult.

My mother was nothing like this woman before me on the train. I found myself staring at her polished shoes, wondering how she got them so shiny. I was sad when she marched us out of the carriage at a little station in deepest

Devon, but I needn't have worried, because I went straight into the arms of a kindly farmer's wife who treated me as if I were her most precious dolly.

I was used to being put to bed in my knickers at our house, in a freezing back room with a pillow like a rock and bedbugs for company, but suddenly I found myself dressed in a beautifully embroidered nightgown, tucked up like a little princess under the softest quilt in a bedroom overlooking a walled garden. Mum always moaned that my long ginger hair was a bleeding nightmare because it was so thick and unruly and hung like rats' tails. I screamed every time she tried to get at it with the brush.

Now it was washed by caring hands, gently combed and plaited; my old clothes were thrown away without comment and replaced with cosy knitted jumpers, flannelette liberty bodices and smart pinafores. I'd never seen clothes like them, not to mention my own pair of brand-new shiny shoes for the village school and stout walking boots for playtime. It didn't matter to me that some of them had come second-hand from the posh kids up at the manor house. Winter brought mittens and woollen stockings rather than freezing fingers, chilblains and blotchy legs like corned beef. The farm was full of excitement, with animals to play with and the smell of pies cooking on the range. I was in heaven.

My schoolteacher, Mrs Mills, took quite a shine to me and I was invited to tea at her neat cottage most evenings after school. There, by the warmth of the fireside, she taught me to read. On Saturdays, she ran dance classes at the village hall and I took my first, tentative steps into a world which made me feel alive. It was as if I was born to dance. My limbs felt light, and I practically radiated happiness, like a little sunbeam, as I threw myself into those lessons with gusto.

Mrs Mills could be terrifying to the other girls from the village, peering over her half-moon glasses at them or rapping them on the backs of their legs with her ruler when they got their steps wrong. But with me, she was kind and gentle, as if she knew that I was a little flower trying to grow up between the paving cracks in London. All I needed was care and attention, and she lavished that on me. We learned country dancing, the waltz, the foxtrot and how to curtsey like young ladies.

'Oh, I ain't got it right, miss!' I'd cry when I faltered.

'Oh no, not *ain't*, Zoe,' she'd say, softly. 'It's *isn't*. There's a good girl.'

Those four years were the happiest of my life, and when the war ended, I must have been the only person who went round looking as if someone had died.

The village tea party for VE Day was a huge affair, with a table stuffed full of buns, cakes and treats for all the children, but I could barely eat a bite. I knew what was coming, with a sense of doom that took away my appetite for life: the East End of London and Mum.

Victory had made it inevitable. Nothing could save me. Not even Mrs Mills and her promises to write to me often.

I was going home.

Mum was there to greet me as I stepped off the train at Paddington. I had grown into a strapping, healthy, country girl, fed on the cream of Devon cows and nurtured with kindness. She was raddled with drink, smaller and bonier than I had remembered, with two high-coloured patches of rouge on her cheeks.

'Hello, Mother,' I said, reaching out to her, with a brown paper parcel containing gifts of home-made cakes and jam from the farm. 'How do you do?'

She snatched the parcel with one hand and pulled the ribbon from my hair with the other, bringing tears to my eyes.

'Oh, Miss Hoity-toity! Don't worry, I'll soon knock that out of you.'

I caught my breath as we made our way to the tram, looking at bombed-out buildings, filthy pavements and miserable hordes, walking with their gas masks slung in cartons over their shoulders, as if they weighed a ton.

Limehouse welcomed me with spit in the eye from the grubby rascals who careered around on planks of wood with stolen pram wheels attached and shouts of 'Wotcha, ginger nut!' It was a far cry from ring-a-roses on the village green.

They started calling me 'Posh Zoe' to mock me and so I lived up to it, walking to and from school with my nose in the air. Throughout the rest of my school years, my beautiful cardigans from Devon grew smaller and smaller but I refused to give them up, even though they sat inches above my midriff. My woollen stockings were threadbare and my skirt barely covered my backside. But my clothes were a reminder of the life I'd lived before – the life I was meant to have, surrounded by beauty and kindness and nice things, rather than fly-blown ceilings, dog shit and bus tickets.

My pink satin ribbons were my most prized possession. I insisted on wearing them in my hair even though, as the years passed, they blackened with the filth of the East End. I couldn't let them out of my sight to wash them and hang them on the line, or Mum, the spiteful cow, would have thrown them on the fire. She delighted in telling me so, taunting me in one of her toothless rants. She was dropping her knickers as often as her aitches with anything that had a pulse, in order to buy the booze she needed to numb the pain of her pathetic life, because Dad had never come home from the navy. He was too busy getting his leg over with a woman he'd met in Southampton. Mum's health had suffered and every blow she struck me – and there were quite a few – only made my accent grow even more plummy, just to wind her up.

By the time I was fifteen, they were calling me Mad Zoe in our street, because although I spoke like the queen, I had developed a mean right hook for anyone foolish enough to cross my path. The other children whispered about me and called me names, but I cared not a jot. I didn't have any friends because I didn't want any. What did I have in common with these cockney ruffians?

One day, not long after my sixteenth birthday, just after New Year's Eve, Mum announced she was going into hospital to be treated for 'women's troubles', which I knew full well was a bad bout of VD she'd caught off a travelling salesman. The time had come for me to escape, to a better life, away from the poverty of the East End.

'You think you're too good for the likes of us,' she spat, anger blazing in her eyes, which were like two fiery little coals. 'Well, you'll learn, my girl.'

I sullenly spread some margarine on a stale slice of bread for my breakfast.

'Don't you dare burn the house down with your nose in a book while I'm away or you'll be for it.' She glared at me.

'I won't. I can take care of myself,' I muttered. 'Not that you give a damn.'

The minute I heard the front door slam, I leaped to my feet.

I felt hot with excitement as my fingers crept over the rusty old lid of the tea caddy, where I knew she kept her takings for the week. I had to rootle around a bit in the tea leaves before I pulled out a crisp pound note, neatly folded. How many men had she slept with to earn that?

And how much had I put up with while she plied her filthy trade? That was more to the point. My childhood was punctuated by the grunts of strange men in her bed at night, their heavy footfall on the stairs waking me from a half-sleep; the lifting of the latch at dawn as they crept away, back to their homes and their wives and their unsuspecting girlfriends. What's more, the contempt she bore for me, her only daughter, was written all over her face every morning and delivered in slaps and punches every night.

She owed me for everything she'd put me through since the end of the war, and as I clasped that money in my hand, I felt I was only taking back what was mine.

I glanced at my reflection in the hallway mirror. My face still had a smattering of the freckles I'd had since childhood, but the girl staring back at me was on the brink of becoming a woman.

'Zoe, you are going to make a better life for yourself,' I said, firmly.

God knows, I'd tried to swallow the reality of living in our grim house with its horrid scullery, but I couldn't help dreaming. No matter how hard Mum hit me, she couldn't beat hope out of me – and that only made her rage more intense. It was simply *because* I wanted more than she could ever give me that she hated me with such a passion.

The war had smashed houses to heaps of rubble and wooden splinters, but it had given me a glimpse of another world.

It was a world I didn't belong to – yet – but I was determined that once I got my foot in the door, there would be no turfing me out this time.

Chapter Two

ZOE
Soho, 1957

I wanted to be where the posh folk were, so I hopped on a bus up to Piccadilly, and strolled through the Burlington Arcade, pressing my nose against the shop windows, gawping at jewels and furs and so much finery. They still had the Christmas decorations up and everything looked so warm and inviting inside. The stuff in those stores was beyond my wildest dreams and though my fingers were turning blue with cold, I lost myself in a daydream, thinking about how people would swan about their gorgeous houses, dripping with gold and fancy clothing; what nice conversations they'd have about all the books they'd read by the blazing hearth. All I got for my trouble was a clip around the ear from a few shopkeepers for leaving smears on their pristine glass and dirty looks from snooty women who clearly thought I was a guttersnipe.

I followed a girl my age, who was wearing a woollen coat with a smart velvet collar. She was chatting to her mother about the beautiful things they'd been buying. They carried an armful of neatly wrapped parcels each.

'How do you do?' I ventured, just as she was hailing a cab.

I thought if I could just strike up a conversation with her, she'd see that we spoke the same way and I knew how to behave in decent company, and then perhaps we could be friends.

'Stay away from us, you dirty little beast!' she shot back. 'Mother! I think this horrid girl is trying to rob us!'

And she slammed the cab door in my face.

That was like a punch in the stomach. I reeled down Piccadilly, lured by the lights and the rush of people, all with somewhere to go and money to spend. The evening was drawing in, the temperature had dropped, and the quid in my pocket suddenly felt like very small beer indeed. People stared at me and my threadbare, too tiny clothes and filthy ribbons. I shivered a little.

They didn't care that beneath the surface I could be like them, if only someone would give me half a chance. I was just another scumbag from the slums looking to steal, as far as they were concerned. A little knot of anger began to form in the pit of my stomach at the unfairness of it all.

Theatreland was ablaze with a thousand neon lights winking in the darkness, and I craned my neck to take it all in. There were endless streams of traffic; buses nudging their way past huge, glossy black cars which pulled up outside the foyers of gilded theatres. Women and men dolled up to the nines stepped out into the crush of people queuing to get in.

Street entertainers were working the crowd for pennies, and as a woman with an accordion squeezed it for everything she was worth, a cheer went up near the front of the queue, where a magician was pulling coloured handkerchiefs from the sleeve of another man's jacket.

As I inched closer, I caught sight of that girl I'd seen before down Piccadilly – the one who was getting into the cab with her mum. It was a split-second decision to speak to her, just to explain that I hadn't meant to scare her, but that she had no right to treat me like I was dirt. So, I took a deep breath and tapped her on the shoulder. Just as I did, she slipped her hand into the pocket of an old gent who was transfixed by the magician taking a budgie from a top hat. Quick as a flash, she pulled her hand out, as if she'd been scalded.

'What's your game, then?' she hissed, spinning around to face me.

I found myself staring into a pair of blue eyes, frosty like icicles, which belonged to a girl who was probably only a few years older than me. They bored into me, and I realised then that I'd made a terrible mistake.

'Do excuse me,' I said. 'I didn't mean to frighten you, only I thought you were someone else.'

She burst out laughing, shaking her head full of dirty blonde curls.

'Blimey, don't you talk proper?'

She spoke like she came from round my way, in Limehouse, but she was dressed like the posh folk, with money to burn at the theatre.

She looked me up and down, taking in my threadbare clothes, the great expanse of leg protruding from my too-short skirt and the grimy ribbons in my hair. A few women in the queue sniggered at the sight of me. I knew then, I looked ridiculous, and that only made that little knot of anger in my stomach tighten more.

A broad grin spread across the girl's face.

'Hopping the wag, are you?'

I didn't want to confess to being a runaway, down on my luck with nowhere to go, but my appearance told its own story.

14

'No, I'm just visiting the theatre, like everyone else,' I murmured, shuffling my feet on the pavement.

''Course you are!' she laughed. 'Got money for a ticket?'

I shrugged my shoulders and pulled out my pound note.

'Yes, I have.'

She smiled at the sight of my money.

We were nearing the front of the queue now, and the snooty doorman in his peaked cap and gold epaulettes was looking right down his nose in my direction.

She linked arms with me.

'I'm Rose.'

'Zoe,' I said. 'Pleased to meet you.'

'Save your money, the show's like watching paint dry,' she giggled, as the doorman shot her a filthy look. 'Come on.'

She pulled me from the queue and steered me up a dark side street, where raucous laughter rang out from grimy doorways and the most delicious smells of cooking wafted from exotic-looking restaurants, which were a world away from the pie and mash shop or the local chippy round my way. My head was spinning as I tried to take it all in and I couldn't stop my stomach from rumbling.

'You're a right card, Zoe, but I like you,' Rose chirruped as we wandered through a warren of backstreets. 'Do you need somewhere to stay?'

I hesitated for a split second. The pavement looked cold and hard, and it was covered in pigeon shit.

I nodded.

'Well, Zoe,' she said. 'I reckon you've landed on your feet. Welcome to Soho.'

We turned into a garden square illuminated by hissing gas lamps and Rose pulled me down some concrete steps and past an old metal sign saying 'Air Raid Shelter'.

She pushed open the door, and through the gloom I could just about see a group of people sitting around a large wooden table, chatting as trinkets were held up to the light of a candle. An old woman sat at the head of the table, in a rocking chair.

The whole place fell silent. I could almost hear my heart pounding.

'What've you got there, Rose?' said the woman, her mouth pressing itself into a thin, hard line. The temperature dropped several degrees.

Someone flicked a switch and a single electric bulb hanging from a dusty cord in the ceiling spluttered to life, revealing walls of cracked plaster and peeling paint. The woman looked like a granny from the olden days, with her steel-grey hair parted down the middle and worn in a neat bun. She peered at me over a pair of round spectacles, her eyes flashing with indignation.

'This is Zoe,' said Rose proudly, puffing her chest out like a strutting pigeon. 'She's a new friend I've just picked up around Theatreland. I reckon she could come in handy.'

You could've heard a pin drop.

'Well, you reckoned wrong,' said the woman, swiping a pile of gold chains from the table and shoving them into a beautiful wooden sewing box before I could get a closer look at them. She slammed the lid firmly shut.

'She looks like Raggedy Ann's younger sister. This is the Underworld, Rose. It ain't a charity, you know that much,' she said, coldly.

I felt tears prick my eyes. It was true – I looked like I belonged in the workhouse. I didn't want to sleep on the streets, and I had nowhere else to go, but my voice had deserted me.

'Sorry, love,' said the woman, with a shrug of her broad shoulders. 'We're stuffed to the gunnels already. I've enough trouble as it is, trying to stop the drunks from Piccadilly coming down here to use our place as a public convenience. You'll have to sling your hook. Now, hoppit.'

She picked up a silver-topped cane which was resting against her chair and tapped it, as if she meant business.

'Please, Maud,' said Rose, a crestfallen look sweeping across her features, 'give her a chance, you'll see . . .' Her voice trailed off.

I glanced around me.

You couldn't call it a palace – in fact, far from it – but there were oil lamps glowing beside jam jars filled with fresh flowers on the table, and candles flickering on tea chests in the darkest corners, where rows of iron bunk beds left over from the blackout still stood. But, oh, those beds looked so nice and comfy, with soft quilts, blankets and plump pillows. There were other homely touches – antique clocks, some fine china, a rail full of dresses and furs, and a few rugs scattered about the concrete floor. Maud had truly made it feel like home. I really did want to stay, even if the whole place did smell of damp.

Rose nudged me so hard in the ribs, it almost winded me.

'Speak up, or you'll be out on your ear.'

Maud was getting up now, and walking towards me, to send me back up the staircase and into the cold night. She was tall, and the way she moved reminded me of a train intent on reaching its destination.

'Good evening,' I said, lowering myself into my best curtsey and extending my hand, as if I were being presented at Buckingham Palace. 'How do you do? I'm Zoe, and it is a pleasure to meet you. I am only looking for some work and a place to stay for a while. I promise I will pay my way.'

I produced my pound note with a flourish, and offered it to her.

Her mouth fell open in astonishment.

'Very posh indeed, ain't we?' she laughed. 'Such lovely manners! Where on earth d'you learn to speak like that?'

She snatched the pound note away in a trice and stuffed it down her blouse before I'd even had time to explain myself.

'I had elocution lessons during the war when I was an evacuee,' I said, quietly, feeling the faintest hint of a blush creeping up under my collar as she had a proper look at me, peering closely at my hair in its filthy ribbons. She hadn't said I could stay and now she had taken all my money. 'But I really grew up in the East End.'

She broke into a grin.

'Oh, you sound just like one of those Mayfair ladies with hot and cold running servants, you do! I bet the East End never heard anything quite so fancy. Never mind a plummy accent, you sound like you've scoffed the whole fruit bowl, dear.'

The whole room erupted at her joke. A couple of girls who'd been snoozing in the bunks sat up and rubbed sleep out of their eyes.

'Wakey wakey!' Maud boomed in their direction. 'Come and meet Zoe, she'll be staying with us for a while.'

They clambered out of bed, pulling on their clothes with a yawn, and shuffled over to greet me. Just then, the door to the air raid shelter was pushed open and the magician I'd seen earlier doing tricks at the theatre strolled in, with a white cat at his heels.

'Evening, David,' said Maud. 'You're just in time to meet our newest recruit, Zoe, who speaks beautifully, la-di-dah.'

David reached up his sleeve and pulled out a bunch of paper flowers, which he presented to me before sauntering off towards a battered leather armchair in a dark corner of the shelter. I clasped them tightly. It was such a kind gesture.

'David's one of the finest magicians in the business,' said Maud. 'At least, he was until someone pinched most of his act and started poncing off his skills. So, he works with us now, because we appreciate his special talents.'

David smiled to himself, took off his top hat and settled himself in the chair. He reached inside his jacket pocket and fished out a bottle of gin, which he put to his lips. Maud glared at him for a split second and that was enough to make him change his mind.

'He was drunk in a Soho doorway, down on his luck when I found him,' she whispered to me. 'I like to think I help keep him on the straight and narrow.'

I was so happy in the Underworld that I gave Maud a little hug. She recoiled a bit.

'No offence, love, but when was the last time you had a bath?'

I stared at the floor. It was true, my face only had a passing acquaintance with a dishcloth.

'Our old tin bath had more leaks than the *Titanic*, so I never really bothered with it,' I replied, shuffling my feet in shame. 'And my mum refused to give me money for the local baths, so I just managed as best as I could with the sink in the scullery.'

A couple of the other girls chortled with laughter, and Maud reached over and clipped them round the ear.

'Shut up, you lot!' she barked. 'It ain't Zoe's fault she's poor. We've all come from somewhere and don't you forget it. We don't ever poke fun at girls from slums, do we?'

They shook their heads.

Her face softened, and I found myself gazing into her eyes, which were green, like emeralds.

'Now, don't you worry, I will get Rose to take you up to Marshall Street tomorrow morning and I'll give you a sixpence for a nice hot bath,' she said. 'All my girls get a good wash once a week at least. Just because we live down here, don't mean we lack certain standards.'

Her black blouse was starched and buttoned up over her ample bosom and her skirt was old-fashioned, reaching to just above her ankles, showing off an inch or two of thick woollen stockings above her sturdy lace-up shoes. It was hard to guess her age because she was almost fizzing with energy as she spoke to me, but I thought she must be old enough to remember the Great War, and maybe even earlier than that.

She gestured to the row of expectant faces gazing at me.

'These are the Piccadilly Commandos, a fine bunch of young ladies, and we all work together to put food on the table and share what we've got, because London can be a very tough place when you're on your own, can't it?'

There were murmurs of approval.

'What kind of work do you do?' I asked.

A few of the girls exchanged glances.

'Second-hand sales, mostly,' Maud cut in. 'There's always demands for trinkets and china, watches or small leather goods up in the markets. Ain't that right, Rose? And there's always plenty to be had, if you know where to pick them up.'

'Oh, yes,' said Rose, smiling sweetly. 'People love a bargain.'

'And by working as a team, we find it easier to get by. It's just like one big happy family,' said Maud, beaming at me.

She leaned over and whispered in my ear, 'I'll tell you what, Zoe. If you like, you can call me Ma.'

Chapter Three

NELL

Soho, January 1957

Why is it that whenever a woman gets herself nicely set up and is running her life exactly as she pleases, a fella always thinks he can go one better and starts interfering?

Did Cleopatra need help when she was ruling Egypt and telling blokes how to build the pyramids? You can bet your last farthing she did not. Did brave Queen Boadicea ask a man to help her drive her chariot into battle against the Romans? No, of course she bleeding well didn't.

So, why the hell does my Jimmy keep sticking his oar in? He is becoming a right royal pain in the backside lately. I thought he was keeping busy with his mob, the Friday Gang, relieving unsuspecting factory owners of their weekly pay, but apparently it ain't enough to keep his mind focused. Instead, he's getting very fixated on trying to cut back the amount of time I spend out shopping with the Forty Thieves and running my club, Rubies.

These days, he's always giving me that slow smile of his and his boy-next-door look: 'You look tired, Nell. Why don't you knock off early tonight, love?'

And then Lou the barman starts polishing the glasses frenetically, because he's all excited at the prospect of running the show without me.

I must admit, my Jimmy's still a real bobby-dazzler of

a bloke. His blue eyes crinkle at the corners when he laughs and he wears his sandy blond hair slicked back, so it shows off his handsome features. He's always loved new threads, but he's grown into his role as a gang boss and his handmade suits and silk ties from Bond Street give him the edge. Sometimes when he walks into the club and puts his arms around me, it takes my breath away.

But I know the real reason Jimmy wants me home early. It's to have more time with me indoors, so he can get me in the family way. He seems to think that if we have another child, it will make it more likely that he can make an honest woman of me.

We had our tenth anniversary last summer. When I say 'anniversary', I mean I have refused his offer of marriage ten times. It's quite romantic, in its own way. Every year, on VE Day, he gets down on one knee and makes a big show of presenting me with an engagement ring, just as he did when we were first courting. And every year I turn him down flat. We live together, love each other and drive each other up the wall, so why change a good thing?

It don't matter to me what the neighbours think – I do not want to be Mrs Jimmy Feeney for all the tea in China. I am quite happy being Nell Kane, Queen of the Forty Thieves and boss of Rubies. God knows, it was quite a struggle to get here, and I am not giving that up for anyone.

My name is on the licence for this club, and I don't see why I should change a thing. A wedding ring is a band of gold, but to me it feels like a shackle. Don't get me wrong; I love a bit of tomfoolery as much as the next hoister, but I can pinch my own, thanks.

Jimmy dotes on our little girl, Ruby, and she is the apple of his eye and she's our world. But I worry I just ain't got the time at the moment for the patter of tiny feet again. I mean, I have my club to run, and I have to keep an eye on my gang, the Forty Thieves. I'm not saying I never want another one – of course I do. It's just that the time ain't right for me just now. But you try explaining that to my Jim!

The problem is people have got short memories where women are concerned. They have forgotten all the work that we were expected to do in the war, and how we proved ourselves while men were away fighting. Women stepped up and were driving buses, digging fields and mending engines as well as any fella. Next thing, it's all done and dusted, peace is declared and it's back to the kitchen sink, ladies, with barely a thank you. Well, I, for one, am having none of it.

What's more, the minute you walk down the aisle people start getting properly nosy about when you're going to be expecting, how many little darlings you are planning to have and what you are making for your husband's tea. Do I look like I give a fiddler's damn about what Jimmy has for dinner? No, I do not. You can tell by the look of him that he ain't exactly half-starved.

During the day, I'm out hoisting with my girls in the poshest stores in the West End – Selfridges, Marshall and Snelgrove, Gamages and maybe a quick ride over to Bayswater to check out the stock in Whiteleys. From there it's only a stone's throw down to Kensington, and Derry and Toms. Sometimes we go further afield, to Birmingham or down to Brighton, but that takes a bit of planning, being off my manor.

Most days, I make sure I'm home to see Ruby after school, and once she's tucked up in bed, I've got my mate Iris back at Queen's Buildings to babysit while I go out to the club.

There's one rule about money that Soho has taught me: if folks have got it, they want to spend it. They don't want to think about their grotty, rented homes, the rising damp or the nagging wife. They want a slick place with chrome and glass, crisp white tablecloths, a slap-up dinner, and drinks with girls who are fun and easy on the eye. And that is where both my businesses collide, quite happily.

Some of the Forty Thieves' best customers are household names – the women you see in the films, who have desires for beautiful dresses which outstrip their pay packet from the studio. People think starlets are made of money, and they certainly dress like they are a worth a million, but let me tell you, I know exactly where they get their clothes from. And that is because I am nicking them to order.

Take Diana Durbidge, the blonde bombshell from Dagenham, who is England's answer to Marilyn Monroe. She's a regular at Rubies and men love her, for two obvious reasons, but she leaves it to me to find her nice things to wear. I almost feel as if I've got shares in her next film, because she owes me half her wages. She's a sweet girl and being seen in Rubies helps make my gaff popular with the in-crowd, so I am prepared to overlook the fact that most of her wardrobe is on tick and she's behind with a few payments. Well, that and the fact that she always invites me and Jimmy along to the premières in Leicester Square. I do enjoy getting my glad rags on – and mine, by the way, are bought and paid for. No hoister with any self-respect wears the clothes she steals. Besides, I make it a rule of the gang that everything that is pinched gets fenced on and the girls are then free to spend their earnings on whatever they please.

Part of running a club is about being seen, making sure everyone's enjoying themselves, and you'd be surprised at the people I rub shoulders with. Lawyers, actors, politicians, cozzers – they are all out for a good time after dark. I'm the soul of discretion and what goes on within these four walls stays right here. Although, you can't stop the gossip mongers, and there's one reporter in particular who's always on the hunt for a bit of tittle-tattle to make a headline. My Jimmy thinks he's decent enough, because he likes to prop up the card tables at one of our spielers over in Ham Yard, but there's something about him that don't quite fit as far as I'm concerned.

Maybe it's the way he's always licking his stubby little pencil and making notes in that dog-eared notebook of his, or the fact that his eyes are small and beady, like a shark's.

Make an innocent comment about the weather, and those cold eyes will look deep into yours as he takes out his pencil and notebook and says: 'Tell me more . . .'

My girls in the club complain that he stinks of booze and fags and he never wants to take his grimy mackintosh off, even in the height of summer. I'd hate to be Duncan Swift's landlady, having to wash his greying string vests and God knows what else.

So, I thought Duncan Swift was just a fly in the ointment as far as my life in Soho was concerned but then Lou came running in with a copy of the *London Evening News*. There was a massive picture of me and Jimmy plastered all over the front page. It had been taken at the première of Diana Durbidge's last film. There we were, grinning like a pair of fools under a huge headline.

And that was when the penny dropped.

SECRETS OF THE KING AND
QUEEN OF SOHO!

He's the tough businessman whose empire is rumoured to have been built on violence, and she's the woman whose club Rubies is the top nightspot for London's most glamorous film stars. Today reporter DUNCAN SWIFT goes where few dare to tread, behind the glitz of Soho after dark, to ask the troubling question on everyone's lips.

What is the truth about clubland's most powerful couple, Jimmy Feeney and Nell Kane? Is there more to their success than meets the eye? In this rare interview, the man rumoured to be the "Boss" of gangland offers a tantalising glimpse into their world.

Jimmy Feeney is wearing his trademark Savile Row suit as he leans across the table of a smoke-filled Soho pub to take me into his confidence: "People want to call me the Boss, or the King of Soho, who am I to say otherwise?"

He breaks into a grin. It's a look that many police officers know only too well. Especially those who have searched his premises after a tip-off and traipsed back to the station empty-handed. Soho is in the grip of lawlessness, with wages robberies, smash-and-grabs, illegal gambling dens and prostitution on the increase, and many politicians are saying "enough is enough". So, what does one of the area's most powerful businessmen have to say about the situation unfolding on his doorstep?

"As I was saying to a constable only the other day, you'll find me a very honest man to talk to. Ask me anything you like. My accounts are all up to date. The used car business is very lucrative, and my head office here in Soho means I'm always on the spot if there's a new business opportunity. Can

I help it if I make a lot of money? What's a man to do? Why does anyone have a problem with that?

"These are boom times for us here in London after those gloomy war years, and I have got my eye on some exciting new projects for the future. Bigger and better things. Watch this space."

When I point out that Mr Feeney isn't everyone's cup of tea and there are those who remember his days on the wrong side of the law, there's no sign of his famous temper; the attacks which earned him the nickname "Jimmy the Razor". So, perhaps the rumours of this boss ruling Soho with an iron fist are just that – rumours.

"Oh, I'm not claiming to be a saint," he smiles. "Now and then anyone who runs a company has to bang a few heads together to keep things running smoothly. People do look up to me and they come to me with all sorts of problems. Being called the King of Soho suits me, to be honest.

"And I'm not denying my past, but I have paid my dues to society. Many fellas had a misspent youth and I'm no exception. But these days, I'm a family man, with my daughter Ruby and my lovely lady Nell, who is famous in her own right in London, as the owner of the classiest club in town, Rubies, which attracts the right sort of clientèle and is the place to be seen."

Certainly, I'm intrigued by Nell Kane, the fiercely independent woman who rose from the slums of Waterloo to be the self-styled queen of her manor.

She keeps herself extremely busy. Those in the know say her sense of fashion is legendary, and she loves going shopping but, strangely, not every store manager in Oxford Street is pleased to see her when she does. The housewives of South London have a very good idea why that is, and they are not complaining, but they remain tight-lipped. Ask a question about Nell Kane and you'll get a door slammed in your face, or worse. Some of those women from the Elephant and Castle seem very well dressed considering they are living on their husbands' factory pay. And perhaps they have Nell Kane and her associates to thank for that, or perhaps those are just silly rumours, too?

Mr Feeney also plays his cards close to his chest as far as the lady in his life is concerned. He offers a mere hint of what makes their relationship tick.

"Nell is the light of my life, and she puts up with a lot, but I can't speak for her," he says. "Anyone who knows Nell knows she is her own woman. She's no wallflower, and what of it? She runs her businesses and I run mine, and that works just fine for us. We both work hard and have been very successful."

It certainly is an unusual set-up, but then, not many things about this couple are conventional, as Miss Kane and Mr Feeney have yet to tie the knot!

"People can think what they like, we don't give a damn," he says, a flicker of anger clouding his brow.

So, what about her line of work? Many men and women – might feel it is wrong for a mother to spend all day out at the shops and then all night running a club.

But not Mr Feeney!

"Nell is a wonderful mother, and she is certainly the Queen of Clubs with Rubies, but as for anything else, I really don't have the faintest clue what you are talking about. She's certainly a snappy dresser, but if you're suggesting anything illegal, it must be a case of mistaken identity, and I'm beginning to feel like you are being rude in a way I don't appreciate."

At this point, Mr Feeney glanced at his very expensive watch and seemed to grow tetchy. He put his hand in his jacket pocket. Remembering his reputation, I felt it would be a good time to draw the interview to a close.

So, with that, dear reader, I made my excuses and left. My exclusive story reminds us all that Soho is not for the faint-hearted, but this roving reporter is dedicated to bringing you all the news from the underbelly of London, where other journalists fear to tread . . .

Oh. My. God.

Jimmy. My Jimmy.

Never mind being the King of Soho.

He was the biggest flaming idiot who ever had the misfortune to walk the streets of London town. I'd lost my heart to him long ago, even though he wasn't the brightest button in the box, but with all his experience on the wrong side of the law, I'd have thought he'd know by now to keep his big mouth shut. Instead, he'd trusted that bleeding reporter and fallen right into his trap. That slimy guttersnipe had all but outed in me in print as the Queen of Thieves, and Jimmy had blown the lid on our Soho operation. What's more, that article made it look as if Jimmy was enjoying the limelight in a way that could only lead to trouble. It went against all the villain's codes that we lived by. Even if the reporter had made it all up, people would think Jimmy had said it, and that would go down like a cup of cold sick in gangland. We'd been stitched up by Fleet Street.

My mind was whirring. I needed to act fast, to try to make it right – put the word out that we'd been played for fools. It was still early – barely past five o'clock – and so most of the regular faces wouldn't be in town yet. I knew just where I'd find Jimmy, though – bellied up to one of the gaming tables round the corner in Ham Yard. It was always cards in the spieler for him, but he kept an eye on the gaming tables which we ran with dice for the poorer punters. They liked it – that and betting on the gee-gees, so who were we to deny them a flutter?

I was pulling on my coat to go and tear a strip off him and plan our next move when there was a heavy footfall on the staircase and the sound of shouting.

Lou the barman read the look of horror on my face and charged like a raging bull towards the door to block it. He was a miserable git, Lou, but loyal to a fault.

But he was no match for what was on the other side of it.

Half a dozen of London's burliest cozzers came rampaging through the door, truncheons raised, and set about Lou until he lay in a bloodied heap by the bar.

'Stop it!' I cried, as they put the boot in, but they ignored my pleas.

I picked up a chair and slowly backed myself up against the stage. Now, I wasn't the sort of woman who would shy away from a bit of a punch-up, but I knew against this mob I was completely outnumbered.

Hearing the commotion, some of the dancers appeared, wearing very little, and then, spying Lou covered in blood, shrieked and ran off down the corridor to hide in their dressing room in a tangle of feathers and sequins. They really were about as much use as a chocolate fireguard.

The boys in blue were busy smashing the bottles of spirits above the bar with their truncheons, glass splintering everywhere. There were still a few balloons and bits of tinsel around the place from our New Year's Eve party, and a huge cardboard cut-out of Father Christmas. They even wrenched that down and stamped on it, as if he was a wanted man.

When they'd done their worst to the decorations, they started overturning tables and destroying my beautiful club. The velvet curtains above the stage were torn to shreds

31

and the footlights were smashed. The piano was upended in a clatter of notes. I would have cried, but what was the point? They were unstoppable. I stood there, dumbfounded.

When they started to move towards me, I knew I was as good as done for. They were going to work me over like poor Lou, who was lying on his side, groaning, in a pool of crimson.

'If it's money you want, there's plenty in the safe out the back,' I said, my voice faltering. 'Come on, boys, why don't we all calm down and come to a sensible arrangement?'

I was shaking like a leaf inside, but years of experience had taught me to hide my fear. God knows I was doing my best, but I felt all the blood rushing to my head, and I thought I was going to faint.

Out of nowhere, a reed-thin fella with a face like a rat sauntered in from the stairwell, his mackintosh tightly belted, a smile playing on his lips.

'I'll pretend I didn't hear that, Miss Kane,' he said, surveying the damage and nodding, as if it satisfied him. 'Because that would be bribing a police officer, which is a serious offence. Very serious.'

I racked my brains. He wasn't on my list of straightened cozzers. The bungs we'd been paying the top brass were eye-watering, but Jimmy usually saw to it. Who the hell was this geezer and why wasn't he on our payroll?

I forced a weak smile.

'I'm Nell Kane, owner of this establishment, and it's a pleasure to meet you.'

I reached out to him, offering my hand, as if it were the most mundane thing for my club to be smashed to bits before my very eyes.

'I'm Detective Chief Inspector Walter Munro, head of the Flying Squad,' he said coldly.

'Are you new? It's just, I like to think I know all the most important policemen in Soho . . .'

I lowered my voice as he drew nearer. 'Couldn't we have sorted this in a more reasonable manner, Detective Chief Inspector? Jimmy Feeney can be very accommodating. I can arrange a meeting for you, if you like?'

Before I had time to clock what he was up to, he pulled something out of his pocket and then clapped me in a pair of handcuffs.

At the same time, the other plods were picking up Lou, who was semi-conscious, and dragging him across the club.

'Seems you fell while you were resisting arrest, mate. We'll have to charge you. Come on, there's a good boy.'

Munro put his face next to mine, so I could see right into the depths of his steely grey eyes and smell his bad breath.

'I'm a new broom, someone who has been appointed to clean up the filth of Soho, and after the article in the paper, I'm starting at the very top. You know how it works, Nell. Word will get round and suddenly all of the gangsters will crawl back into their holes in South London or over in the East End, where they belong, and stop polluting the air in the West End.'

He spoke with a reassuring Scottish brogue, as warm as a malt whisky, but the message he was delivering was about as welcome as cancer.

Somehow, I found the courage to laugh.

'This is all a big mix-up. You can't believe all the nonsense you read in the papers, Detective Chief Inspector, surely?'

He didn't find that funny.

He grabbed hold of me around the waist, his bony fingers digging in, and began to frogmarch me across the club.

'You aren't refusing to come quietly, are you?'

I fought the urge to spit in his face.

'This is a proper business,' I gasped. 'I've got my licence and everything . . .'

He squeezed harder, pinching my flesh, making me want to cry out.

'Oh dear, looks like you are trying to get away from me, aren't you?'

'No, Detective Chief Inspector,' I said, fighting back tears as his fingers dug harder into my side, winding me. I nearly tripped over in my high heels. 'You've got me all wrong. I'm delighted to help you in any way I can.'

He smirked at me and relaxed his grip.

'Good.' he said, running his hands down over my hips, smoothing my dress in a way that I didn't appreciate. Jimmy would have chopped him into mincemeat if he'd seen that.

'This is going to be a special year for Soho, I can feel it,' he said, propelling me towards the doorway, with his palms dangerously close to my backside.

He dragged me up the stairs and out into the street, where a crowd had gathered. And at the front of it all was that upstart reporter Duncan Swift, grinning like the Cheshire Cat, with a gang of photographers beside him.

The flashbulbs went off all around me, as I was shoved into the back of Munro's shiny black Daimler.

'Happy New Year, Miss Kane,' he said, climbing into the driver's seat. 'I hope you've made a few nice resolutions, because you are going to spend the night telling me all about them.'

Oh, Jesus wept.

Chapter Four

ZOE

Soho, January 1957

I awoke to the sound of raucous laughter and poked my nose out from the eiderdown, where I was snuggled up against the cold.

Maud was clapping her hands with glee, and her girls, the Piccadilly Commandos, were screeching like hyenas, as Rose stood on the table in the middle of the air raid shelter recounting her story.

'And then the cozzers beat the hell out of that fat lump Lou the barman while Nell cowered in the corner. They done her club over good and proper, that's what I heard. There weren't one piece of glass left in the place after they'd finished, and Nell just about pissed herself with fear when they took her off down the station. Queen of Thieves, my arse. Queen of Cowards, more like!'

That brought more hoots of mirth.

'Tell it to me again!' said Maud. 'Start at the bit when that stupid idiot Jimmy shot his mouth off in the papers about being King of Soho and the top brass decided they'd do a raid.'

I sat up in my bunk, rubbing sleep out of my eyes.

'What's happened?'

Maud stood up and waved at Rose to get down.

'On second thoughts, let's save it for later. It'll make a nice bedtime story.'

She came over to my side.

'It's just gangland gossip, love. Nothing for you to worry about, but we do like to have a little joke about it. Sleep alright, did you?'

'Like a log,' I said, scratching my head as I searched in vain for my clothes, which I'd tucked down the bed beside me when I nodded off. 'Where are my things?'

'Oh, we sent them off to the launderette, love, just to get them a bit of a wash, but don't worry, I've got plenty of nice stuff you can wear.'

'But I want my clothes,' I said. 'They're—'

'Full of holes?' Rose cut in, winking at me from across the room. 'Ten sizes too small?'

Tears started to well up. 'That's not funny! You don't understand, they are my things. I want them back.'

Maud's face softened. 'There, there, don't cry. It's alright, love. You'll get them back soon enough, and we ain't going to let you go about starkers in the meantime, are we?'

She gestured to the rail in the corner, stuffed with dresses and coats. There were some really beautiful things hanging up there. Posh clothes, properly expensive stuff which looked warm, and stylish, too. But when I thought of my old Devon cardigan, my little skirt and knitted socks, I couldn't quite get rid of the lump in my throat or the desire to cry.

Maud grabbed a particularly lovely silk kimono from the stool by one of the other bunks and handed it to me.

'You can put that on for now,' she said.

I shrugged it on and wiped away a tear.

'It's all very emotional, leaving home and finding yourself in a new place, ain't it?' she soothed.

36

'Oi!' cried a voice. 'That's mine, that is!'

'Share and share alike,' said Maud firmly, slapping away the scrawny hands which had popped up on the other side of my bunk and were making a grab for the kimono.

Maud turned to me, her green eyes sparkling. She almost crackled with energy.

'Now, we'll get you togged up and you can go up to Marshall Street with Rose for a nice bath after breakfast, and then I'll show you around Soho. I'll meet you at Bianchi's at noon. How does that sound?'

Bath and breakfast. Those two words had not featured much in my Limehouse life, it had to be said. And Maud had already shown more motherly care than the woman who'd raised me on sufferance, so I had to count my blessings.

'Thanks, Ma,' I murmured.

I pulled myself together and clambered down, wincing as my toes touched the freezing floor.

'And we'll find you something nice and warm to keep your toes all toasty,' she clucked.

Shoes and boots were hurriedly pulled on to the feet of half a dozen Piccadilly Commandos, in case they were left barefoot by another fit of their leader's generosity.

'It all sounds like a dream come true,' I replied.

I clambered down from the top bunk and Maud took me over to an alcove, where I stood in front of an old mirror.

Maud had put one of those modesty screens beside it, like they do in shops, and I went behind there with some underwear which she'd pulled from a basket. It was a silk brassière, the finest thing I had ever felt, and I put it on, although I didn't have much to fill it. Next, she gave me a pair of knickers and a suspender belt and some stockings. I fiddled with those because I wasn't used to doing

37

up fancy underwear, although I'd seen my mum wearing stockings which were full of ladders.

After that came a checked wool dress which I pulled on. It clung to my slender waist and the way the full skirt swished around my legs made me look different – more grown-up. She even gave me a pair of leather gloves and a beautiful swing coat to wrap myself up against the cold.

When I stepped out and turned to face my reflection, I couldn't quite believe it was me. I flinched when she produced a big brush and started to pull the dirty ribbons from my hair.

'Can't we do this later?' I said, biting my lip.

'I just want to take them out and wash them with the rest of your stuff, love,' she said reassuringly.

I nodded.

'Might as well give your mop a bit of a brush through as well, while we are about it?'

Maud was so persuasive, I was like putty in her hands. She started to work through the tangles in my hair and after ten minutes, it was smooth, and I barely recognised myself.

She produced a velvet bow which I tied around my thick red locks, making a ponytail.

'Putting on the posh does suit you!' she smiled, as I admired my reflection in the mirror. 'Now, I've got to get myself dolled up, too.'

She opened a trunk and started to rifle through it, pulling out a jacket, with braiding and epaulettes. It looked like a uniform. She put it on over her blouse, buttoning it up to the neck. Next came a massive blue bonnet, which was tied with a ribbon under her chin. Then, she rummaged again and pulled out a hymn book, which she tucked under her arm.

Rose started to hum 'Onward Christian Soldiers', giggling as she did so.

'You may well laugh, my girl,' said Maud. 'But when I found myself on the streets, with nowhere to go a few years back, it was the Salvation Army that gave me a cup of tea and a sandwich and helped me get back on my feet. And I've never forgotten it.'

'Or given the uniform back,' tittered one of the Piccadilly Commandos.

'I still like to keep up the good fight, when I feel moved to do so,' she said curtly. 'The Lord moves in mysterious ways. Now, you can't be hanging around here all morning. Off you go!'

And with that, she shoved me and Rose towards the staircase out of the Underworld.

'Wait for me!' I gasped, as Rose marched off towards Marshall Street baths.

Maud had insisted on me wearing high heels which I could barely walk in.

'They're all the rage, love,' she'd told me. 'Every young woman should know how to walk elegantly in heels, so it's about time you started. Besides, they finish off the whole outfit.'

As I took my first faltering steps, I overheard Rose giggling that I had the gait of a navvy, but by the time we'd reached Carnaby Street, I was getting the hang of it, and I felt a bit more ladylike. What's more, I was now standing a head taller than most women in the street, giving me a bird's-eye view. Soho was jam-packed with shops, delivery vans, people cleaning windows and chatting to one another. A couple of workmen stopped digging up the road and gave me a wolf whistle. I wasn't used to that kind of attention, and I blushed beetroot.

Rose appeared by my side again.

'Come on, slowcoach.'

She pulled me towards a doorway and a sign saying 'Sunset Club'.

'I thought we were supposed to be going to the baths,' I said.

'There's plenty of time for that later,' she laughed, pushing open the door. 'And I won't tell if you don't.'

We descended into the dank basement, and I was hit by the overpowering fug of cigarette smoke and the insistent beat of a drum.

Rose pushed the door open, and I stumbled in the half-dark into a room full of young people dancing in a way I'd never seen, while a brass band blared out from a tiny stage in the corner. Sweat poured from the musicians as they played, and anyone who wasn't dancing was swigging Coca-Cola and lemonade from bottles. Stronger stuff was poured in from hip flasks. In gloomy recesses, couples were caught up in clinches, away from the prying eyes of the rest of the room.

The girls wore long, swishy skirts or cropped trousers and tight-fitting blouses, and they were being swung and twirled around by the best-looking blokes I had ever seen. They were dressed in the sharpest suits and the way they moved was captivating.

The whole place was glowing with energy, and nobody seemed to notice or care if their hair was escaping from their ponytails, or their blouses got untucked while they danced. I had visions of Mrs Mills from my lessons in the village hall tutting loudly and giving everyone what for with her ruler for forgetting their manners. I wasn't sure what she'd make of the condensation, which was dripping from the ceiling.

'It's jazz!' yelled Rose, over the din. 'An all-nighter. I was worried they'd have finished by the time we got here. Come on, we're jiving!'

She handed me her coat.

In an instant, she was swept into the arms of a tall, handsome man, who seemed to know her, because a smile of recognition had spread across his face when we came in.

They set off, pushing their way into the middle of the dance floor, and I watched as he picked her up and twirled her around. My feet started tapping in time to the beat; I couldn't help it, it was so catchy, and I hadn't danced in years.

Rose spun back around towards me, her face flushed, and her fella held out his hand to me.

'Errol,' he said. 'What's your name, sweetie?'

He reminded me of the GIs who had visited our school in Devon once, with presents of chewing gum and chocolate for the class. But his accent was so different because he was from the Caribbean. It was warm and mesmerising all at the same time.

'Zoe,' I said, batting my eyelashes at him. 'Pleased to meet you.'

He leaned over to me, and I caught a whiff of his aftershave, which was delicious, like lemons.

'Rose here likes to dance with me, but you gotta keep it secret from her Auntie Maud, OK? Rose comes here sometimes to relax when she is supposed to be working. I thought she wasn't going make it and that would have broken my heart.' He clasped his chest.

Rose grinned up at him, as if he was her world, and all the frostiness in her blue eyes melted away. I didn't blame her – he was gorgeous.

'I won't tell a soul,' I said. 'Promise.'

'We won't stay long,' said Rose. 'I knew I could trust you, Zoe. Why don't you come and join in?'

'No,' I said. I didn't think my foxtrot and waltz would cut it down here. 'I'd prefer to watch. I'm fine, really.'

So, I stood there, watching the entire room having the time of their lives, feeling like a bit of a gooseberry, until someone whispered in my ear: 'Want to dance?'

And that is how I met him.

I turned around and found myself gazing into the eyes of a bloke who was a dead ringer for Elvis. Now, I'll let you into a little secret. I'd been harbouring a secret crush on Elvis for a few months, after I heard some of his tunes on my mum's radiogram before she hid it from me out of spite. I'd also seen some posters of him plastered all over the local cinema. I'd spent hours in the rain, gazing up at him because I couldn't afford a ticket.

Now I was standing in a club, dressed up to the nines, with my very own Elvis asking me to dance. It was a dream come true. His hair was a shade lighter than the real thing, but he'd greased it back and he was wearing a jacket that was different from everyone else's, which made him stand out in a way I think Elvis would have approved of. It was longer, drapey, a bit old-fashioned-looking, and he had narrow trousers which showed off his legs. His tie was tightly knotted at his throat, even in the heat, and he exuded confidence as he held out his hand to me.

I quickly shrugged off my coat and put it on a chair together with Rose's. Then I let him lead me to the dance floor, with several girls looking daggers at me. He was probably the best-looking bloke down there, it had to be said, but I knew from the way they were staring, he was something special.

I faltered a bit in my high heels, so I kicked them off, enjoying the freedom to move. He reeled me out and back into him, and even though I hadn't a clue what I was doing, I was a fast learner for dance steps, so I kept smiling and he didn't seem to mind. I copied some of the other girls and moved my body the way I wanted to, changing things, throwing in a little twist or a shimmy. Before I knew what was happening, people were whistling their approval and clapping our moves. And do you know what? I loved it. All the applause and the attention spurred me on. It was as if I was born to dance, and we just clicked together.

When the song came to an end, he kept tight hold of me and whispered in my ear.

'I'm Vinnie. Give me three guesses to get your name right, and if I win, I get a kiss, OK?'

That made me giggle as I caught my breath.

'Gorgeous,' he said.

I shook my head and the band struck up again. We set off around the dance floor. I was more confident now; I was beginning to understand what jiving was all about and I loved it.

He moved in close.

'Diana, like Diana Durbidge, that actress, 'cause I reckon you'd be a dead ringer for her if you dyed your hair.'

'No,' I laughed as he swung me from side to side and our feet tapped in time. 'It's your last guess now.'

'Angel,' he said. 'Because you look like an angel.'

It was the nicest thing anyone had ever said to me. I

43

was dumbstruck by it. We paused there, standing still in the middle of the dance floor.

And when he bent his head towards me, I didn't try to stop him.

Our lips met.

He pressed me tightly against him and I knew in that moment I wanted him as much as he wanted me.

'It's Zoe,' I murmured.

'I'll call you Angel,' he said, his eyes twinkling. 'Because that way I win, and I get to kiss you again.'

I ain't ashamed to say I forgot all about Elvis after that. Vinnie was steering me towards a dimly lit alcove, when a shout went up at the other side of the club.

'He's got a knife!'

The crowd parted, girls running pell-mell and screaming, and Errol stood there, his face twisting in anger, with a crowd of his mates lining up behind him. A bloke who was dressed identically to Vinnie was squaring up to him. From the back, I could have sworn it *was* Vinnie, but when he turned his head, his build was heavier, and his face was rounder.

'You don't talk to me like that!' spat Errol, brandishing a flick-knife. 'I get enough of that shit up there.' He jabbed his finger upwards to make his point. 'We don't put up with it down in our club.'

Rose shrieked and threw herself between the pair of them.

'Stop it! Stop it! It ain't worth it! Someone'll get killed!'

But this other guy just laughed and shrugged her off, pulling his fists in front of his face, like a boxer, with a look in his eyes that spelled trouble. Errol's mates jeered at him.

'Teach him some respect, Errol! Come on!'

In a split second, Vinnie had left my side and was in the thick of it. I followed close behind, running to Rose to comfort her. She was sobbing in disbelief at what was happening.

'Victor, leave it out, mate,' said Vinnie, grabbing him by the shoulders and shaking him.

'I'll take both of you, don't matter to me,' scowled Errol. 'Do you think I should go home back to my own country, too, like this jerk-off?'

Vinnie put his hands up. 'Look, mate, I want to apologise on behalf of my brother Victor, who can be a proper prick. Whatever he's said, he regrets it, don't you, Vic? I know he didn't mean it, honest. It was his mouth running away with him. He gets like that sometimes. Maybe you trod on his toes when you were dancing?'

Victor glared at Vinnie for a split second, but his jaw was set firm, as if the only thing he was focusing on was the fight ahead of him.

'Victor, listen to me,' said Vinnie. 'We don't want this. It ain't right. Now is not the time.'

He put his hands on his brother's shoulders.

That made Victor back down and he lowered his fists. He stared at the floor for a moment and when he glanced up, he looked different – calmer.

'Yeah, I'm sorry,' he said to Errol, who still had tight hold of his flick-knife. 'I lost my temper. I didn't mean any of it. The words came out wrong. I think it's the drink.' He didn't sound in the least bit sorry, and Errol didn't look convinced either.

The blokes behind Errol started laughing in Victor's face, jeering at him, but he took it, smiling at them.

'Yeah, I know, I was a bit of a prick. Big deal. Get over it. It was a misunderstanding, that's all.'

45

Errol lowered his voice and put his face next to Victor's.

'It's all the same with you boys. We have every right to be here, and we aren't leaving. This is *our* country, too, so you'd better get used to it. See? Our dads and uncles came over from Jamaica in the war when you needed us to fight. Without us, you'd all be talking German, you prick.'

Then Errol said to Vinnie, pointedly, 'This club is ours, and don't you forget it.'

He flicked his knife closed and put it back in his jacket pocket.

Victor turned on his heel, scowling, and stalked out of the club. Vinnie stayed put. People started milling about; musicians picked up their instruments again, but the atmosphere had changed. Nobody seemed to be in the mood for dancing any more. Vinnie gave me a quick peck on the cheek as he walked past.

'See you around, Angel.'

And with that he headed back over to the other side of the room, where Errol was standing with his mates.

'No hard feelings?' he said, stretching out his hand.

Errol shook it – reluctantly, as if he wasn't quite sure he trusted him.

'Nice club you got here' said Vinnie. 'I like what you've done with the place. I'm often in the area. Let me buy you a drink next time and we can have a proper chat.'

He sounded so warm and charming, just as he had been with me.

But as he left, I couldn't help noticing that his eyes weren't smiling.

Chapter Five

NELL

Soho, January 1957

'Just answer the question!'

Munro slammed his hand down on the table in front of me, almost making me jump out of my skin. I must have nodded off for a moment, my eyelids half closing, and the bastard did it to shake me up and bring me back to reality.

'I've got nothing to say,' I croaked. 'There's nothing to tell you. My business is all above board.'

I'd lost track of time and my mouth was parched, like the desert, because I'd barely had a cup of water to drink all night.

He'd forced me to answer hour upon hour of his pointless questions about my club, Rubies, and Jimmy, and how we earned our money. I gave nothing away, nothing that could drop us in it, no matter how hard he pushed me. The comforts of Paddington Green cop shop were few and far between and I knew Munro was trying to put the frighteners on, but God, I could feel myself wilting.

'Oh dear, I think I need to make sure you aren't concealing a weapon,' he said, putting his face so close to mine that I got a whiff of his rancid breath.

He pulled me to my feet, with my hands cuffed in front of me, and started running his hands all over my body.

'It's razors you girls like to carry, isn't it?' he whispered

47

in my ear. 'I know your type. You could be hiding it anywhere.'

His hands wandered places that they should never have been. I was all woman; I had a good figure and I dressed to show it, but that didn't give him the right to mess with the goods, did it? Inside I was dying of shame, as he stood right next to me, putting his hands up my skirt, fingers creeping over the tops of my stockings, brushing between my thighs.

'Are you sure there's nothing you want to tell me about?' he said, raising an eyebrow.

'Nothing.'

I held his gaze through it all, vowing that one day I'd get even.

All I could think about was my little girl, Ruby, and how she'd be worried sick about why I hadn't come home to tuck her up in bed and read her a story, like I usually did. I could see her now, her beautiful dark hair pulled into plaits and her little round face all serious, asking me, 'Why are you late, Mummy?'

And Jimmy . . . Christ – he'd be beside himself.

When he'd finished, he shoved me back down into the chair and handcuffed me to the edge of the table, just to make things more uncomfortable. He loomed over me, peering down the top of my dress. It was my newest outfit, which I'd bought from Gamages for Christmas. Don't get me wrong, I'd gone hoisting in Selfridges first to nick the stuff to pay for it, but this dress was my most prized outfit for the club's festive party season and it didn't disappoint.

It was satin, midnight blue, with a sweeping neckline that showed off my collarbones and framed my bust beautifully. It had three-quarter-length sleeves and a pencil skirt which clung to every curve. Jimmy said I looked like a film star in it. Now, after Munro had put his greasy paws all over it, I wanted to tear it off and burn it. At least he'd stopped short of a full strip search, which I had to be thankful for, I suppose.

Word got round Soho fast, so I half-expected my Jimmy to blast his way into the police station brandishing a sawn-off shotgun to rescue me. It had been pitch dark outside when Munro brought me in for questioning on some trumped-up allegations: receiving stolen goods, resisting arrest and operating a nightclub without a proper licence. That was a load of old cobblers and he knew it, but it was done to make a point. He could make my life very difficult. I got the message, loud and clear.

Now, I watched the sky turning red, as the thin winter sun rose through the bars on the window high above the desk. The dawn chorus started up and I knew Covent Garden would be springing to life, with all the barrows piled high with flowers and delivery boys wobbling about on bicycles, as another day began in the heart of London.

All I wanted to do was sleep, but Munro was perky as a spring lamb, fuelled not only by the thrill of intimidating me, but by endless of cups of tea brought to him by a smirking bobby who behaved as if they'd collared Dick Turpin red-handed for highway robbery. What a pair of tossers!

In the end, it was a whey-faced lawyer in a cheap suit who came to save me. He tapped politely on the inter-view room door, walked in and whispered a few words in Munro's ear. The detective chief inspector shrugged his shoulders and said, 'It seems your partner in crime Jimmy Feeney has got you off the hook with the help of a friendly judge, who is threatening to kick up a stink if I keep you here any longer without charging you.' Munro eyed me laconically. 'Which is a shame, isn't it, because we were so enjoying the pleasure of each other's company, weren't we?'

'If you say so, Detective Chief Inspector,' I said.

I gave him a weak smile. I wasn't going to shout or make a fuss; that would only give him more of a thrill. At least Jimmy still had enough clout to pull a few strings in high places.

Munro undid the handcuffs, and I rubbed my wrists, which hurt like hell.

Then I got up, without saying another word, and walked out of that room, with what was left of my dignity.

'See you around, Nell,' he said to my departing back.

Jimmy was waiting for me outside the police station, standing beside the Bentley, smoking furiously. He threw away the half-finished ciggie when he saw me and bounded up the steps, enveloping me in a hug.

That's when I crumpled, sobbing into his arms.

He cupped my face in his hands, covering me in kisses.

'Oh, Nell, did they hurt you? My duchess, I swear to God, I will make them pay for this.'

We both knew we had enough put by to repair the damage to the club, but the pounding our gangland reputation had taken was another matter. The article was a disaster, but having a police raid was enough to scare away the punters and put the kibosh on our reputation as Soho bosses. Rubies acted as an unofficial labour exchange for anyone looking to do a bit of villainy. No face worth their salt would want to be seen dead in it for a while, in case the likes of Munro came calling.

'It's alright, Jimmy,' I sobbed. 'It was just a bunch of idiots smashing up the place and trying to put the frighteners on. I didn't tell them anything.' I kept quiet about the humiliation of Munro feeling me up, or we'd be looking at a murder charge. 'All I could think of was Ruby and you and how much I missed you. Is she alright?'

'She's fine. Iris put her to bed and promised you'd be back by later today because you had some work to do at the club, that's all,' he said. 'She sends you her best love.'

I fought back tears. I was such a fool for spending time away from my daughter, but it had always been that way, ever since she was born. I'd known poverty when I was younger and there was something in me that would never let me stop working. I needed to earn my own money, to have something put by, because no matter how much I loved Jimmy, I was scared to rely on any man. It was like a dark pit of fear inside me. No matter how much I stole, how much cash I rang through the tills at Rubies, it was never enough to fill that hole. And now I'd been banged up in the nick for the night and forced to be apart from my flesh and blood because of it.

'I'll get even, Nell, don't you worry about that,' Jimmy said, holding me close, stroking my hair. I could feel the strength of him pressed against me like that, so warm and reassuring.

'It was all my fault, this whole stupid cock-up. I thought I was just having a friendly chat with that bloody hack, and the next thing I know it's front page news.' He laughed nervously, in the way that he always did when he'd put his foot in it. 'But I've got my fellas on it, and they'll make him pay. There's no stone in Soho left unturned as far as Swift is concerned.'

'What about Lou?' I snivelled. 'He tried to defend me, but they kicked the shit out of him. He looked in a bad way when I saw him, the poor sod.'

'They let him off with a caution and three broken ribs,

so he'll live,' said Jimmy. 'It ain't the first time he's taken a beating, it won't be the last. He'll be dining out on it with the punters for weeks, you'll see. In the meantime, me and the boys'll move our spieler from Ham Yard to be around in Rubies a bit more, just in case. Come on, let's get you home.'

We glided through the backstreets of Soho in the Bentley, with him whistling slightly off-key, like he always did. Shopkeepers were busy sweeping up rubbish from the clubs which sat cheek by jowl with their stores; barrow boys were wheeling out their fruit and veg stalls, carefully arranging the freshest apples and oranges at the front to lure the punters, while cafés were already doing brisk business. The dark alleys where the brasses plied their trade were quiet for now; the neon signs were dimmed, and tramps were snoozing in doorways under heaps of rags. I spotted a fella in a crumpled suit, still pie-eyed from the night before, staggering along the pavement. Going one over the eight was just part of life in Soho – no one gave him a second glance. It all looked the same as it had yesterday and the day before that, but in my heart, I knew that something had changed.

'Munro means business,' I said flatly. 'We ain't seen the last of him.'

'Don't worry your head about that, sweet,' said Jimmy. 'I've got a plan.'

'What plan?'

'It's going to go off soon,' he said. 'It's the big one – the job that's going to give us enough to retire, to get out of all this. I want us to be able to live life the way it should be lived, away from all this hassle and the Munros of this world.'

I bit my lip.

'You alright, princess?'

'Fine,' I lied.

I wasn't being disloyal to him – not my Jimmy.

But those words only made my heart sink even further.

Chapter Six

ZOE

Soho, January 1957

'And what time do you call this?'

Maud was sitting at a table in the gloomiest corner of the Italian café, her lips pursed and her face darker than the storm clouds hanging over Covent Garden. She was still wearing her Salvation Army uniform, but had taken the bonnet off, and was glaring at us in a way which would have made the Devil himself feel uncomfortable.

'Sorry we're a bit late,' said Rose, going red as the tablecloth. 'The attendant at the baths got narky about the hot water being all used up, so we had to wait ages.' She pulled off her coat.

Maud's eyes glinted.

'And you,' she said, tapping her cane on the floorboards, eyeing me. 'What've you got to say for yourself? I've been here for over an hour waiting for you both.'

'I'm sorry,' I said.

I didn't want to lie, but I didn't want to drop Rose in it either. We'd spent ages dawdling through Soho after we left the club. Rose was pretty shaken up, so we stopped off at a café for a reviving cuppa. There had been a bit of a queue at the baths and before we knew it, the morning had whizzed by.

Maud's face softened, and she looked more like that

homely granny who'd been so kind to me earlier this morning.

'Come and sit down.'

She patted the chair beside her and beckoned Rose to sit. I was taking my chair opposite when Rose squealed. Maud had hold of Rose's arm and was twisting the flesh, hard.

'Don't lie to me, my girl,' she said, in a whisper. 'I know you've been spending time with the fellas again instead of working for me, haven't you? I have got spies everywhere in Soho, you silly little cow.'

Rose nodded, tears rolling silently down her face. Maud still had a tight grip on her.

'I thought as much!'

'It was me,' I blurted. 'I wanted to go dancing. I told you I love dancing and I wanted to show Rose what I can do. I got carried away on the dance floor and we lost track of the time. It was all my idea. I'm sorry.'

'It's true! She's an amazing dancer,' Rose gasped. 'She had the whole place watching her. I've never seen anything like it.'

Maud relaxed her grip.

'I admire your loyalty, Zoe,' she said. 'The thing is, you'll learn pretty quickly that it pays to be loyal to one person in this gang of ours. And that is me.' She gave me a look that could curdle milk.

A waiter brought us three plates of the strangest-looking food I have ever seen and plonked them down in front of us. Maud took Rose's plate and tipped the contents onto her own.

'Get your coat on and get out to work,' she said, icily 'And don't come back without something special for me, or there'll be hell to pay.'

With that, she pushed Rose out of her chair.

Rose stumbled to her feet, clutching her arm, which had a deep red welt on it. Without a word, she quickly pulled her coat on and left.

'Well, don't just sit there catching flies,' Maud said, leaning across the table, as I looked on open-mouthed. 'I expect you've worked up quite an appetite jigging about or jiving, or whatever it is you youngsters do these days. Tuck in. It's good stuff – spaghetti. We're quite continental around these parts, don't you know? Bet you don't get that in the East End.'

I tried to copy her, winding the spaghetti around my fork, but I ended up spilling most of it on the table. Once I got the hang of it, I managed to shovel some into my mouth. She was right. It was good, and I was starving hungry.

'So, Zoe,' Maud said, licking her lips, 'we've got to work out how best you can earn your keep, haven't we? All my girls have their own special talents. Take Rose – she's very light-fingered.'

She paused for a moment, watching me closely.

So, I hadn't imagined it. Rose *had* put her hand in that gentleman's coat pocket to steal something the other night in Piccadilly. All those necklaces I'd seen Maud and the gang admiring had been pinched.

'But I'm not a thief!'

'You're telling me that quid you gave me just fell into your hands, did it?' said Maud, with a laugh. 'I don't think you're in any position to judge the likes of us, are you? Just because you talk all hoity-toity. You weren't living in a castle the last time I checked!'

'No,' I murmured, stung by her words. 'I just meant I wouldn't be any good at it. I took that quid from my mum's tea caddy, that's true. But she owed me it, just the same.'

Maud rolled her eyes, as if she wasn't in the least bit convinced by my story.

'Oh, pull the other one, love, it's got bells on. I don't carry passengers in this gang, in any case.'

She made to get up and leave.

It was pointless arguing with her. I was going to have to do something to earn my keep if I was going to stay in the Underworld, even if it meant breaking the law. Right now, I didn't have anywhere else to go.

'Just give me a chance, I will do something – anything,' I said. 'I didn't mean to cause trouble with Rose. I just wanted to have some fun, and I didn't think going for a bit of a dance would hurt anyone.'

'I know it was her idea to go dancing, not yours – she's got previous where that is concerned,' she said softly, sitting back down. 'And I'm not asking you to pick pockets. That's a skill that takes time to learn. But you can at least help by distracting the punters while we go dipping. I'll show you how. It'll be fun.'

I nodded. It sounded more fun than sleeping rough, but that was about the sum of it.

Maud gazed into the distance for a moment, an idea forming.

'But there is something else you might be able to help me with, using those dance skills of yours.'

'Anything,' I said. 'Whatever it takes, I'll do it.'

'There's a club which is in a bit of trouble lately, from what I hear. And that might present a bit of an opportunity for me and my gang.'

There was a fire behind her eyes when she spoke, as if anger was slowly burning away inside her.

'It's run by a woman called Nell, who let me down badly a few years back. And the thing is, when people are on the ropes, that is the best time to hit them, hard.'

'What did she do?'

'You don't need to worry yourself about what she did or didn't do,' said Maud coldly. 'I just want you to do what you are told. Nothing more, nothing less.'

'Of course,' I said, getting a bit hot under the collar.

Just sitting near Maud when she was talking about this other woman was enough to make me uncomfortable. I could almost feel her hatred.

'I want you to get a job as a dancer and then flirt with her fella, Jimmy – make her jealous, drive a wedge between them. That shouldn't be too difficult for a pretty girl like you, should it?'

'But I've never—'

'I ain't asking you to take your knickers off, love. Just lead him up the garden path. He likes the ladies, if memory serves. I'm pretty sure their relationship is like a house of cards. It just needs a little push to make it collapse.'

'It ain't right to break up a man and wife,' I said, feeling flustered.

'They ain't married,' said Maud, drily. 'So your conscience is clear on that.'

'What if he doesn't fancy me?'

She threw back her head and laughed. 'Take a look in the mirror, Zoe. You must have seen how men look at you, especially now we've smartened you up a bit. And once you open your gob and you start talking proper, you'll have all the fellas in Soho eating out of your hand.'

I gazed at my reflection in the mirrored tiles on the wall behind her. It was true. The young redhead sitting there was striking. I could hardly believe it was me.

'But don't go getting ideas above your station,' said Maud. 'You come home to the Underworld every night and report everything back to me. It won't be forever. Just a few weeks.'

It was pointless trying to persuade her otherwise. I was going to be a dancer in a nightclub and flirt with the boss to upset his wife, and that was that.

'You'll need a cover story, of course. You can be running away from your auntie down in Surbiton, searching for fame and fortune in the West End. How does that sound?'

'What about my parents?'

Maud gave me a wicked grin.

'They were killed in the war, of course. German bombing raid. Tragic.' She pretended to dab a tear from the corner of her eye with her lace handkerchief. 'It was only out of the goodness of her heart that your dear old aunt took you in, but you are one of these wild youngsters, with your mind set on dancing to that dreadful new American rock and roll music, aren't you? You couldn't keep away from the West End dives and she threw you out on your ear.'

'Yes, Maud,' I said, limply.

I didn't want to call her 'Ma' any more. She wasn't my mother, and she wasn't my friend either.

She pointed to the rest of the pasta, which was congealing in a horrid lump on my plate.

'Eat up, Twinkletoes, and let's hope you don't disappoint me again. For your sake.'

Rain had started to fall as I traipsed after Maud towards the nightclub where I was supposed to seduce another woman's husband. She was like a ship in full sail as we swept through the streets, with me trailing in her wake.

It wasn't the career I'd had in mind when I left the East End, but Maud had made it clear I didn't really have much of a choice. The best I could hope for was that whatever she wanted me to do with this fella Jimmy would be over and done with quickly, and I could just get on with being a dancer and helping her pull off the occasional con. I'd never nicked anything in my life – not even a sweet from the corner shop – and the money I took from Mum didn't count as stealing, as far as I was concerned. But I'd experienced the harsh reality of how wealthy people looked down their noses at girls like me, so perhaps helping Maud nick a few bits and pieces wasn't so bad after all. I can't say it sat easily in my stomach – but maybe that was just the spaghetti.

'Chin up, love,' said Maud, reading the look on my face as we turned a corner and a bright red neon sign saying ' 'Rubies' hove into view. 'London is full of opportunities for a girl like you, but we've all got to start somewhere. I'll leave you here and let you find your own way home later. I'll be waiting for you. And don't get any funny ideas about doing a bunk, either. I have eyes and ears everywhere.'

As she said that, I spotted David, the magician, sauntering along on the other side of the road, with his hands in the pockets of his army greatcoat. He flashed Maud a grin. Perhaps he'd been following me and Rose all along? He lit up a smoke and went into the café opposite, where he took a seat in the window. He was there to act as a sentry; that much was clear.

I managed a weak smile and gave him a little wave, pushing open the door to the nightclub, and my new life as a dancer.

The narrow staircase was dimly lit and I almost bumped into two scrawny girls who were grumbling their way up it.

'It weren't right, Jeanie,' one was saying to the other, as she flicked her fag ash onto the steps. 'She's taking a flaming liberty.'

Her chum nodded in agreement. 'Docking our pay weren't fair! We couldn't have danced even if we hadn't scarpered. The floor was covered with glass and the place was stuffed with cozzers.'

I pressed myself against the wall to allow them to pass.

'Good luck, love – you'll need it,' they chuckled at me.

And the pair of them carried on up the stairs, laughing their heads off.

As I pushed open the door, Rubies was a hive of activity, with workmen hanging a new set of velvet curtains over the stage and an electrician on a stepladder fiddling with the lights. A piano tuner was doing his best, but the piano sounded as if it had seen better days.

In front of me, the bar was being restocked by a burly bald-headed bloke who was sporting two black eyes, which wasn't what you'd call good for business. A couple of young lads were sweeping up around the tables and, over in the corner, a group of fellas were deep in conversation, their shirtsleeves rolled up, cards on the go and drinks in their hands, even at this hour.

A woman with her black hair cropped short, like a pixie, was perching on a bar stool in a sequined bra and tiny skirt, her long legs dangling. She looked like she'd been sucking a lemon. I guessed she was the only dancer who'd decided not to walk off the job that day.

Presiding over it all was a blonde standing behind the bar. She was immaculately dressed and made up like a film star, with her hair falling in perfect waves to her shoulders. At her throat she wore an enormous ruby on a gold chain. Her crisp white blouse was tucked into a pencil skirt which accentuated her hourglass figure. She was possibly the most beautiful woman I had ever seen in my life, but there was something imposing about her, too, which was a bit scary.

She glanced over in my direction.

'Can't you see we're busy, love?'

She took a drag of a cigarette and blew smoke rings in the air, waiting for me to turn and leave.

'I've come about a job . . .'

'Well, we're not advertising for staff,' she said with a wave of her hand, the diamond rings on her fingers twinkling under the electric light. 'So you've had a wasted journey. Now, off you pop.'

'I heard you'd lost a couple of dancers, that's all,' I said. I didn't want to sleep on the streets tonight – or any night, for that matter – so I wasn't going to give up that easily. 'I met them on the stairs. I thought you might be in a bit of a tight spot and require some assistance.'

She raised an eyebrow and mocked my posh accent.

'Oh, I say! You thought we were in a tight spot, did you? How very *kind* of you to offer to assist. Does Buckingham Palace know you're here?'

I stood there, smiling through gritted teeth.

She laughed at her own joke and took another puff of her ciggie.

'Anyway, you could hardly call that pair of good-for-nothings dancers, love. It was me who told them to sling their hook – ain't that right, Alma?'

The grumpy pixie swivelled to face me. She looked me up and down.

'Might be worth a try-out, Nell. Good height on her. Look at those legs!'

As she spoke, the fellas at the card table stopped playing and glanced over towards me. One of them whispered to a handsome man with swept back sandy-coloured hair, and the pair of them laughed uproariously.

The blonde woman shot them both a look of irritation.

'Alright,' she said, 'I'll give you an audition. Alma here will get you kitted out.'

I practically skipped across the floor towards the bar, with my hand outstretched.

'I'm Zoe,' I said. 'It's a pleasure to meet you.'

She didn't shake my hand.

'I'm Nell,' she said. 'I run the club and I'm the boss. So you can call me Miss Kane.'

This was the woman I had to betray. And now there was no turning back.

Chapter Seven

NELL

Soho, January 1957

There are times in life when you know someone has got that extra something – the charisma that's going to make them a hit with the punters.

So, when this skinny, lanky redhead strode into my club that freezing January afternoon, I knew she was special because she was so different from all the rest. Her skin was soft and smooth, like alabaster, and she had a freshness about her that comes with youth and inexperience. I've been in this game long enough to know that men would throw money at girls like her.

The way she spoke had an appeal all of its own, too – as if she'd been to finishing school, but had taken a wrong turn on her way to Chelsea and ended up in a Soho nightclub by mistake.

But there was no way on God's green earth that I was going to let on about it, because the next thing you knew, she'd be demanding a ridiculous salary or behaving like a poor man's Ginger Rogers. It was going to be a case of 'treat them mean to keep them keen' as far as this girl Zoe was concerned; I'd made my mind up about that.

As Alma took her backstage to find her some dancing shoes and a suitable outfit, I was secretly praying she hadn't got two left feet. I'd just lost a couple of my best dancers, and with the word out that Munro and his mob were going to keep giving us a hard time, I needed fresh faces to lure my regulars back. The fact that Jimmy and his mob were already drooling over her like a bunch of pathetic schoolboys hadn't exactly escaped my notice either. That was a good sign.

Zoe emerged about ten minutes later, her face so red with embarrassment that it almost matched her hair. She was wearing a gold satin bra and shorts that were cut so high, her legs looked like they went on for miles. In her stiletto heels, she was slim as a pin and as tall as most men. She looked perfect.

Alma had given her a huge feathered fan, and as every bloke in the place turned to stare, Zoe kept trying to cover herself with it. In the end, Alma lost patience with her and snatched it from her grasp.

'You are going to have to get used to being looked at, so you might as well start now. Never be ashamed. It's how you earn your money. The only ones who should be embarrassed are the men who are prepared to spend a week's wages just for a glimpse of what we've got.'

Zoe nodded and shuffled her feet a bit. It wasn't exactly an inspiring start. I poured myself a drink.

We had a little record player at the side of the stage, for rehearsals, and Alma put on some upbeat swing, the kind of stuff that girls could really show off their moves to.

'Just follow me, Zoe,' said Alma, stepping lightly across the boards in time to the music. 'And five, six, seven, eight . . .'

Alma had the dead-eyed look and rictus grin of a professional who'd spent years hoofing it in the limelight, going nowhere fast. I made sure she had a decent salary, but most of it went on drink, fags or pathetic men who promised her the earth and fleeced her nightly. In the cold light of day the lines on her face were worn deep, but in the evening, with a few sequins and a good layer of face paint, she was a sex kitten who could tease the punters and put on a show to remember.

Alma never faltered in the spotlight, no matter what was going on at home, and I was in awe of the way she could swivel her hips and kick her legs all the way up to her head and still keep smiling, God love her.

Zoe set off dancing beside her, and what happened next was extraordinary. She wasn't actually watching what Alma's feet were doing; it was as if she was feeling it. She was bang on the rhythm, but she put something extra into the movement, something that made the gold outfit she was wearing really sparkle. Her whole body seemed to come alive with the music, the muscles on her lean legs flexing as she stepped and shimmied.

As the song was finishing, Alma turned her back to the audience and unclasped her bra, shaking her hips with the most seductive wiggle.

Then Alma turned around, clasping her bosom in one hand, twirling her top with the other before she chucked it on the floor.

She motioned for Zoe to do the same.

Zoe hesitated.

'Come on!' Alma hissed through gritted teeth.

When Zoe copied her, I could feel every male pulse in the room quicken. Some of Jimmy's fellas were on their feet, clapping and cheering. And Jimmy? Well, he was drinking her in, mesmerised, as she stood there naked from the waist up, her long hair swishing over her breasts, which she covered with her hands. What's more, she was gazing right at him, as if there was no one else in the

66

room. Perhaps she wasn't such a wallflower, after all. I was pleased about that. I needed her to be able to flirt with the punters.

Jimmy caught my eye. I winked at him, and he blushed.

Whatever this girl had, I knew one thing – it would sell like hot cakes.

'That'll do, thanks, Zoe,' I said. 'You did well.'

She smiled nervously and bent down and picked up her top.

Jimmy followed her every move, even though he knew I was watching him. I wasn't the jealous type and, if anything, I thought it was funny, how blatant he was about ogling a pretty girl. I'd give him a bit of a hard time about it later, just for the sheer hell of it.

'Put your clothes on, love,' I said to her. 'You're hired. Can you start tonight?'

Everyone jumped when the door to the club was pushed open a few moments later. I think we were still all on edge after the police raid. But we had nothing to fear from the band of good-looking women who strutted their way in, swathed from head to foot in the most luxurious furs. They were my girls, the Forty Thieves, and they'd just been shopping, by the look of them.

'Come on then! Where's the party?' Em shouted, pulling off the most ludicrously big fox fur stole. God only knows how she'd stashed that down her drawers without getting caught. Patsy pulled a bottle of champagne from her carpet bag, nicked from Fortnum and Mason's, no doubt.

'We thought you could probably use a bit of cheering up after what you've been through,' said Em, wrinkling her button nose at the sight of Lou's shiners. 'We went for a spree around Bond Street, because everyone needs a new fur in the winter, don't they?'

She took off her coat and revealed a chinchilla jacket underneath it, with the tags still on. I burst out laughing at the sight of it. She handed it over to me and I felt the softness of the fur; it was stunning and worth a fortune.

'Well done,' I said.

The Partridge twins, Madeline and Laura, who were a willowy pair of raven-haired beauties, produced some lovely fur-lined mittens from secret pockets in their coats. The Partridges looked like pure class and their favourite technique was distraction. It was only when they opened their mouths that you realised they'd been born in a slum, so they usually kept talking to a minimum when they were on the shop floor.

Patsy, my deputy, was more solidly built than the rest – which did come in handy if you wanted to block a doorway. But she had the most beautiful hazel eyes, which twinkled with mischief, and I'd lost count of the men who'd fallen for her charms, including a few store detectives.

She also knew how to turn on the tears, making herself vulnerable, when she needed to. That was a rare talent. I always said she could have had a career treading the boards up in the West End if she hadn't been a hoister.

'Blimey, you've cleaned up, ladies,' I said, pulling my best champagne flutes from under the bar counter.

Lou popped the cork, and I flung the fox fur around my shoulders.

'Let's have a toast – to the Forty Thieves!' I said, pouring some fizz into the glasses.

'And to Nell, the Queen of Clubs!' said Em, taking a sip.

'Sod the cozzers!' cried Patsy, downing her glass in one gulp. 'I wish I'd been here to clobber them one.'

I nodded in agreement, but I was glad that none of them had gone through what I had with that creep Munro.

'Give us a song,' said Em, raising another glass to me.

'Yeah, come on,' said Patsy, flushing from the drink. 'You know we love a knees-up.'

I tried to make a few excuses, because my throat was still hoarse from the hours I'd spent being interviewed by Munro, but my girls were having none of it. The piano was still in pieces after the police raid, but I was confident enough to sing unaccompanied. I'd started as a club singer, many years ago in Soho. It was my first proper job – well, that and the hoisting. But the thing is, singing was something I did for fun these days, and the punters seemed to enjoy it, too, which was a bonus.

I put down my drink and went over to the stage, just as Jimmy was returning to his game of cards with the fellas. There were a few wolf whistles as I swayed my hips and I blew Jimmy a kiss, as I began to sing.

While I was singing I spotted my new dancer, Zoe, watching us all, unable to contain her amazement at what she was seeing. I could have invited her over to join in the fun, but there was a pecking order and I needed her to realise that she was at the bottom of the heap as far as I was concerned. She'd have to win my approval before I offered her a glass of water, never mind champagne. But she had potential.

I gave her a little wave as she headed out of the door.

I kept going with the song, but Jimmy didn't have eyes for me in that moment. His gaze was glued to her backside.

When I finished, the fellas applauded me wildly and I took a little bow.

'Thank you, that's your lot!'

'Nice-looking girl,' said Em, when I went back to the bar to crack open another bottle of bubbly. 'Who's she?'

'Just a replacement for a couple of my hoofers who I fired earlier,' I said.

If I'd known who and what she really was, I would have locked the door behind her and thrown away the key, to stop her taking another step into our world.

But it was already too late.

Ruby was playing hopscotch with the other kids when Jimmy and me arrived home at Queen's Buildings.

I hated to admit it, but I was dead beat after my all-nighter down at the cop shop. All I wanted to do was put the kettle on and put my feet up. For once, the appeal of being just a housewife was overwhelming.

'I might give the club a miss tonight and stay home with Ruby for a change,' I said. 'Turn in early.'

Jimmy beamed at me. 'That's a lovely idea, Nell. She'll be over the moon with that. Me and Lou can keep an eye on things at the club tonight, no worries. You need a break.'

My little girl spotted me as I climbed out of the Bentley and her face lit up. I ran towards her, my arms outstretched, sweeping her up and covering her with kisses.

'Mummy's home, darling!'

A frown crossed her face, as she snuggled to my chest.

'Where were you? You didn't read me a story or kiss me goodnight like you always do!'

Those words were like a knife in my heart.

'I'm sorry, sweetheart,' I said, putting her down and taking her by the hand. 'I got held up at work, that's all. Now, shall we go and get some tea? It's freezing out here.'

A right old pea-souper of a smog was already descending, and the hoots of the barges from the River Thames were muffled in the early evening air. I didn't like her getting too cold. Last winter she'd had a bad bout of flu and it sat on her chest for months.

'Why did you have to work so late, Mum?' she said, skipping up the stairs to our flat, two by two.

Jimmy shot me a sideways glance.

'It couldn't be avoided, petal,' I said, 'but it won't happen again, I promise. Not ever.'

Iris was making beans on toast for Ruby's tea when I pushed open the door, and she rushed over to give me a hug.

We'd known each other since we were at the fur factory together during the war, and she'd been by my side when I fought my way to the top in the Forty Thieves. I trusted her more than anyone, and she'd repaid my trust by loving my child as if she was her own. Iris had a lot of love to give, because her old man Tommy ended up in the mental hospital a few years after he got back from Burma, where he'd been in one of the prisoner-of-war camps. He never got over what happened to him out there. At least now she was safe from his beatings, but it was sad, all the same.

I did what I could to get her back on her feet, helping her set up her salon down on the high street. Her back room was handy for storing my stolen goods when the need arose, too.

She lowered her voice so that Ruby wouldn't hear.

'I was so worried, Nell. Are you alright?'

'Fine,' I said, giving her a reassuring pat on the shoulders. 'It was just the brass hats down at Scotland Yard wanting to rattle a few cages up in Soho, that's all. It'll all be fine.'

'But the papers . . .'

'Are full of lies,' I said, with a laugh. 'You didn't believe any of that garbage in the *London Evening News*, did you, Iris?'

She shook her head, but I could tell by the look in her eyes she wasn't entirely convinced.

'Jimmy would never brag like that about being King of Soho. It was that snake Duncan Swift who made it all up to get a headline in the paper. And I would never let him say or do anything which put the Forty Thieves at risk. You know the rules are we never talk about the gang publicly. And he knows that, too. I swear it.'

She dug her hands into the pockets of her housecoat.

'I'd appreciate it if you'd put the word out around Queen's Buildings that whatever they've read is a load of hot air,' I said.

''Course I will,' she replied. 'I never believed he'd talk about the Forties or brag about being King of Soho or whatever. It just ain't like him.'

I opened my purse and handed her a tenner.

'Treat yourself to something nice,' I said. 'It's just a little extra thanks for being there for Ruby last night.'

She took it but held my gaze for an instant, as if she wasn't sure if I was trying to buy her loyalty.

To be honest, I wasn't sure either. That newspaper article had dented everyone's faith in us so badly, I hardly knew who I was any more.

I got Ruby's face and hands washed while Jimmy had some tea, and then I tucked her up in her bed with her teddy and her hot water bottle, ready for a story. I picked a book of fairy tales because, even though it went on for bloody ages, I knew it was her favourite.

I was just starting the 'Once upon a time . . .' when she piped up.

'Do you know, Mum, the war ain't over?'

She had that serious look on her face – the one which reminded me so much of her dad.

'No, love,' I said, brushing a stray strand of hair away from her forehead. 'It finished a long time ago, before you were born, and you have nothing to worry about.'

'You're wrong,' she said, sitting up. 'It's still going on because I met someone today who is still fighting in it. She had a uniform on and everything.'

Jimmy poked his head around the bedroom door, and I rolled my eyes at him.

'Did she? I bet she looked funny 'cos the war ended in 1945. Was she covered in cobwebs?'

'No!' said Ruby, crossly. 'She was a very nice lady. Her name is Maud.'

'And what did she say to you, this Maud?' I said, stifling a laugh. 'Did she tell you the moon was made of cream cheese as well?'

I went to tickle her, but she folded her arms and pouted.

'Why won't you believe me?'

Jimmy came in. 'We do believe you, sweetheart, of course we do. Now, Mummy's tired, so let me read this to you now and then it's time for sleep.'

I kissed her cheek and then peered through the crack in the bedroom door, as Jimmy read to her. She was a funny one at times, stubborn, but that only made me love her more. He only got her halfway through 'Rapunzel' before she nodded off.

He crept out into the hallway and put his arms around me, nuzzling my neck.

'I've got a bit of free time before I've got to get back to the club.'

I looked deep into his eyes and said with a smile, 'Still got your dander up after watching Zoe, have you?'

'Oh, don't be daft!' he said, pulling me closer. 'I couldn't help looking, she had it all on display! But she's all skin and bone, not my type. *You're* my type, you know that, Nell.'

His hands wandered downwards over my backside and I felt that tingle of desire that he always gave me. Just his touch was enough to turn my legs to jelly.

But it had been two weeks since I last bled, and if I let him, there was a risk I'd get pregnant. I'd never bothered Jimmy with the ins and outs of my monthlies. He knew well enough when I was in a foul mood. Oh, I gave him plenty to keep him happy, so he had nothing to complain about, but I was quietly very careful about planning the days when I had a headache. That always fell two weeks after my period, if you know what I mean. Jimmy was none the wiser. He just thought we hadn't been lucky enough to conceive yet.

I kissed him, but pulled away afterwards before things got beyond the point of no return.

'Sorry, Jim, I think I'm just too tired tonight. Can we save it for another day and make it really special?'

He looked a bit hurt.

''Course, that's fine,' he said. 'You've been through hell. I shouldn't be pestering you. Get some sleep and I'll see you in the morning.'

He gave me a peck on the cheek.

When I heard the front door bang shut, I flopped onto the settee and flicked on the television, watching it crackle to life in the corner. I was the only one in Queen's Buildings to own a telly, and I can't say I watched it much, but it was nice for company on those rare evenings when I found myself alone.

I poured myself a sherry and kicked off my heels, putting my feet up on the coffee table. Vera Lynn was on, singing live from Hammersmith. Oh, I loved hearing her songs

74

during the war and on any other night, I'd have joined in, too.

It was such a silly thing to worry about, but I couldn't quite get Ruby's imaginary friend Maud out of my head.

There was something about the way she hadn't laughed along with me when I teased her that troubled me.

Was she missing me so much that she was making up fairy stories of her own?

Chapter Eight

ZOE

Soho, January 1957

Flirting with Jimmy was a small price to pay for the thrill of performing as a dancer in such a prestigious club.

The whole room had been transformed, with crisp white tablecloths on every table, stage lights which reflected in the mirrored ceiling above, and a feeling of expectation as people started to arrive, dolled up to the nines.

I peeked out from the velvet curtains, watching Jimmy as he glad-handed his way around the club. He really was very good-looking for an older bloke – broad-shouldered and lean. It could have been worse. Maud could have told me to cosy up to Lou the barman, who looked like something out of a horror film with his bashed-up face. But Jimmy was charming, shaking hands and making admiring comments to the ladies, who enjoyed every moment of his attention. I felt a flicker of something as they clasped his hand for a moment longer than was necessary. Perhaps I was just anxious to have my chance with him, to do the job I had come here to do. But his cheekbones were quite chiselled, and with his hair slicked back, it really showed off his blue eyes.

The drink was flowing, and musicians were warming up by the stage. There was a full brass section, a drummer and the piano, which was now, mercifully, being played in tune. It was exciting to be able to dance with full musical backing. Up to now, I'd only been used to a piano in a dusty old village hall.

A gasp went up as a gorgeous, statuesque blonde with a totally knockout figure sashayed in, wearing a full-length red satin gown, her shoulders covered in the most beautiful white fur wrap. I recognised her instantly. It was Diana Durbidge, the film star, and she had a gaggle of admiring fellas with her. Jimmy showed her to the best table in the house, right in front of the stage. My heartbeat quickened. She'd be able to spot any wrong moves.

'Nervous?'

A voice came from over my shoulder. It was Alma, drawing on a ciggie.

'A bit,' I said, wiping some perspiration from my brow.

It was getting hot, even though in my gold top and shorts, I was barely wearing anything.

'Don't be,' she said, throwing her fag end to the floor and crushing it under a stiletto heel. 'You're a natural. I've been in this game a long time and I've not seen many girls that take to it like you do. If you go wrong, just smile and keep moving.'

Another three girls clattered their way up the stairs at the side of the stage to join us. They were dressed like me, in gold. Only Alma's outfit was different; she had a bra that was encrusted with rhinestones. And her knickers left little to the imagination.

'Doreen, Maggie and Judy,' she said, by way of introduction to the other dancers. 'You are all late. Do it again and I will dock you a shilling each.'

They rolled their eyes.

'This is Zoe, the new girl I was telling you about,' she added.

I smiled at them. They didn't smile back.

The band struck up and a hush fell over the room as the curtains were pulled back.

'Right, ladies,' said Alma, 'move it like your fancy man is out there and he's just bought you a massive diamond ring.'

'Fat chance,' said Doreen through gritted teeth, as we high-kicked our way out to greet the audience.

Once I stepped out onto the stage, moving in time to the music took over from my nerves. Alma had me positioned just behind her, so I could copy her steps, but it all came so easily, and I even remembered to smile.

Diana Durbidge was tapping her feet along, and stood up to applaud Alma as she jumped down into the splits at the end of our first number. Some wag shouted, 'Give us a twirl, Diana!' She laughed and blew them a kiss before taking her seat as the band struck up again. I couldn't help noticing that she spent a lot of time watching Jimmy as he stood at the bar. He was deep in conversation with a tall, dark-haired fella, who was snappily dressed and seemed to command respect. But other than chatting to him, Jimmy only had eyes for one person that night: me.

As we shimmied around, to wolf whistles, there were girls wearing next to nothing, with trays of flowers and chocolates slung around their necks, moving through the audience. It was all to persuade the punters to part with more cash. All the drinks cost an arm and leg, too. When an actor I recognised from a cinema poster strolled in with a beautiful girl on each arm, I began to understand that being seen in Rubies was part of a glamorous world which was a million miles away from the slums.

As we were getting to the end of our third and final dance before the singer came on, Alma turned and clasped me by the hand, bringing me to the front of the stage.

'Remember what we did earlier?' she whispered. 'Well, now it's down to you.'

The lights dimmed and only the piano and the drummer kept playing, as she shuffled me into position.

'Let's hear it for Zoe, our new girl!'

Then a spotlight fell on me. My heart was pounding as I turned my back and kept my hips swinging from side to side. To my horror, I fumbled with the clasp on my top for what felt like an age. Then cymbals crashed as I undid it.

I covered my boobs with my arm and my free hand, slowly turning around, feeling all the eyes in the room watching as I twirled the top and chucked it aside. This is what people had come to see and I wasn't about to disappoint them. The lights went out and when they came back up everyone was cheering and clapping.

It was dizzying, that applause. I wasn't ashamed, not in the least. In fact, I felt powerful and appreciated for the first time in my life. Jimmy was cheering the loudest of all, and I felt my stomach do a little flip as he broke into a huge grin which lit up his face.

The lights went down again and one of the dancers dug me in the ribs.

'Stop hogging the limelight and get off!'

That was the moment when I knew I was destined to make it big in clubland.

But as we took our bows and the musicians took a break, there was someone in the audience who wasn't smiling. He was sitting there at a table of gorgeous-looking women who were vying for his attention. His lips were pressed into a thin line and his eyes burned with anger as he looked right at me.

It was Vinnie.

★

By the time I'd got changed, the dance floor at the front of the stage was crowded with smooching couples, dancing to some slow songs. Diana Durbidge was still holding court, throwing her head back, showing off her gorgeous diamond necklace as she laughed. She nodded at me when I passed, a look that said 'Well done!', as if she knew how hard it was to get up in front of people and give it your all.

I scanned the room but there was no sign of Vinnie. It was daft, I suppose, but I wanted to talk to him, to explain that I didn't just take my clothes off for a living. There was something about the way he'd looked at me that made me feel cheap – there was no other word for it. Alma had told me to feel proud of myself and my body, and standing there, hearing all the applause, I *had* felt good – powerful, even. But the look of anger in the eyes of a man I barely knew had punctured my confidence, in an instant.

'Penny for your thoughts,' said Alma, slipping her bony arm through mine as we pushed our way to the bar.

'It's nothing,' I lied.

'You've got a face like a wet weekend,' she whispered. 'Cheer up, for God's sake! It's bad for business. We are still on duty. We've got to mingle with the punters a bit, smile, make them spend some money.'

'But I was hoping to go home!'

'Home?' She laughed, steering me towards the bar, where a row of fellas were already opening their wallets to buy us drinks. 'It's only just gone eleven! You can sleep later. Let's relax a bit.'

She turned on a smile for the blokes, which was almost electrifying. The years rolled back from her face and the hardness in her eyes softened.

'Dennis!' she cried, reaching out to a porky bloke with thinning hair. 'Haven't seen you in a while! Where've you been hiding? Come and meet my new friend, Zoe.'

'What you drinking, love?' he said, as Lou hovered expectantly.

'She'll have champagne,' said Alma. 'It's our favourite, ain't it?'

I nodded. I'd never so much as tasted a drop in my life. I had sneaked a couple of swigs of sherry from my mum's supply – the secret one she kept under the sink in the scullery – just to try it. Now I watched in awe as the cork popped and Lou poured some into glasses on the bar. I sipped, feeling the bubbles fizzing on my tongue and tingling up my nose, and it made me giggle. It was exactly what Nell and her friends had been drinking earlier. Now I understood what all the fuss was about. It was delicious.

'That's better,' Alma whispered in my ear. 'And it's the most expensive drink in the house, so that'll keep the old misery guts Lou happy!'

Dennis slipped his arm around my waist, and I leaned into his shoulder. He seemed to like that. When another bloke asked me to dance, I accepted. I let his hands wander all over my backside as Alma watched, giving me a knowing wink. I can't say I enjoyed it, but I understood that it was expected of me. I didn't want to upset the punters. Part of my job was to keep them happy.

Jimmy was there, too, drinking with a few fellas, including that tall, dark-haired man I had seen earlier. They were still engrossed in conversation, and I was a bit disappointed when he didn't look over in my direction.

At one o'clock, Alma went to get her coat and I took that as my cue to leave as well, or Maud would start to think I wasn't coming back.

'See you tomorrow, Zoe,' she said, with barely a backward glance.

I went to get changed and then made my way across the club, which was still crowded, climbing the staircase, greasy with spilled drinks and littered with fag butts. The cold night air hit me and, inhaling deeply, I realised that I was a bit giddy after the champagne. The gas lamps were hissing, casting shadows up the shopfronts, which had their blinds drawn. In a few hours' time, everything in Soho would spring to life again, with the dawn chorus of delivery boys on bicycles and newspaper sellers yelling the day's news. By night, a different Soho was plying its trade in underground clubs and drinking dens. Above ground, women dressed in fur coats and high heels called out from doorways to men muffled up in overcoats, their collars pulled high around their throats: 'Fancy a good time, dearie?'

I wondered what lies they'd tell their wives when they finally staggered home.

I had only gone about twenty yards or so when a figure stepped out of an alleyway and grabbed hold of me. I was going to scream, but then I recognised his face in the dim glow of a street lamp. It was Vinnie.

'Been waiting to speak to you all night,' he said gruffly. 'But I couldn't get a look in.'

'For God's sake!' I said, trying to shake myself free. 'You just about made me jump out of my wits.'

But he didn't let go, propelling me back up against the wall, his eyes glinting.

'You didn't tell me you were that kind of girl, Angel.'

His whole body was pushed up against me, pinning me to the cold bricks.

'I'm not!' I protested. 'I'm a dancer, earning my living, that's all.'

He smiled at me, but it was more of a sneer, the corners of his mouth twisting.

'I thought you were different, Angel,' he said. 'We had such fun. I thought you were special – really special. But after that performance, I can see you're just like all the rest.'

'What do you mean?' I said, sobbing with shock. He was making me feel like a tart. 'You can't talk to me like that, and you don't know the half of it, Vinnie! Let me go!'

I balled my hands into fists and pummelled them against his chest.

'Prick-tease,' he said, moving in and kissing me roughly, biting my lip as he did so. I screamed, but he covered my mouth with one hand and shoved the other up my dress.

Then, out of nowhere, there was the sound of shattering glass and Vinnie grunted and fell backwards, clasping the back of his head.

'For fuck's sake!' he gasped.

Jimmy stood there, brandishing a broken bottle in a way that made it clear he meant business.

'Time for you to run home, sunshine,' he said, as Vinnie stared at his hands, which were covered in blood.

Jimmy moved towards him and gave him an almighty push.

'I said, shove off!'

'You're a dead man!' said Vinnie, grimacing as he almost lost his footing.

'You and whose army? You stupid little fucker.' Jimmy put his hand inside his jacket and revealed a gun. 'You're playing with the grown-ups now, sonny.'

Vinnie froze for a split second.

Then he turned on his heel, one hand still cradling the back of his head, and staggered off into the night.

That was when my legs gave way.

Jimmy caught me as I fell.

'You're in shock, sweetheart.'

My whole body was shaking like a leaf as he held me in his arms.

'Just relax, I won't hurt you, Zoe. You're safe now.'

There was something about hearing him say my name that made my stomach flip. I gazed up into his eyes.

'Do you want me to walk you home?'

Home.

That was something I'd never really had not for such a long time. I began to cry – for the life I'd been born into, for everything I'd lost and for where I'd ended up. Once I'd started, I couldn't stop.

He held me closer, so I could feel the softness of his silk tie against my cheek and hear the beating of his heart. He stroked my hair, over and over, until my tears had dried.

And when I looked up at him again, I knew it with all my heart and soul. It wasn't a case of doing what Maud had told me to do, over some stupid grudge.

I wanted him.

'I don't want to go home, not just yet,' I murmured, uncertain of what to do with this feeling of desire.

He put his arm around me.

'Do you want to go somewhere quiet, just to get yourself sorted?'

I nodded. God only knows what a mess I must have looked. My mascara was smudged halfway down my face, I was sure of it, and my eyes were sore from weeping.

'Come on,' he said. 'I've got a room above the spieler. There's a sink in there, and hot water. We can make you a nice brew, or I've got something stronger if you need it.'

I let him lead the way, leaning on him, not to be flirty, but because all the energy in me had gone. I felt hollow, like a straw doll with all the stuffing knocked out, just like I did when I had measles as a kid.

We wandered through a warren of backstreets and ended up in a little courtyard. To anyone looking, we must have seemed like just another couple heading home. That thought thrilled me a bit, if I'm honest.

Jimmy pulled a key from his coat pocket and rattled it in the lock of an old door with peeling brown paint, before giving it a good kick to get it to open. A gloomy staircase lay ahead. It was so narrow his shoulders were almost touching the walls. I followed him up it.

We went into a little room, maybe ten feet square, with a window overlooking the yard below. There was a gas range and a sink with some cups in it in one corner. A battered leather sofa and some armchairs ran the length of one wall, with a low coffee table in front of them. An ashtray overflowed with last night's cigarette ends. There were shelves stacked with booze and fancy glasses, some really heavy-looking ones, and even a cocktail shaker. In the corner, there was a huge safe. God only knows how they'd lugged that up the stairs.

'Make yourself comfortable,' he said, gesturing to the sofa.

I sank into it gratefully, leaning back and closing my eyes for a moment. My head was spinning.

I heard the clink of glasses as Jimmy poured us both a drink.

'I've never tried whisky before. It's a man's drink, ain't it?' I said, as he offered me some of the amber-coloured liquid.

'Try it, just a sip, to calm your nerves,' he said, swirling it around in the glass.

I swallowed some, feeling it slip down my throat, burning me slightly.

He watched me closely.

'Would you like a cup of tea?'

'Please,' I said weakly.

He sloshed some water into the kettle and lit the stove, and then he turned around and came back over to the sofa, sitting down beside me.

'Tell me a bit about yourself, Zoe,' he said, his eyes searching my face.

I didn't want to lie to him. It felt wrong.

'I'm just a girl from nowhere looking to go somewhere,' I said. 'My happiest days were in Devon during the war, when I was evacuated, and then when I came home, my dad went away and my mum . . . Well, she did what took her fancy, if you know what I mean, and so I was on my own, really. 'That's when I decided to try my luck as a dancer.'

He nodded, as if that satisfied him. Perhaps he'd heard similar stories from other girls. How many had he brought up here to this room? I couldn't help but wonder.

'Ambition ain't a bad thing, Zoe,' he said, lighting a smoke, inhaling deeply. 'There's plenty of chances for girls like you in clubland. Don't let what happened with that stupid Teddy boy put you off.'

Just thinking about the way Vinnie had turned like that, after we'd had such fun dancing together, made start to snivel again. Jimmy pulled out a silk handkerchief and offered it to me. I wiped my eyes.

'Don't upset yourself,' he said. 'You don't have to let anyone touch you unless you want them to. I won't let blokes handle the goods too much in my club. Alma knows how to play the game to keep the punters sweet. That kid just crossed the line. He needs a good belting to teach him some manners. If I catch him round here again, that is what he'll get.'

I frowned. 'I know him. At least, I thought I knew him – he's called Vinnie. But we only danced together once in a club, and he seems to think he owns me now. I just don't understand it.'

'Nobody owns you, Zoe,' Jimmy said. 'You should remember that. You're different from the rest. Where did you learn to talk so proper?'

I blushed.

'It was my teacher when I was evacuated. She was very particular about how I spoke. I think she was trying to do something nice for me, to help me get a head start in life. That way of talking stuck, I suppose. And it got my mum's back up, which made it worth it.'

That made me smile, and he smiled with me.

'Folks like us don't get many breaks,' he said. 'It's good to take your chances where you can find them.'

He took my hand and our eyes met.

The way he looked at me then almost took my breath away. It wasn't the look that the fellas in Rubies gave me when I was dancing half-naked, entertaining them with barely a stitch on.

And it wasn't the burning anger that Vinnie had in his eyes, which had terrified me.

It was a kind of longing.

I understood it because I was feeling it, too.

On the stove the kettle started to whistle, and somewhere

below on the streets of Soho drunks were shouting, but I was deaf to all of that.

I leaned across and kissed Jimmy, so I suppose you could say I started it.

But there were two of us in that poky little room.

He kissed me back.

And that's how we began.

Chapter Nine

NELL

Elephant and Castle, January 1957

The hands on the alarm clock glowed four in the morning as the front door creaked open. After a few moments I heard Jimmy creep into the bedroom, and then I felt the familiar warmth of his arms encircling my waist as he clambered into bed. He'd been out later than usual, but I knew he'd got a robbery to plan, and he'd probably spent ages going over the details with his mob. I'd wait until daylight to talk to him about it.

'It's freezing in here,' I whispered. 'Keep me warm, Jim.'

He nuzzled into my neck, murmuring how much he loved me, and we dozed together in the dark, not saying anything much, just being beside each other. I loved those quiet moments in the small hours, listening for the sounds of the day starting outside at Queen's Buildings. We were like any other couple, lying there in each other's arms, with our little one fast asleep in the bedroom next door. Those moments were so precious to me because we could forget all about being King of Soho and Queen of Thieves, all the hassle of Munro and running the club and keeping gangland happy. We were just another family living in the Elephant and Castle, doing what we could to get by, raising our child with a smile on her face.

As his body pressed close to mine, I started to wonder

whether it was fair for me to put off having kids for much longer. Ruby's imaginary friend was playing on my mind. Who was I to deny her a little brother or sister? It wasn't her fault she was making up silly stories – she was just a child, trying to fill her world with something interesting because she was lonely. And Jimmy wanted a baby so badly because he loved me. I began to feel foolish for being so selfish about it all.

His breath was warm as his fingers curled around mine. Jimmy, my Jimmy.

The most delicious smell of frying bacon woke me from my slumber as the thin winter sun streamed through the bedroom curtains. I pulled on my dressing gown and made my way down the hall to the kitchen, to find Jimmy with his shirtsleeves rolled up, creating a full English breakfast.

Ruby's hair was already neatly plaited, and she was chatting to him excitedly about something or other. But when she saw me, she stopped talking and frowned.

'Still got the hump with me for last night?' I said, kissing her on the forehead.

'No,' She pouted.

'Don't be rude to your mother, Ruby,' said Jimmy, sliding some bacon and eggs onto her plate, giving her a wink.

'Sorry, Mummy,' she said.

'It's alright, sweetheart,' I replied, sitting down and tucking in. Suddenly I was ravenously hungry. Jimmy's fry-ups were too good to resist. 'I promise I will make it up to you.'

A smile spread across her face, and it was like the sun coming out in my world. God knows, she had me wrapped around her little finger, that girl, but I loved the very bones of her.

'Now, eat up,' I said, 'or you'll be late for school.'

★

I watched Ruby skipping across the courtyard and then went back to the kitchen, where Jimmy was already doing the washing-up.

'Give it a rest, Jim,' I teased. 'Or you'll be wanting a medal for all that hard work.'

'I don't do nearly enough for you both,' he said, scrubbing away at the pan.

There was something about the sight of him at that sink that turned my legs to jelly. He was my man, helping me out indoors, and there weren't many fellas in Queen's Buildings who'd be prepared to do that.

I lit up a smoke.

'How was the club?'

A muscle twitched in his cheek as he dried his hands on a tea towel.

'Busy, I suppose, which was good.'

'Girls did alright? No dramas on stage?'

'No, no,' he said, avoiding my gaze. 'It all went off like clockwork. Diana Durbidge was in with her usual crowd. Takings were healthy, given what we've just been through with Munro.'

There was a look in his eye that told me something wasn't right, but I knew better than to push him.

I inhaled deeply and then blew a smoke ring and watched it curling around the ceiling light.

'There's been a bit of bad news from Albert and the boys,' he began eventually. 'That job I've got planned has moved forward to this evening, and it can't go ahead unless I get it sorted. And if I don't go through with it, it will be like losing face.'

I sat down at the kitchen table, and he sat opposite me,

91

stress etched on his features.

'Tell me about it, Jim,' I said, stubbing out my ciggie in a saucer. 'We can work it out together.'

He addressed his comments to the table, as if he was ashamed of himself.

'My top wheelman doesn't want to be involved because of what's happened with Munro. He's had his collar felt by the law. A few other fellas had said they were in, to provide backup, but now nothing will persuade them. It's like we're lepers.'

'How many people are you short?'

'A getaway driver, a lookout, someone to carry some of the bullion. Enough people to make a difference. It's such a peach of a job, it's a perfect plan, with minimum fuss, but now it's slipping through my fingers.' He looked disgusted with himself. 'I thought I had a tight team, people I could trust, but with the top brass working against me, it's impossible. I feel like such a fucking fool for talking to that grimy little hack.'

He banged his fist on the table.

'Shhh, Jimmy, don't upset yourself,' I said. 'If you need a getaway driver, I'll do it.'

He laughed. 'You?'

I almost slapped his face for that, but he was looking too handsome.

'Yes, me,' I said, sounding more than a little bit chippy. 'I'm a bloody good driver. And maybe I can get a couple of the girls to pitch in, for a decent cut. Patsy's built like a brick shithouse, she's strong enough to carry stuff.'

And that was when I had a genius idea.

'And Em's little brother's just out of Borstal, and looking for a bit of work. He's keen, and he's been driving her mother up the wall, kicking his heels all day at home. He could be a lookout.'

'What was he done for?'

'The jump-up,' I said. 'Just nicking stuff off the back of lorries and getting caught, the silly twerp. He got six months in Rochester for that, but he's from a solid family and they don't tell tales. Em's one of my best in the Forty Thieves, you know that. Besides, you could do worse than getting a bit of younger blood in the gang to help, Jimmy. It might a light a fire under a few of the old guard, who seem to have lost their guts at the first sight of a cozzer's uniform in our club.'

He leaned over and kissed me, tenderly, on the cheek.

'I don't deserve you, Nell,' he said, almost choking with emotion. 'You are an absolutely blinding bird, and I am so lucky to have you in my life.'

'Well, I was wondering if you had a bit of spare time this morning to remind me just how much you love me,' I replied, batting my eyelashes at him.

A look crossed his face. I suppose it was surprise, that I was giving him the come-on, when he was so used to getting the brush-off.

'You mean . . .?'

'Does a lady have to ask twice around here?' I joked, standing up, putting my hands on my hips and loosening my silk dressing gown, so that he got a tantalising glimpse of what was underneath it.

He pulled me to him, and the years melted away from us both. I started to unbutton his shirt, and the thrill of feeling his taut, muscled chest was just the same as it had been when we first met during the war.

'Oh, Nell,' he murmured, covering my neck with kisses. 'I want you so much.'

He gave me that wolfish grin of his as he took my hand

and led me to the bedroom. Then, he laid me down as if I were the most precious thing he owned. My whole body ached for him in that moment.

'I want you, too, Jimmy,' I whispered. 'More than anything, I want us to have another baby.'

He started crying as we made love, holding me close.

'Oh God, Nell, I want that, too, so much. You are my whole world. I promise you I will look after all of us. Always.'

It was always a pleasure to pop round to Em's house in the next tenement block at Queen's Buildings because her mother Marj was one of my best fences, and she owed me a few quid. She'd been a fence for as long as I could remember, way back to the days of Alice Diamond, the old Queen of Thieves who I'd given the boot. Marj was no fan of Alice's, and had thrown her weight right behind me when I took over, mainly because she was always getting on the wrong side of Alice for trying to cream off a bit too much of a profit for herself. There was no such nonsense with me, and I respected her for what she did. So, we rubbed along just fine.

Business had been brisk and there would be a fat wallet full of tenners waiting for me. The cold snap meant everyone wanted a new fur stole, or at the very least a mink collar and a pair of fur-lined boots to keep out the chill, so we'd been doing very nicely. The Forty Thieves were working extra days to keep pace with demand.

Marj kept an old pram at the bottom of the stairwell to move the loot from street to street, looking every bit the proud grandmother. If a cozzer had peeked under the hood to admire her little one, he would have been in for a shock, because heaps of neatly stacked stockings or tightly rolled furs had taken the place of a gurgling baby.

I climbed the stairs to the first floor and banged on the door. Marj opened it a fraction to check who it was before letting me in, breaking into a big grin.

'Oh, hello, love.'

She bustled me down the hallway, her hair in rollers, covered by a headscarf. She was a dead ringer for her daughter, Em, with the same button nose and eager little eyes, but at her time of life, she was rounder, more homely, with her housecoat straining over her hips. There was something comforting about Marj, and I could never resist her cakes – they were delicious.

Em was busy spreading marmalade on a doorstep of toast, while a young bloke lounged in an easy chair, listening to the wireless. His hair was slicked back to make him look older, but his shaving rash gave away his youth. He stood up when he saw me, out of politeness, brushing a few crumbs from his trousers. His frame was still rangy, in the way that young lads are, and his clothes hung off him, as if he'd yet to grow into them properly.

'This is Derek,' said Marj proudly. 'You remember him, don't you, Nell?'

''Course I do, but you're so grown-up I'd have walked past you in the street!' I joked.

He coloured up a bit at that. I was doing it to give him a bit of a lift.

Em went to ruffle his hair.

'Ah, he's still my little bruv, ain't he?'

'Oh, leave off!' he said, ducking out of her way.

'Well, I wish you were out earning a man's wages,' tutted Marj. 'You can't sit around here all day on your backside, son. You've got to go and get yourself a job, ain't you?'

He rolled his eyes. 'I'm seeing a bloke later down the

95

warehouse, but you know it ain't that easy finding work.'

'It ain't easy sitting here in my kitchen, that's for sure.' Marj wasn't really chiding him. There was a glow about her when she spoke. 'For a fine young man like you, there's bound to be people queuing up to give you a decent pay packet.'

She poured me a cuppa, turning towards me and lowering her voice.

'Ain't he just the image of my Jack?'

'He certainly is,' I said, taking a sip.

Jack had joined the Royal Navy during the war because he thought it would be a cushy life – that's what everyone had said, that it was easier than square-bashing with the army. But he couldn't have been more wrong. A German U-boat put paid to that notion, and he was lost at sea when his minesweeper was sunk. Derek was barely old enough to remember his father, and had grown up the apple of his mother's eye, a constant reminder of everything she'd lost.

Marj dug deep into the pocket of her housecoat and pulled out several rolls of notes, held together with rubber bands.

'Nice work,' I said, unfurling one and peeling off her cut. 'Any problems I need to know about?'

'Everyone round the market's up to date on payments,' she said. 'I think a few of the girls would like more stockings, and there's a thing for petticoats – loads of them, which the younger ones are starching to make their skirts stick out for dances. Lord only knows what they'll think of next, but I reckon we could make a bit more by selling those?'

'Gamages have lots, and they're such a dozy bunch there, it'll be an easy hoist,' said Em, in between mouthfuls of toast. 'Do you want me to get the girls to give it a go?'

'They're cotton, not silk, so we won't go overboard,' I

96

said. 'We can charge more for high-end stuff, but if they're easy to swipe, I won't complain if a few of them find a way into our hoisters' drawers.'

Providing what people wanted and stealing to order was all part of the success of my gang. I liked to give the punters what they were after. If I didn't, the tallyman would be hawking them off the back of his van before we knew it. He was such a bloody pest.

I glanced over to Derek, who was pretending to listen to something on the radio but had his ears pricked for what the Forty Thieves were up to.

'How long've you been out, Derek?'

'A few weeks,' he said, scuffing his feet.

'And he ain't never going back,' said Marj firmly. 'He's eighteen now, in any case, so it would be prison next time. I want him to go straight, Nell, keep out of trouble. My heart can't take it.'

She clasped her chest. There was nothing wrong with her ticker, as far as I knew, but I understood a mother's desire to keep her only son out of the nick.

'The thing is,' I said, 'I might have a bit of work for Derek later on today.'

Marj respected me enough not to say it out loud, because I was Queen, but I could tell that the idea wasn't particularly welcome. She got up and started clanking pots and pans in the sink.

'What kind of work?' said Derek.

'It's being a lookout, not actually doing anything to get yourself in trouble with the law—'

'Oh, I don't think he wants to . . .' Marj cut in, unable to contain herself.

I raised an eyebrow in her direction.

'I mean, I am not gainsaying you, Nell. You know I

respect what you and Jimmy say round here, but he's only just got out . . .'

'It's an opportunity for him,' I said firmly. 'It's a sign of how much we trust this family by asking him. It's not doing the actual villainy, it's just helping keep a lookout and warning those who are taking the biggest risks. The money will be very good – much more than he could earn in a month down the warehouse, and he can still keep a straight job.'

Marj glanced at her carpet slippers.

'Well, if you put it like that . . . I s'pose.'

'I'm interested,' said Derek brightly. 'Definitely.'

'That's good,' I said, smiling at him. 'You'll need to pop across the water to Rubies this afternoon to have a word with Jimmy. He'll be expecting you. And if the warehouse manager can't find you a vacancy, you could always let me know and my Jimmy will go and have a word in his ear. It's amazing what opportunities can open up for you.'

Marj pursed her lips but didn't say any more. She knew when she was outranked.

'I might need a few of my best girls to help out, too,' I said, turning to Em. 'How do you fancy doing something a bit more exciting than hoisting for a change?'

'Oooh,' said Em, twirling one of her blonde curls around her fingers. 'I've always fancied myself with a big bag of swag slung over my shoulder. I reckon I'd make a great bank robber.'

She broke into a fit of giggles. She was game for anything, standing barely five foot three, but an absolute gem of a girl, with the heart of a lion as far as breaking the law was concerned.

'I've always said, it's best not to let the fellas have all the fun.' I laughed. 'Times are changing. There's no rules that say women can't get involved, and it's a massive bit of work if we can pull it off. I was hoping you'll get Patsy on board for us, as I need her to help do some of the heavy lifting. We're planning it for this evening.'

Em's eyes gleamed with excitement.

'You might even say, it's going to be pure gold,' I added.

I took out another ten-pound note and offered it to Derek, who accepted it as if he'd just been handed the crown jewels.

'Not a word to anyone, but you're working for Jimmy now,' I said, ignoring the pleading look in Marj's eyes.

She was his mum, but I was the Queen round here, and she knew there was no arguing with that.

Chapter Ten

ZOE

Soho, January 1957

My whole world had changed overnight. It didn't matter that I was waking up in a disused air raid shelter – I felt like a princess, because of me and Jimmy.

It was my first time, but knew I wanted more.

I was already planning ways of letting Jimmy know that I thought he was special, so that we might get together in that room above the spieler again. Maud wanted me to drive a wedge between him and Nell, and the fact that they weren't married made everything feel that bit easier. But I'd enjoyed being with him so much, I was hatching some plans of my own.

Nell was foolish enough not to have made him walk her up the aisle, wasn't she? I mean, he was a wealthy, successful bloke, and I had a space on the third finger of my left hand. I wanted a better life, and maybe, just maybe, he was the man who was going to provide that for me. I'd be happy to work hard – I wasn't expecting everything to be handed to me on a plate – but I'd already shown I was a good dancer with a career ahead of me, and he seemed to like that.

Maybe he'd just grown tired of Nell and wanted someone younger, with fewer worries and a bit less attitude? She did seem like a bit of a ball-breaker. I'd realised what men like

Jimmy needed to make them happy, and I was prepared to give him whatever he wanted because I enjoyed it. After the way we were together, I could feel myself falling for him. And if that meant my life got better along the way, where was the harm in that?

He'd whispered such sweet things about me, how beautiful I was, and he was so gentle with me, there was no question of him taking advantage of me. I wanted him.

Nell was older, tough and more experienced, and they had history together, but a girl like me . . . Well, I was young and pretty and easy-going. So, why wouldn't he want to spend more time with me?

'Penny for your thoughts, daydreamer,' said Rose, as I lay in bed, grinning like a fool.

'Oh, nothing,' I lied. 'I'm just pleased with how the dance went. It was so exciting to be on stage and hear all that applause.'

'Well, don't get too used to it,' she scoffed. 'Maud won't like it if she thinks you're enjoying yourself too much. Just play it down a bit, for your own sake.'

I wiped the smile off my face, with some difficulty.

I murmured. 'Is everything alright after the way she tore a strip off you yesterday?'

Maud in a bad mood was properly terrifying.

Rose stifled a laugh. 'Oh, she'll forget about it in time. I had a good day dipping around Covent Garden, lots of wallets and a few silk hankies.'

She lowered her voice. 'But I ain't giving up on seeing Errol.'

'Not even after how angry she got?'

'Sometimes when you love someone, you've got to take risks,' she said.

I knew exactly what she meant, but I couldn't tell her

– not about me and Jimmy.

'Do you love him?'

I sat up and we put our heads together, so that the other Piccadilly Commandos couldn't overhear us. They were a right bunch of earwigs.

She blushed. 'We've had a few moments together, if you know what I mean. And he swears he loves me and is making plans for us to be together when he gets enough money from the club.'

'Maud will never allow it,' I said flatly.

'There are parts of London she don't ever go,' she whispered. 'Notting Hill, where Errol and his mates live, isn't her manor. But us being together over there is a long way off. Meanwhile, I just try to see him around Soho when I can. And anyway, she's been off with a bee in her bonnet, chasing after some grubby reporter over in the East End, from what David told me. So she's too busy to bother about us at the moment.'

'What do you mean?'

'Oh, she's after the bloke who wrote that story in the newspaper about the club bosses the other day. She got David to help her track him down over in some pub in Petticoat Lane, and it must have been important because she gave him her best gold fob watch as a reward for finding him.'

'But why?'

Rose shifted uncomfortably and her eyes narrowed.

'Why do you need to know? Stop asking so many questions, Zoe. You're new here, remember? Maud don't like people poking around in her business.'

'I'm sorry,' I said. 'I didn't mean to be nosy . . .'

I just couldn't help wondering why it was that Maud hated Nell so much.

'What about you and that fella, Vinnie?' said Rose, changing the subject.

I shrugged. 'Turns out he wasn't very nice to me.'

'What do you mean?' said Rose. 'I thought he was sweet on you. The way you were dancing together, you lit up the whole club! So, what happened?'

'He just got sort of jealous last night about me performing in Rubies, and when I was leaving, he put his hands all over me in a way I didn't very much appreciate.'

That was putting it mildly. I still felt sick about what he'd done. I just didn't understand why he'd flipped his lid like that.

'Fellas can get all chippy about their birds,' she said. 'Sometimes it's a way of showing how much they care. They're idiots, 'cause they just can't say how they really feel.'

Vinnie had left me in no doubt about that, but the strange thing was, I felt guilty, as if I had been the one who had let him down, not the other way around. I pushed that thought away.

I was already planning what I was going to say to Maud, and I had decided not to mention Vinnie, or the truth about Jimmy and me. I would just make out that things were progressing nicely, Jimmy had flirted with me and made plans for us to have a quiet drink together when Nell's back was turned. That would keep her happy. Maud wasn't the only one who could play games with people. I'd show her that, for sure.

I looked around the Underworld, but Maud was nowhere to be seen.

'Did she come home last night?' I asked.

'Nah,' said Rose. 'She must have stayed over in the East End. And while the cat's away, the mice will play!'

She started pulling on her clothes and smoothing her hair down.

'Errol's invited me to a boxing match this afternoon in Solomon's Gym off Great Windmill Street. All the regular faces will be there. Do you want to come? We can hop into Marshall Street for a quick bath first, to freshen up. I want to look my best, and it ain't easy, living in this fleapit.'

'Love to,' I said.

There was a chance that Jimmy might turn up, and that thought gave me butterflies.

I climbed down from the bunk and pulled on my clothes.

Rose looked at me for a moment.

'You seem different – happier than yesterday. Soho suits you, girl!'

That made me laugh.

'It's probably just the dancing. It's put some colour back in my cheeks and made me feel alive again.'

That was a lie – and the first of many I'd tell, but I'd already decided that my secrets were worth keeping if it meant I could spend time with Jimmy, the man who'd stolen my heart one night in Soho.

A crowd was already gathering outside Solomon's Gym when we arrived.

Smartly dressed blokes were jostling to get in, with bookies taking bets left, right and centre. I got the impression that in Soho, they'd lay money on anything that had a pulse. Girls our age let them push past, out of respect.

We paid a penny each to get in, and as we surged through the double doors into a room with a boxing ring in the middle of it, I was hit by the smell of stale sweat mixed with the fug of cigarette smoke. There was a sense of excitement and the hum of so many people chattering in a small space, with rows of us crammed in around the ring. I'd never seen a boxing match before – not a real one, anyway. There were the usual fist fights in my street in Limehouse, when boys would scrap with each other to settle scores, and I once saw a couple of housewives clobbering each other with their rolling pins when they'd fallen out, but I don't suppose that counted, really, although it was quite entertaining.

A big fella with his black hair swept to one side, like a thatch, rang a bell as we took our seats, and a cheer went up. He had a cigar clamped between his teeth, but somehow managed to address the crowd.

'Welcome to Solomon's Gym, the most prestigious boxing establishment in the city! We're offering you the very best of London's young sporting talent and we'd appreciate you giving them your full support today. I thank you!' The way he said it, through his teeth, sounded like '*ithangew*', and that set me off in a fit of giggles.

A bunch of lads strutted out into the crowd, stripped to the waist, wearing shorts and soft boots laced up to their calves, with their hands encased in boxing gloves. They were already glistening with sweat, as if they'd been sparring, and a couple of them were nursing cuts and bruises. In the middle of them, glowering, was Vinnie's brother Victor, with blood congealing in a cut on his lip. And at the back of the line, without a scratch on him, standing a head taller than the rest, was Errol.

'Oh, ain't he gorgeous,' whispered Rose, giving him a wave.

He nodded in her direction and blew her a kiss, before clambering through the ropes into the ring.

My stomach lurched as I scoured the room for any sign of Vinnie, but I couldn't spot him anywhere. Rose dug her hands into her pockets and pulled out a packet of Parma violet sweets, offering me one. I popped it into my mouth and tried to ignore the sick feeling I got every time I thought of Vinnie. He had a physical effect on me. My legs went weak, and my heart started to beat faster. I tried to shake it off, but when Victor got into the ring with Errol, he looked so like his twin, that only made it worse.

A hush fell over the room before the fight began, because the doors were pushed open again and a couple walked in. All heads turned to stare. It was Jimmy, wearing the most razor-sharp suit and polished shoes, with Nell on his arm, looking like they owned the place, because, let's face it, they probably did.

I wanted to spit in her eye for being with him, but more so when she brushed past me, giving me a smug little smile of recognition, which put me in my place. I opened my mouth to speak but no words came out. And that was when it happened.

Jimmy looked through me, like I was nothing to him.

Maybe it was just to hide the fact that we'd spent the night in each other's arms, or maybe it was because they were a couple, no matter what Maud had said. I was just his bit on the side, another dancer who he'd got his leg over with. The way he looked at Nell as if she was his whole world when he showed her to her seat made me feel so worthless, small and stupid. All my daydreams about us walking up the aisle together and living happily ever after vanished into thin air.

Rose nudged me in the ribs.

'Errol's about to fight. Come on, Zoe, we're supposed to be rooting for him!'

''Course I am!' I said, fighting back tears.

The bell rang for round one, and the pair of them

squared up to each other for a split second before they were on their toes, flinging punches. Victor was more determined, but Errol was lighter on his feet, so that Victor only seemed to give him a glancing blow now and again. People were cheering and shouting at them both: 'Come on, stop dancing and fight!'

That seemed to annoy Victor, who got more frustrated and lost focus. Errol caught him with a punch, right under his jaw, sending him flying into the ropes. The referee stopped the fight for a moment or two, while Victor spat blood onto the canvas.

That was when my heart skipped a beat, because Vinnie strolled in, cool as a cucumber, carrying the most enormous bunch of red roses.

And he was heading in my direction.

'I've been looking for you all over Soho, Angel,' he said, presenting me with the blooms, as Rose squealed with excitement. 'I wanted to apologise for everything I said and did last night. I was a total idiot, a fool. I was drunk and stupid and jealous. I don't know what came over me. Please, please forgive me.'

I froze. My heart was pounding, and blood was rushing in my ears. He smiled at me. Then I blushed as red as the flowers.

'Oh, Vinnie, you were bang out of order,' I began, falteringly. 'It isn't that easy to forget what happened.'

He looked crestfallen.

'Don't be so hard on him, Zoe,' said Rose, pouting at me. 'He's only gone and bought you the biggest bunch of roses I've ever laid eyes on! That's got to count for something, ain't it?'

'I'm sorry, Angel, truly. I showed you no respect and took a liberty,' he said shamefacedly. 'It will never happen again. I want to show you who I really am, if only you'll give me a second chance.'

He was so full of remorse, I didn't know what to say. I felt flustered and embarrassed by it, to be honest. On the other side of the ring, I spied Jimmy, his eyes boring into mine. He was bristling with barely suppressed rage because I was speaking to Vinnie.

That was enough to make my mind up.

'You're right, Rose.'

I accepted the flowers and gave Vinnie a peck on the cheek, just to show Jimmy that he didn't own me. Who did he think he was, to waltz in here with Nell after what we'd done, and not even give me a smile or say hello?

'It was all a silly misunderstanding, wasn't it?'

'That's right, Angel,' said Vinnie. 'I promise I'll treat you right. I want to take you out to dinner and dancing, and show you that I know how to behave properly . . . if you'll give me a second chance?'

His eyes twinkled with anticipation. I could already picture us, laughing together as we danced in some of the top nightclubs. Besides, it would drive Jimmy up the wall, which was a bonus. Maybe by making Jimmy a bit jealous, he'd be more prepared to treat me with the respect that I deserved. And who knows where that might lead? I was hedging my bets by stringing them both along. It was fun because it made me feel kind of powerful, like a real woman, who was desired by men. It was just like Alma had told me – men are only after one thing, and we have something they want. So, they could bloody well pay for it and dance to my tune.

'I'd love that,' I said, staring in Jimmy's direction. He had a face like someone had just died.

The clamour of cheers for the boxing match started up

again as Errol and Victor set to against each other, in a flurry of punches.

'Now, if you'll excuse me a minute, I just need to give my brother a bit of a gee,' said Vinnie, heading to the front of the ring.

I watched him as he drew closer to the side of the ring, so that Victor could hear him. Vinnie's face changed to a determined look as he said something to his brother. In that moment, Victor was filled with renewed energy, as if someone had just plugged him into the mains. He flew at Errol, raining punches to his body and his face, driving forward with such power that Errol lost his footing.

The audience gasped.

Victor didn't stop. He belted Errol so hard that he fell over, and then he was down and still Victor kept going, pummelling his face, until blood was spurting from Errol's broken nose.

The referee rang the bell to end the fight and stood over them, shouting to halt the bout, but Victor didn't hear him, and he continued raining blows, like he was possessed. A hush fell over the room and Rose screamed.

Vinnie leaped between the ropes and grabbed hold of his brother, pulling him off Errol, who lay there with his eyes closed, his face a bloody mess.

Vinnie raised his brother's arms aloft.

'The winner! Victor Graveney!'

Victor stumbled a bit, as if he was just coming round from some kind of stupor, then he relaxed and smiled, lapping up the adulation.

That was when the applause started, and everybody cheered. Everyone except me and Rose. Tears were rolling down her face.

'Oh my God, he's just about killed him!' she mouthed to me.

Rose lunged forward, to try to climb into the ring to help Errol, but I stopped her. Errol was surrounded by some of the other competitors, who were pulling him to his feet, wiping the blood from his face with a white towel which was rapidly turning scarlet.

'You can't go in there to help him, Rose,' I said. 'Let them look after him, they know what's best. He wouldn't want you making a fuss in front of his mates either.'

She slumped against me, crying softly.

The boxing promoter stepped into the ring and clapped Victor on the back. Vinnie stood beside him, grinning like the Cheshire Cat.

'We may have a future champion in our midst by the looks of it!' he cried. 'That was a fierce fight. But to the victor, the spoils!'

He produced a crisp pound note and gave it to Victor.

'Now, on to the next match, ladies and gentlemen.'

He glanced over towards me and Rose as we were getting up to go.

'And please, ladies, if you are expecting a tea party or a mothers' meeting, you've come to the wrong place. Boxing is a man's sport.'

A ripple of laughter ran through the crowd as the promoter chimed, 'Ithangew!'

Chapter Eleven

NELL

Soho, January 1957

I'm no fan of boxing matches, but I went along to Solomon's Gym with Jimmy for the sake of keeping up appearances on our manor. Some of our best fellas were too lily-livered to come in on Jimmy's bit of villainy he had in the offing, and it was more important than ever for us to put on a united front.

But when that young thug Victor Graveney beat the hell out of one of the guys from the jazz club up the road, I must admit I nearly lost my breakfast. It was more like a blood sport. I don't know what got into him, but the way his twin Vinnie spoke to him had given him the strength of ten men.

Jimmy was bothered by it, too, in a way I hadn't expected, because I knew he was no stranger to spilling the claret. He watched in silence, his jaw clenched, and his hands clasped firmly together. To anyone in the crowd, it would have looked as if he was just concentrating on the fight, but I knew something was up.

'What's the matter?' I whispered. 'It's only a boxing match, Jim. You look like you've been shot.'

'It's those bloody upstart Graveneys,' he muttered. 'They're trouble. And that Victor looks like he's got a screw loose, if you ask me.'

'They're just a pair of bombsite kids trying to fight their way up from the streets,' I said, patting him on the knee.

I'd seen them around Soho, wearing their silly drainpipe trousers with their crêpe-soled shoes and sporting their hair in ridiculous quiffs, with the rest of the Teddy boys in their gang. They wore clothes that were so different from everyone else because they wanted to stand out, to be noticed, but that was enough to give the pinstripe suit and bowler hat brigade heart failure. Frankly, having grown up during the war, when life was all about rations and making do and mending, who could blame them for wanting to push against authority and be different from their dads and uncles? And so what if they liked loud rock and roll music? It wasn't a crime.

I thought they looked a bit daft with their drapey jackets, but that was about the sum of it. They'd occasionally give each other a clump with a bike chain, or scrap over a girl, but they were still wet behind the ears. They were trying to make something of themselves, just like we did when we were their age. I found it funny, if anything, like watching puppies biting each other in a play fight. Victor was overstepping the mark in the boxing ring, but maybe they'd had unfinished business with each other. That's what I reckoned.

'The Graveneys are more than just a couple of no-good kids, Nell,' he said, fixing me with his piercing blue eyes. 'I think they're a bloody menace and I don't want them getting above themselves.'

'Blimey, Jim,' I whispered. 'Anyone would think you were dealing with a pair of Mr Bigs, rather than a couple of snotty-nosed tearaways from Notting Hill. What have they done to rattle your cage, then?'

He didn't answer, but he wasn't really watching what was going on in the ring any more. He was far more interested in ogling that new little dancer of mine, Zoe, and her mate as they pushed their way through the crowd and out of the club.

Call it a woman's intuition if you like, but I made a mental note to keep a closer eye on Zoe in the future.

Going hoisting came as such a relief after all that blokes' stuff in Solomon's Gym that I found myself walking with a bit of a spring in my step.

Me and my girls from the Forty Thieves were plotting to make a real afternoon of it in all the big West End stores – Selfridges, Gamages, Marshall and Snelgrove, and a quick trip to some of the furriers down Bond Street if we had time, before we met Jimmy and his fellas for their bit of work. I fancied picking up something for Ruby as a treat – perhaps some mittens and a nice scarf to keep her warm.

Of all the shops I'd hoisted in, Gamages on High Holborn was my favourite because it was always a bit chaotic, with lots of clothes rails crammed tightly together, dark corners, staircases and dozy assistants. We always made rich pickings in there. Years ago, I was first caught by a great big lump of a store detective from Gamages called the Hunter and that sent me for a spell in Holloway. The real person behind it all was Alice Diamond, the old Queen of Thieves. I repaid the favour and put her inside by conning her into getting even with her hated brother, the gang boss Billy Sullivan, by striping him one with her razor blade when there were cozzers waiting to pounce on the pair of them. It was priceless. And she hasn't been heard from on my manor since.

I took my time wandering up through Soho, towards Holborn, stopping to gaze in the window of a few jeweller's shops that caught my eye. Maybe it was a sixth sense, or perhaps it was the fact I'd had my picture splashed all over the front page of the *London Evening News*, but I just got the feeling I was being followed. I stopped at a bakery store and a man in a well-cut Italian suit sidled up beside me, taking a peculiar interest in some iced buns. He was dressed like a Chap – one of the fellas about Soho – but his shoes gave him away. They weren't hand-made and they had crêpe soles – the kind that are good for sneaking up on people. The kind that only a cozzer would wear.

I turned to face him and smiled. He coloured up, a blush rising to the roots of his blond hair. He was fresh-faced, probably not long out of university, and I could tell his hands had never done a hard day's graft, which was another telltale sign that he wasn't really a gangland face.

'Well,' I said, turning to go, 'I'm watching my figure, so I'm not going in there today.'

I hurried off down the street until I reached a pub on the corner. When I glanced back over my shoulder, he pretended to be peering at a bookshop. I marched up to the bar, paid for a port and lemon and sat down to drink it, taking my time. I'd only been in there five minutes when his eager little face appeared at the other end of the bar, and he got himself a pint of bitter, gazing at me as he took a sip.

He wasn't even disguising the fact that he was on my tail. Maybe that was part of Munro's plan – to be a total pain in the neck with his ghost squad boys, to wear us all down and make life impossible. Well, I'd had just about enough.

A gaggle of half a dozen office girls came in and I followed them as they went off to the ladies, hooting with laughter at some shared joke. Once we were in there, I opened my handbag and pulled out my favourite long black wig and a pair of horn-rimmed glasses, while they looked on in astonishment. I liked to carry disguises for hoisting, in case of emergencies.

'How d'you fancy a lovely new fur?' I said, pulling on the wig and taking off my coat. It was beautiful – a sable I'd pinched a few weeks ago from Selfridges.

The office girls couldn't believe what I was offering them.

'Just give me your coat, and you can take mine,' I said, as the tallest shrugged off her hound's-tooth woollen coat to try on the fur that was worth at least six months' wages to her. 'But one of you has got to stay behind here for the next ten minutes or so, wearing it, while I slip outside with the rest of you and into the street. There's a bloke at the bar who's hassling me, and I need to get away from him. Got it?'

'Is it a real fur?' said one of them, who was skinny as a waif, with a swishy skirt and petticoats that almost drowned her.

I gave her one of my steely looks and flashed my diamond rings in her direction.

'Do I look like a woman who'd wear a fake fur?'

Her mate cooed as she felt the softness of the fur, twirling around as she admired herself in the mirror above the sink.

'It's real. It feels like heaven!'

Disguise was my best friend. In fact, it took Em and Patsy a few moments to work out who I was when I tapped on the window of the Bentley, which was parked outside the store with its engine running.

Laura, one of the Partridge twins, was sitting behind the wheel, while her sister Madeline was tucked up in the back with Patsy and Em. They'd driven the car up from my lock-up in the Borough. Back in the old days, we'd always have a fella as a wheelman, but I didn't like men getting involved in our operation. Once you'd got the hang of it, driving was easy, even if Jimmy and his mob did find it hilarious to see a bird in charge of a car. I'd have them laughing on the other side of their faces later, when I became their gang's getaway driver for the night.

'Afternoon, ladies,' I said, banging on the window and making Patsy jump. 'What's going on 'ere, then?'

'Oh, Jesus, Mary and Joseph, I could have walked past you in the street and not recognised you, Nell!' She hooted. 'You just about frightened the life out of me. What's with the hair?'

'I'm not taking any chances after that story in the paper,' I said, pulling my coat collar closer around me, against the cold. 'Now, shall we go shopping?'

Patsy, Em and Madeline climbed out, looking for all the world like they were wealthy housewives from Mayfair, in their furs and high heels. I gave a nod of approval.

'Em tells me we're branching out into a proper bit of work later,' said Patsy. 'You can count me in. I've always fancied buying myself a caravan down in Margate for the holidays.'

I gave her a little squeeze of appreciation.

'That's the best thing about the Forty Thieves,' I said, as we pushed open the shop doors. 'I can always rely on my girls. And you know I will never let you down.'

We headed up to the third floor, to start hoisting in ladieswear, where the shop assistants were an idle bunch. By the mid-afternoon, some of them were known to have a quick doze in the store cupboard, and those on the shop floor were usually so bored that they'd chat to one another and ignore the customers.

Em pointed out a rail full of huge, frothy petticoats, the kind the youngsters were so keen on for their dances. True to form, there was a gaggle of girls rifling through them. I elbowed a few of them out of the way as I sidled up, while Em screened me from view. I held one petticoat up above the rail, while I was busy snatching others off the hangers with my free hand, out of the line of sight of the shop assistant, who was chewing her fingernails. They found their way into my carpet bag, and while Em kept the shop assistant busy showing her some silk blouses, I headed off to the stairwell, where I met Patsy.

She was carrying the exact same carpet bag as me and we swapped, and she headed off downstairs to deposit my loot in the Bentley before returning to the store. It was one of the oldest tricks in the game because it was one of the most reliable.

From there, I sauntered over to the furs, which always made my heart beat a little faster. I grew up working in a fur factory, so I was no stranger to the touch and feel of the pelts when I started out as a hoister. And I knew how valuable they were. To every woman on my manor, having a decent fur coat, or at least a mink stole, was a matter of honour. It didn't matter how you came by that fur – once you'd put it on and felt the softness and warmth, there was no going back.

Who in their right mind wanted to shiver through a London winter in a thin woollen coat when you could be swathed in fur? It didn't matter that you only lived in a tenement or a two-up, two-down row of terraces. When you had your fur on, you felt like you were somebody special.

It was even more tempting if me and my girls could provide it for you at a decent price, or with weekly repayments that didn't involve sky-high interest. Oh, I hated moneylenders with a passion. I'd seen the damage they could do to people, and I made a point of never charging interest on repayments because that was just punishing people for being poor.

Em was already busy rolling a beautiful sable on the hanger by the time I got there. She had it rolled in a tight little bundle and was clouting it – shoving it down the waistband of her skirt and into her hoister's drawers, while she peered over the top of the clothes rail.

You couldn't leave the hangers behind, because that was a dead giveaway that stock had gone walkabout. The assistant came over to see what we were up to. She was young, maybe seventeen, and she had her hair pulled up in a fashionable ponytail. I fixed her with my most glacial stare, and she paused and pretended to tidy up a heap of gloves, before retreating to the safety of her counter.

'Three seconds,' said Em, with a grin. 'I think you might be losing your touch, Nell.'

I loved pretending to be a haughty posh woman, giving the impression that I'd tear a strip off any assistant who bothered me. I'd got it down to a fine art, raising an eyebrow and scowling at them, or tutting loudly. It had been enough to stop this young girl in her tracks.

'Nonsense!' I laughed. 'It only took her two to change her mind. You're counting it all wrong.'

Em picked up a fox-fur jacket and carried it over to the changing room, with the assistant hot on her heels. That gave me a chance to roll a mink coat and shove it down my hoister's drawers. They were silk, because it was easier to slide stolen goods down them, and they were elasticated at the knee so that nothing fell out while you were leaving the shop.

The fashion for swing coats was a real bonus for us hoisters, because it made it easier to hide what we were carrying. Some days I was laden down with stuff when I left a shop. People had started calling us the Forty Elephants because of the way we looked, lumbering along with furs down our bloomers – that, and the fact that we mostly came from around the Elephant and Castle.

But now we were about to become more than just shop-lifters. I liked the idea of showing the blokes we could be as good as them at their own game. Don't get me wrong, we were earning a nice living, but me and the girls all liked to live the high life. What with that and the club, I didn't have much put by for a rainy day.

I was beginning to wonder whether Jimmy was right about us earning enough to get out of gangland if we needed to, especially with the likes of Munro and his mob on our tail. If I was going to have another baby, I wanted to be secure – to know that I could provide for it, no matter what.

I was pondering that, watching Em fussing around in front of a mirror, pretending to admire herself in the fox fur to give me time to get away, when I spied Patsy, looking flustered in the doorway. She was waving a newspaper at me.

I smiled through gritted teeth and gave her a wave of recognition. Whatever she had to say, I didn't understand why it couldn't wait until we were safely in the car. She was putting our hoisting mission in jeopardy.

But then, as I got closer, I realised there was a massive picture of me on the front page.

And the headline screamed 'WIFE OF CRIME!'

The car engine thrummed as we sat huddled in the back of the Bentley, with the newspaper spread out on our laps.

'Duncan Swift is dead meat,' I said coldly, surveying the page before me.

My whole life had been laid bare for the world to see: things I was ashamed of; things that kept me awake at night. Everything about me and Jimmy and the mistakes we'd made when we were younger was on the front page of the *London Evening News*. It was bad enough that I'd lived it, but now it was all there again in black and white, chewed over and spat out by that stinking hack Duncan Swift to make a story. I felt vomit rising in my throat and wound the window down, breathing in a blast of freezing air.

Soho's Queen of Clubs, Nell Kane, has a sordid past which is at odds with her glamorous existence rubbing shoulders with film stars at her night spot, it can be revealed today. She adores fine clothes and jewels, and is often seen in the company of film stars including the beautiful Diana Durbidge.

But behind all the glitz and the glamour is a tawdry tale of a reckless young woman who broke the law and turned her back on motherhood. Nell Kane gave birth while serving time in Holloway Jail for theft in the late 1940s. The father of that baby boy was none other than fearsome gangland boss Jimmy Feeney.

It seems jailbird Nell and the young thug Jimmy "The Razor" were more bothered about their criminal pursuits than behaving like decent folk. For Nell gave the baby away without a second thought.

One source, who did not wish to be named, said: "She couldn't wait to get rid of that child because she felt being a mother would get in the way of her ambitions."

And what ambitions might those be, dear reader?

I have it on very good authority that her lifestyle is funded in the most unconventional manner, and she is no stranger to the company of criminals. Her past prison sentence is proof enough of that!

"Jimmy and Nell have a little girl, Ruby, who they are raising despite the fact they are not married," said the source. "I don't think Ruby has any idea about her baby brother, who is being raised by decent folk, who took him in out of the goodness of their hearts." But as far as Jimmy and Nell are concerned, you have got to wonder what kind of parents would keep one child and give the other away, haven't you? It's all just another chapter in the seedy life of the Wife of Crime!

'You've been stitched up,' said Patsy, lighting up a smoke. 'They've gone for all your dirty laundry, ain't they? First Jimmy, now you. It just ain't your week.'

Madeline and Laura gazed straight ahead, not daring to speak, and Em put her arm around me in sympathy. Yes, I'd given my baby boy away, but not in the way that the newspaper portrayed it. I couldn't argue with the fact that I'd done time in Holloway for theft, and everyone knew of Jimmy's violent past – that was how he'd built his reputation as the King of Soho. But they'd made us sound like we didn't care about our own flesh and blood, and nothing could be further from the truth.

All the wind had been taken out of my sails. Suddenly, I was seventeen again, standing in the governor's office at Holloway Prison, beside a posh couple who were offering my baby Joseph a loving home, knowing that I didn't have a choice, because I was an unmarried mother from a London slum. The governor, the prison matron and that couple had all the power. I knew I couldn't keep my baby – the governor had made that clear – and I signed the adoption papers. I had regretted it every day since, especially on his birthday, when I would go for a long walk by the Thames on my own and cry until my eyes were sore.

Back then, I hadn't believed Jimmy when he said he wanted to marry me and look after me and the baby. He had offered; he even got down on one knee and proposed properly with a ring and everything, but I'd rejected him and then I'd ended up behind bars. Matters were taken out of my hands. I suppose I didn't believe he really wanted to marry me, not then, partly because Jimmy was a bit of a Jack the lad, and mostly because of Alice Diamond and the pack of lies she'd spun me. She had a lot of answer for, that evil cow, but I'd got my own back on her in the end. That didn't make losing Joseph any easier, but it was the best I could hope for.

'Well, what are you going to do?' said Patsy, eyeing me up coolly.

Being the leader of the gang meant I couldn't show weakness, not even to my deputy. There was no question of crying or running away to lick my wounds. A knot of rage tightened in my chest. It was a feeling I knew well. There were times when being Queen meant being tougher than any bloke who dared to cross me.

'I'm going to get even,' I said, digging my hands into my coat pocket, feeling my chiv, wrapped in a lace handkerchief.

I knew who was going to get acquainted with that when I finally caught up with him. And that was if Jimmy didn't get there first – in which case there probably wouldn't be much left for me to stripe.

Patsy nodded, as if that satisfied her.

'But first,' I said, 'we are going to pull off the biggest robbery London has ever seen.'

★

We drove in silence to Jimmy's lock-up under the railway arches around the back of Euston Station, where his fellas were already getting the vans ready for the raid.

I knew by the look on his face that he'd read the headlines. He pulled me into his arms, and I choked back tears.

'Stay strong, princess' he whispered. 'We are going to be richer than you could ever imagine by tomorrow morning, and then we can start cracking heads together in Fleet Street.'

'I won't let you down, Jimmy,' I replied, feeling the softness of his jacket against my cheek as I leaned on him for strength.

Em climbed out of the car with Patsy and went over to her brother, Derek. He was hanging around with a couple of Jimmy's men, looking pleased as Punch with himself. They were laughing and joking, teasing him about this being his first proper job.

'It's all stuff they don't teach you about in Borstal,' said Jimmy's right-hand man, Albert Rossi. He leaned over and fastened the top button of Derek's shirt. 'You need to look smart, son, if you are going to be one of us – remember that.'

Albert was from an Italian family who had helped run Soho before the war, but half of them got interned once the fighting started, and what was left after that was a spent force. But not Albert – he had managed to carve his niche on the racetracks and support Jimmy in his clubs. He always had a smile on his face and was known for smoothing things over when there were spats between rival factions, which led some to call him the United Nations of Soho. But the truth was, Albert could be just as vicious as my

Jimmy when he needed to be. The only difference was he never raised his voice and he didn't like getting blood on his shoes.

We went into the lock-up, where Jimmy briefed us all about how it was going to work. There were three identical vans; I was driving one, Albert would take another, and one of his men, Peter, would be in the third.

'The KLM Airlines company is expecting a big delivery of gold this evening at their offices in Jockey's Fields,' he began. 'We've shadowed them on a previous delivery, and there's usually only the driver and one bloke in the back to unload. Albert will come in at the top end of the street to block it with his van and take care of the driver and anyone else who tries to get in the way, while Nell will already be waiting for us. Peter will follow the KLM van and block the other end of the street.'

He turned to me.

'You'll be parked up a few yards down from the KLM office, with me, Em and Patsy in the back. When the delivery van drops his tailboard, you'll have to reverse fast, right up to the back of the van. He won't be expecting that. We'll jump out and get the bullion loaded on to our van while you keep the engine running. Peter will move his van out of your way at the crucial moment so you can get away.'

'What about the bloke in the back of the KLM van guarding the gold?' said Derek, scratching his head. 'Won't he try something?'

Jimmy pulled open his jacket and revealed a revolver.

'This should take care of it. We don't want any have-a-go heroes, do we? No one needs to get hurt – it's just about being sensible, and I'll explain that to him. But if I have to, I will give him a clump just to keep him quiet.'

Derek nodded.

'And, Derek, your job is to get up the other end of the street from Albert's van and keep a lookout. If anyone's coming, you give me a wolf whistle or just shout, and I will take care of it.'

Jimmy threw everyone knitted balaclavas.

'I'm not putting that on!' said Em, pulling a pair of stockings she'd just nicked from Gamages out of her pocket. She gave one to Patsy and they pulled them on over their faces, giggling their heads off. They looked such a pair of daft ha'porths.

'I suppose that counts as a disguise,' he said to them.

I took my black wig out of my handbag and plonked it on my head.

'If it's good enough for the walkers in the West End stores, it's good enough for this blag,' I said, tucking some stray strands of my blonde hair out of sight.

Jimmy laughed. 'I quite fancy you with dark hair, Nell.'

I blew him a kiss.

Albert was grinning from ear to ear.

'It's a great plan, Jim.'

'We'll all meet back here,' said Jimmy, 'and Albert and Peter will drive the gold up to the barn in Bedfordshire, sharpish. Then it's happy days because we will all get paid – and handsomely.'

'Got it,' said Patsy. 'Sounds sweet.'

Jimmy straightened his tie, beaming at me. It was a simple job, clever and lucrative, with the minimum of fuss and no need for violence, if the lorry driver and his mate saw sense. His other fellas were fools for not being game enough to come in on it.

'It's not got the same hallmarks as the Friday Gang,' he said, 'which is all about the wages snatch and coshing people, so I'm hoping the cozzers might look elsewhere to start with, which should buy us some extra time. But it's important for you and me to be seen in the club as soon as we can, to keep up appearances and to hold our nerve, even if Munro pays us a visit.'

'Lou and Alma and the girls will give us an alibi, there's no worry about that,' I said, with a laugh. 'In fact, other than the boxing match, I don't think we set foot outside Rubies, did we?'

Half an hour later, I was gripping the steering wheel, as I waited for the bullion van to show up. The minutes ticked by. I wound the window down to get some air, and I could hear the faint hiss of the gas lamps in the gloomy street. A man wobbled past on a bicycle, and a couple walked briskly in the evening air, muffled up against the cold, their footsteps echoing on the pavement. After that, the street was deserted, which was perfect for our plan. I only hoped it would stay that way, but Jimmy had reassured me it was a quiet side road.

I glanced at my watch, feeling butterflies in my stomach. This was nothing like hoisting. I began to wonder if I was up to it, but I couldn't let Jimmy down – not now. A clock chimed five, which was right when the delivery van was due to arrive.

Then I saw the van coming down the road towards me, with Peter following close behind in his lorry. The delivery van pulled past me and slowly drew to a halt a few yards away. Meanwhile, in the wing mirror, I saw Albert's van appearing at the other end of the street. It stopped suddenly at a crazy angle, as if he'd been trying to turn it and the engine had stalled. I spied Derek sauntering along with his hands in his pockets, looking like he hadn't a care in the world. We were all in place.

The driver got out and opened the back doors of the lorry. I watched the fella inside lower the tailboard, and when the first of the wooden cases was about to be unloaded, I reversed, hard.

'Oi!' said the driver, leaping out of my path.

I kept the engine running and opened the door and climbed out.

'I'm so sorry, it's all my fault . . .'

Just then, the back doors of my van flew open, and Jimmy leaped across, knocking over the bloke in the back of the delivery lorry. The man gave a shout of protest, but Jimmy opened his jacket, showing him his gun.

'Stay down!'

Albert appeared at the side of the delivery van, grabbing the driver and pinning his arms behind his back before he could stop him. Peter rushed over, climbing up into the delivery lorry to help Jimmy, who was already handing down crates to Patsy and Em, who between them managed to carry them into my lorry.

We'd got about half a dozen loaded in the space of a few minutes, when Derek started running towards us, yelling 'Cozzers!'

Jimmy glanced up at me.

'Get back at the wheel.'

That was when the bloke he'd knocked over got his second wind. He got up and lunged at Jimmy, pulling the revolver from Jimmy's jacket.

Jimmy's reaction was instant. He smacked him, hard, right in the jaw – harder than Victor Graveney had hit his opponent in the boxing ring. I heard the bone in his face crack and the man screamed and fell backwards, blood spurting from his mouth.

The gun flew out of his grasp and landed on the pavement, by Derek's feet. He picked it up.

Albert had kicked the driver where it hurt, and he was doubled over by some railings. Peter scarpered to his van and got the engine started. In seconds, it was careering off down the road, but Albert's vehicle was blocking the way, so he gave the delivery driver another clump for good measure and then ran to his van. They both took off, tyres screeching.

Em and Patsy were already in the back of my van as I clambered into the driver's seat, but Jimmy was still on the pavement as a burly policeman came running towards us, blowing his whistle.

I watched in disbelief, leaning out of the window, as Derek raised the gun. He pointed it at the cozzer, who was no more than six feet away from him.

'Leave it!' shouted Jimmy. 'Let's go!'

'Put that down, sonny,' said the cozzer, moving slowly towards Derek. He was a big bloke with a grey moustache, and he was sweating from the effort of sprinting up the road. 'Put it down, now. Don't be silly.'

There was a thud and the lorry rocked as Jimmy jumped up into the back. He shouted, 'Just give it to him, come on!'

That was when I heard it.

A shot rang out. My blood ran cold.

The policeman crumpled to the pavement, and Derek threw the gun away and ran like hell. In his panic, he ran in the opposite direction, away from us. It was too late to stop him. But in my wing mirror, I could see other cozzers heading towards him. He darted across the road to try to evade them and leaped over some railings.

'Drive!' Jimmy yelled, as more policemen appeared at the other end of the street.

I put my foot down on the accelerator and sped away into the night, my heart pounding, and Em's screams for her little brother filling my ears.

London Evening News

OUTRAGE AS POLICEMAN SHOT BY MASKED GANG IN BULLION ROBBERY

Suspect arrested, gun found, as Prime Minister vows "We will punish culprits."

Special report by Duncan Swift

The streets of London descended into terror and bloodshed last night, when a brave police constable was gunned down as he tried to prevent a half-a-million-pound gold bullion robbery.

The city is reeling from the attack, which has drawn condemnation from the Prime Minister, all sides of the House of Commons, and the top brass at Scotland Yard. It marks a new low in London's growing trend for gangland violence, and the authorities have promised the culprits can expect harsh sentences.

Speaking today from Number 10 Downing Street, the PM praised the courage of PC Stephen Morris, who had served in the force for more than twenty years on his beat in Clerkenwell before he was shot in the leg and wounded by the cowardly gunman. He is currently recovering in a London hospital. His wife told the London Evening News: "Stephen loves his job and was just doing his bit when this thug pointed a gun at him and pulled the trigger. He feels lucky to be alive. I don't know what the world is coming to."

The policeman is believed to have been trying to halt a raid on a KLM delivery van at Jockey's Fields, in which gold worth at least £500,000 was stolen in a daring and carefully planned heist. The van driver and his guard were badly beaten by their attackers, who drove off in three lorries at high speed after ramming and robbing the delivery vehicle. One of the robbers was heard shouting "Just give it to him!" moments before the shot was fired. Police believe the assailant was being encouraged to shoot the officer, in order to secure the getaway.

In a startling development, witnesses say a woman with dark hair and glasses was driving the van, and she had two female accomplices who were masked by stockings who helped steal the gold. The brutal trio are now being hunted by every force in Britain. They were assisted by several male criminals, one of whom was armed. The men assaulted the guard and the driver, who bravely tried to stop the robbery before PC Morris came to their aid and was gunned down. It is believed that a younger man acting as a lookout fired the shot.

"We will leave no stone unturned to bring the perpetrators of this heinous crime to justice,' the Prime Minister said. 'The time has come for those who rule the Underworld to realise that they have gone too far, and no decent society will tolerate such an outrage. They can expect to feel the full force of the law.'

Angry crowds gathered outside Paddington Green Police Station, where suspect Derek Brown, 18, is being held following the robbery. He was captured several streets away after attempting to flee. The weapon was recovered in the gutter about twenty yards from where PC Morris fell. Brown, who has previously spent time in Borstal for theft, is expected to appear before magistrates tomorrow morning.

A source who knows the young man, who lives at Queen's Buildings, Elephant and Castle, said: "His father died a hero in the war, and he'd be spinning in his grave. He went off the rails a few years ago and got mixed up with the wrong sort.

His mother and his sister are no good, if you ask me. They are also to blame for what he's done."

Detective Chief Inspector Walter Munro, head of the force's Flying Squad, told the London Evening News: *"I have a message for communities who are shielding these cowards: Turn them in. And to the gangsters who are behind this: you are not above the law. Your lives are going to get a lot tougher. I will make it my mission to bring you down. You are not the law on these streets, and you are about to find out who is."*

Chapter Twelve

NELL

Elephant and Castle, February 1957

We'd been living on a knife-edge ever since the bullion raid. Jimmy knows how to keep a cool head in a crisis and, together with Albert, he made sure that the gold sped away from his lock-up in Euston and off to a safe house in the countryside, where the smelters got busy. But in the weeks that followed, as the police stepped up the search for the loot and Derek was in custody, our nerves did get the better of us both, and we began backbiting over what had gone wrong.

In the immediate aftermath of the robbery, I had my hands full trying to calm Em down because she was hysterical about her little brother. She sat on a crate in the lock-up, weeping uncontrollably, and she wouldn't let me near her, shouting that me and Jimmy were to blame. Jimmy started looking a bit twitchy about that. In his world, bad things happen to those who can't get a grip of themselves, but she was my responsibility, as one of the Forty Thieves. And I gave him a look that said as much.

Patsy was a complete rock. I knew I could trust her to make Em see sense – that Derek had been foolish and there was no need for him to fire off a shot like that, or even touch the bleeding gun in the first place. But we wouldn't turn our backs on him. In fact, we'd find ways to support him on the inside and make sure his mum was looked after, too.

Jimmy and me managed to put on a show of normality for the inevitable visit from that rat-faced twerp Munro and his men. I could have won an Oscar for my performance that night. They stormed their way in through the doors, to find the dancers sharing a few lovely cocktails with us before the show started.

'Fancy a drink, Detective Chief Inspector?' I chimed, twirling my cherry on a cocktail stick. 'You seem to be in a hurry. Whatever's the matter?'

He gave me a look that could curdle milk.

'As if you don't know!'

They'd already been told by half of Soho that me and Jimmy had been to a boxing match late morning, and Alma and the others stuck to their story that we'd been in the club ever since.

Zoe was particularly enthusiastic, swearing blind that Jimmy had spent ages chatting to her about why she wanted to be a dancer, so he couldn't have been anywhere else. He seemed a bit embarrassed about it. Anyone would have thought she was worried he was about to be arrested and carted down the nick. Lou and me had a good giggle about that when she went off to rehearse her steps, but I could have sworn I detected the faintest hint of a blush creeping up above the collar of Jimmy's white shirt.

'Got yourself quite a fan there, Jim,' I teased.

He didn't laugh at my joke, but then, none of us were in a mood for comedy after that total balls-up by Derek.

Derek's mum Marj was a trickier nut to crack, even more so once the word went round that the cozzers were treating him as a punchbag. The one saving grace to the whole disaster was that the constable he shot had survived.

But the way Marj treated me, you'd have thought I'd made Derek pull the trigger, even though I paid her plenty and made sure that he had the best defence solicitors in London.

To be blunt, I wasn't sure I could rely on her silence, and that worried me.

'We'll pay him a wage for every month he's in prison and you will want for nothing, I promise you. Jimmy will do what he can to make sure he's protected. He's one of Jimmy's men now,' I said, as I stood in her scullery, which felt gloomy, like a morgue.

Em sat silently in the chair by the wireless – the place where Derek used to sit to have a smoke. The teapot was on the table, just as it always was, but I wasn't even offered a cuppa.

Marj looked at me, her face haunted and haggard. She whispered, 'I just wish you'd left him out of it, Nell.'

'I'm sorry, Marj, truly I am, but if he'd stuck to the plan, none of it would have happened.'

'He's just a boy!' she shouted, so loudly it almost made me jump out of my skin. 'The papers say someone told him to shoot the policeman, to let him have it! What on earth were you thinking?'

Em put her hand on her mother's arm.

'That's enough, Mum.'

Marj glared at me, her bottom lip trembling.

'He's just *my* boy . . .'

Em went on, 'You'd better leave it for now, Nell. I'll take care of her.'

'My door is always open to you, Marj,' I said, feeling about as welcome as a snowstorm in July.

Jimmy had been telling Derek to drop the gun, to let the cozzer have it, because we were going to get away from there. He wasn't telling him to shoot. But it was pointless trying to explain that to Marj.

And just when I thought life couldn't get any worse, my Ruby started behaving like a little hooligan.

Oh, I could have belted her one for breaking the corner shop window, and she was surly and rude about it, too, glaring at me like a proper little madam when the shop-keeper marched her home. But I'd always vowed never to lay a finger on her in anger because of my dad and what a vile bully he'd been to me as a kid. That had left scars which ran deep, and I didn't want my girl suffering in the same way.

As she stood there in the hallway, her chin tilted towards me in defiance, I began to worry that she was misbe-having to get attention because me and Jimmy had been so distracted dealing with the fallout from the botched robbery. We'd been raising our voices to each other in a way she'd never heard before. And we'd both been putting in long hours at the club, for the sake of appearances. I'd just expected her to cope with it all, but kids are funny like that, aren't they? They pick up on things and it can make them act out of character. Don't get me wrong, she was no angel, but she'd never been in that kind of trouble before.

Now I had Mr Jones spitting tacks because of what she'd done to his business.

'It's a flaming liberty! I won't have my premises damaged by kids larking about with bricks. Do you hear me? I didn't fight in the war for this.'

I grabbed my purse from the table in the hallway and started counting out ten-pound notes to shut him up.

'You were in the Home Guard, Mr Jones, from what I recall.'

His eyes were bulging out of their sockets.

'There you go,' I said, handing him a wad of cash, with a tight smile.

I knew I was being overly generous, but I didn't want any more bad feeling in the neighbourhood. Not right now.

He stuffed the money in his trouser pocket and turned on his heel, muttering under his breath, 'You lot think you can just run amok round here – well, you can't. Decent folk have had enough of the likes of you.'

On any other occasion, I would have given him a clump, or sent the girls round to have a quiet word with him after hours about the need to find some manners. But this whole situation was about as welcome as a hole in the head, so I was prepared to let it slide. That's the thing with being Queen: you've got to know when to pick your battles.

It didn't sit easily with me, though. There was a change in the air on my manor and I didn't like it one bit. I'd get things back on a better footing, let them all know who was boss, once Derek's trial was over. But for now, I wanted to smooth things over and keep the peace.

'You take care, Mr Jones,' I said, icily, to his departing back. 'And Ruby is very sorry.'

She wasn't. She poked her tongue out at him, the little minx.

Once he'd slammed the front door shut and gone on his way, I turned to her and stood there, with my hands on my hips.

'Well? What have you got to say for yourself?'

I could see there was something going on with her because her eyes were red from crying, but she didn't look remorseful. And she didn't say a word.

I kneeled down beside her, my tone softening.

'Sweetheart, I know things have been difficult indoors lately, but you've got to promise me you won't ever do anything like that again. It's causing headaches we don't need.'

She looked up at me, her eyes blazing with anger.

'I hate you! You gave my brother away!'

A huge pang of guilt hit me, almost knocking me sideways. I'd been praying she'd never find out about Joseph. Nobody round here would dare to breathe a word of the story in the paper, out of respect for me and Jimmy, surely? But now the cat was out of the bag.

'Oh God,' I said, pulling her to me. 'Who told you that?'

'It was my best friend, Maud.'

I rocked back on my heels. I'd had just about enough of this make-believe Maud.

'I suppose she told you to throw a brick as well, did she?'

'Yes!' she cried. 'She did. It was Maud. It was all her idea. She said it would make me feel better.'

'You can tell me the truth, Ruby,' I said. 'I won't be angry. I need to explain things to you properly, but you've got to start by coming clean about who has been filling your head with all this stuff, and why you threw that brick. And please stop blaming it all on this imaginary friend of yours. You are getting too old for fairy stories.'

'It *was* Maud,' she said, tears springing to her eyes. 'She's my best friend in the whole wide world and she's looking after me because you are just too busy, and I hate you!' She ran down the hallway to her bedroom and threw herself on the bed, sobbing. 'I want my brother!'

I watched her for a moment and then shut the door. I'd let her cry it out and we'd talk about it later. I tried to convince myself that this was just another one of our little spats, but I knew it was more – much more – and I didn't have the strength to cope with it. I couldn't think straight, and my knees had gone weak. I had given her brother away and I would never forgive myself for it. Now my little girl hated me as much as I hated myself for what I'd done, and it was like a knife in my heart.

I clung to the wall for a moment, making my way into the kitchen, my hands shaking. I grabbed a packet of cigarettes and lit up, inhaling deeply, thoughts swirling around my head. Then I opened a cupboard, pulled out a bottle of sherry and poured myself a large glass.

As I sipped, the life I'd lived before flashed before me. I wanted to go back in time, to change the way things had turned out, but it was useless, and I found myself staring at the bottom of an empty glass. I refilled it, trying to drown out all the shame of what had happened, and what I'd done. Every time I emptied the glass, I refilled it and drank some more. Me and Jimmy had a long history, but it wasn't a great start when I found myself unexpectedly pregnant by him. Not long after that, I'd ended up in Holloway on a shoplifting charge after the Queen of Thieves, Alice Diamond, got me arrested as a test of my loyalty to her and the gang. No one expected me to be jailed for a first offence, but the court came down on me like a ton of bricks because it wasn't that long after the war. I had the baby, my baby Joseph, while I was in the nick. My head was swimming now, but I kept drinking. I tried to recall Joseph's face, but with every passing year it grew harder to see him in my memory. But I remembered very clearly the day they took him – how I fed him one last time, and felt his fingers curling around mine. Then his cot in the prison nursery was so cold and empty, and I was broken up inside. And that pain had never left me.

He'd be eleven years old, big enough to ride a bike. I only prayed that the couple who'd raised him had kept their word to love him as their own and give him the best of everything.

I put my head in my hands as I downed the last of the bottle, because I knew there were more secrets for Ruby to discover – things a mother should never have to tell her daughter.

Jimmy loved her. She was the apple of his eye, his little girl.

But he wasn't her father.

I'd always known it, from the moment she was born, but the look in her eye tonight – when she was so full of rage – almost made my heart stop because she was the image of her real father. It was a secret I carried with me every day and it weighed heavily, deceiving Jimmy like that. But I decided long ago that you had to make the best of the hand life dealt you.

Jimmy and I were meant to be together, no matter what had happened in the past. We'd overcome so many obstacles and we'd clawed our way to the top in gangland. We belonged side by side.

But every time I looked at my Ruby, I remembered the night of passion I'd spent in her father's arms.

And the worst thing was, try as I might, I had very few regrets about it.

Chapter Thirteen

Zoe

Soho, February 1957

I stared at my reflection in the dressing room mirror, pushing my mouth into a pout, just as I'd seen Diana Durbidge do when she wanted someone's attention.

Then I threw my head back a little, like she did when she was laughing.

'What the bleeding hell's all that about!' scoffed Alma, standing in the doorway. 'Fancy yourself as a film star, do you?'

'Just practising a few looks for the fellas in the club,' I lied. 'To make them buy me a drink.'

Her eyes narrowed, like a cat's. 'Pull the other one, it's got bells on. I've seen you walking down Carnaby Street arm in arm with that Teddy boy. It's all for him, ain't it?'

I giggled.

She took the top off her lipstick and started to apply it, before blotting it with a tissue to make the colour stay put.

'I've seen the way he looks at you, Zoe, and I don't think you need to put on an act. He's smitten.'

I felt a warm glow inside. It was true. Vinnie had been treating me like a princess, buying me flowers, taking me to dances, hanging on my every word, and being as sweet and gentle as a puppy. He was as good as his word that day in the boxing match when I'd forgiven him. There'd been no repeat of his brutal behaviour the night I started at Rubies. He was like a totally different person. We'd kissed each other but he hadn't tried anything more than that.

'I respect you too much, Angel,' he'd said. 'We can wait until the time is right. I want you to know I'm not that kind of a bloke.'

But the feminine charms I was trying to perfect in the mirror weren't for him. Not really. They were for the one man I couldn't quite get to notice me – not for the past few weeks, anyway: Jimmy.

The whole atmosphere in the club had got really tense since the police paid us a visit to ask about a bullion robbery. Alma told us girls to back up whatever Nell and Jimmy said, and Lou had paid out extra that night, so there were no questions asked, we just did what we were told. I did my best to stick up for Jimmy when the policeman questioned me because . . . well . . . it felt right somehow. I hadn't seen any gold in the club, and I had no idea if they'd been involved, but given Jimmy was the boss in Soho, I guessed they must have had a hand in it, even if it was just paying the guys who did it.

There were whispered conversations in corners between Jimmy and Albert, or Albert and Nell, or sometimes all three of them. It was all a bit shady. Jimmy made a big show of putting on card games during the day for his fellas, being really generous with the drink. It wasn't long before the club was buzzing with gangsters. Nell was always wreathed in smiles, but when she and Jimmy thought no one was watching, the mask slipped, and they kept sniping at each other.

Nell still went out shopping with her girls, the Forty Thieves, but there were a few faces I didn't recognise. When Alma told me that the young lad who'd been collared for shooting the policeman was the brother of one of Nell's gang, I thought that was pretty suspicious. I made sure to pass that on to Maud, who was pleased with what I'd learned. She was behaving more secretively than ever, whispering to David as they sat together at the table in the small hours of the morning, when she thought we were all asleep. She was more preoccupied with her own murky business deals than what I was up to with Jimmy.

I kept fobbing her off that Jimmy was too preoccupied to flirt with me, and I was convincing because it was true. The more he ignored me, the more I wanted him. I didn't breathe a word of that to anybody. It was a secret I carried alone and nurtured like a little flame at night in my bunk in the Underworld, when everyone else was asleep.

'Well,' said Alma, finishing off her face, 'it's another night in our glad rags for the punters! Don't dawdle too long, I'll see you out the front.'

She flounced off up the corridor. When she was gone, I pinched some of her lippy and powder and I was just admiring my reflection one last time when there was a gentle knock.

Jimmy was leaning on the door frame.

'Mind if I come in?'

'Suit yourself,' I said, pretending to fluff up my hair, and pushing my mouth into that little pout again.

He put his hands on my shoulders and I almost melted at his touch.

'I wanted to apologise,' he began.

I stood up and spun around. 'No need, Jimmy.'

'I can't stop thinking about you,' he whispered.

'You've got a funny way of showing it. You've barely said two words to me in the past two weeks!'

He shrugged. 'You know it ain't easy for me, and I

know you've been busy with someone else.'

'I'm just having some fun. I'm single,' I said, airily. 'Vinnie's quite devoted to me. Seems he knows how to treat a lady, after all. Maybe you beat some manners into him.'

He laughed. 'I'd like to think so.'

His eyes creased at the corners. He really was quite irresistible.

'I know I've got no claim on you, Zoe,' he said. 'I'm never going to stop you doing what you want, with whoever you want. But I like your company and I think you like mine, so I was wondering whether we might get some more time together at my office at some point in the near future?'

I could see us, making love on the sofa in that little room above the spieler; lying together in each other's arms afterwards, not wanting him to leave.

His breath was warm on my face. I leaned forward and kissed him, very gently, on the lips. I imagined what Diana Durbidge would say to one of her many admirers.

'Perhaps,' I said.

Vinnie was waiting for me outside after the show.

'I've got something special I want you to see,' he said, pulling me into a warm embrace.

'Aren't we going to that new coffee bar, the one everyone's talking about?' I replied sulkily.

Rose said she'd had some of the best evenings there.

'We can go another day, but first, I've got some place I really want to show you.'

His whole face lit up, like a kid at Christmas.

He put his arm through mine, and we wandered along through some backstreets, until we came to a row of shops with all their blinds drawn for the night. Old newspapers were blowing about and there was even a tramp snoozing in the doorway opposite.

'It doesn't look that impressive,' I said, with a shrug. 'Now can we go?'

My feet were killing me from the performance, and I just wanted to sit down and have a laugh with him over a frothy coffee. Rose said they tasted like heaven.

He produced a shiny new key from his coat pocket and put it in the door beside the shop. It opened. The lights were on in the hallway. I followed him up the stairs. Everything smelled of fresh paint.

'What is this place, Vinnie?' I said

He pulled me into a living room, which was thickly carpeted, wall to wall. It was a kind of luxury I'd heard about but never seen. My heart skipped a beat.

There were two cream-coloured sofas covered in pink fluffy cushions, a huge gilt mirror over a gas fire, some pink lamps which gave off a lovely soft light, and in the corner, a record player with a neatly stacked pile of discs beside it.

'It belongs to my boss, Mr Smeets, but me and Victor can use it. It's our base in Soho. His main business is over in Notting Hill and he don't come over here very often.'

I sank into the sofa and kicked off my heels.

'What does he do, this Mr Smeets?'

'Property investment, mainly,' said Vinnie, loosening his tie. 'A bit of this, a bit of that. Me and Victor have been helping him and he's shown us his gratitude, financially.' He flicked through the records and selected one by Elvis. 'You like him, don't you?'

'I suppose,' I said.

I wasn't going to confess to having a massive crush on him. That would have made me sound like a silly schoolgirl, and I was a woman now. Besides, I had two fellas interested in me, so I didn't need to fantasise about a crooner any more.

The record crackled to life and Elvis began to sing his hit, 'Don't Be Cruel'.

And Vinnie pulled me into his arms. We swayed in time to the music, and I let him kiss me, his tongue exploring my mouth, so softly.

'You won't ever be cruel to me, will you, Angel?' he said.

'Of course I won't, Vinnie,' I replied.

He looked at me, and it was as if he was looking through me.

'Are you sure?'

My insides started to feel all floaty. It was funny, the effect he had on me. It wasn't like Jimmy, who made me hungry with desire. Vinnie made me feel weak – helpless, even. I found it hard to think straight when he turned on the charm.

'Yes,' I said. 'I promise.'

He smiled at me, and we rocked from side to side, his arms around me. I tried not to think about Jimmy earlier, and how much I'd enjoyed flirting with him, because that seemed a bit disloyal after I'd promised Vinnie never to be cruel. I knew it was a promise I could never keep, but I loved being with him and all the fun we had together. And now he was dancing with me in this gorgeous flat with its own record player. I just couldn't help myself really.

'Good, because you are so precious to me,' Vinnie replied.

I laid my head on his shoulder.

'You can stay here, if you like,' said Vinnie, after a while. 'Mr Smeets says I can have people I like to stay and help look after the place. What do you think?'

I swallowed, hard. I hadn't told him about Maud and the Underworld, other than to say I had an old aunt I was staying with, who laid down the law about me seeing boys. So, I always made Vinnie kiss me goodbye a few streets away from the air raid shelter, and I checked he wasn't following me before I went down there.

'I don't know, Vinnie,' I said, biting my lip. 'I might like to, but what would my Auntie Maud say? I can't upset her, not at her time of life.'

'You're right, sweetheart,' he said, kissing me on the cheek. 'There's no pressure, but any time you feel like it, you can come here.'

Just then, there were voices in the hallway and Victor strolled in, with his arm around a girl, thin as a rake, but very beautiful, with bottle-blonde hair and eyes as wide as saucers.

'Evening, all,' he joked.

She simpered at me. 'I'm Sandra. What's your name then, love?'

'I'm Zoe,' I said, straightening my skirt and slipping back into my heels, so that I stood a few inches taller than her. 'Pleased to meet you.'

'It's not Zoe, it's Angel,' said Vinnie firmly, giving me a little squeeze. 'That's the name she should have been given, because she is an angel – aren't you, sweetheart?'

It seemed rude to disagree with him, so I nodded.

'Pleased to meet you, too, Angel,' said Sandra.

'She's that dancer I've been telling you about,' said Victor. 'She's smashing, ain't she?'

'Gorgeous,' breathed Sandra. 'And she talks lovely, too.'

She looked me up and down and whispered something to Victor, who nodded.

I'd been happy dancing with Vinnie, but I still hadn't got over what Victor had done to Errol in that boxing match. I didn't want to spend much time around him, out of loyalty to Rose, who was still cut up about it. Poor Errol had spent a week in the hospital recovering and his face was still all smashed up, so she'd heard. He'd been lying low in Notting Hill and hadn't been in the dance club either. Some people said it was under new management now.

'I'd better be getting home, Vinnie,' I said. 'Auntie Maud will go off her rocker if I stay out too late. Her lumbago's been playing up something terrible.'

'That's fine, Angel,' he said.

'Oh, but I was hoping we'd have a little party!' said Sandra huffily.

'There'll be plenty of time for that another day,' Vinnie replied smoothly. He handed me my coat. 'Come on, Angel, I'll walk you home.'

As we were going down the stairs, he turned to me and pulled another key from his pocket.

'This is for you, Angel,' he said. 'Just to show you I'm serious about us.'

'Oh, Vinnie!' I cried, throwing my arms around him and kissing him. 'Do you really mean that?'

''Course I do.'

It wasn't just a posh flat in Soho; I felt like I was getting the keys to a castle.

For me, the fairy tale was just beginning.

I've never had much time for the papers, but I couldn't help noticing people were hanging around the news-stands and the corner shops on my way to Rubies the next day, so I stopped to have a look.

The whole world and his wife were talking about the policeman who'd got shot in the bullion robbery. Copies of the *London Evening News* were selling like hot cakes.

'Read all about it!' yelled the newspaper seller. 'Policeman dies a hero!'

'The poor man,' said a woman in a headscarf. 'He only got shot in the leg, but it says here he got a blood clot after the operation to remove the bullet and it went to his heart and killed him.'

I paid a few pennies and took my copy, folding it under my arm and scurrying off. It felt important to tell Jimmy about it all. By the time I got to the club, I was out of breath and a bit flustered. Nell was nowhere to be seen, but Jimmy and Lou were deep in conversation, with a copy of the paper spread out on the bar, so I was too late. Lou glanced up at me, giving me a look which said 'hoppit', and so I forced a smile and made my way across the club to the dressing room.

It was still early and there was no sign of Alma or the others. I'd barely got my coat off before Jimmy appeared, striding towards me.

He pulled me to him, and I didn't resist when he kissed me.

'Things have got a bit complicated, Zoe,' he said, brushing some stray hair away from my face.

'Is it the policeman?' I replied.

It felt so good, the two of us being there together and the fact that he was confiding in me.

He nodded.

'The less you know the better, but I might not be around much for a while, just until things calm down about this robbery. But I want you to know that you are someone I care deeply about, even if I can't show it. So, I got you this.'

He pulled a ring from the breast pocket of his jacket.

It was a gold band, studded with emeralds.

'It's nothing too showy, because I don't think you want people asking questions about where it came from. But I thought the stones would go nicely with your red hair.'

'It's beautiful, Jimmy,' I gasped, slipping it on for a moment.

It fitted me perfectly, but I knew I could never wear it. It would remain a secret, like our affair.

He turned on his heel. 'You're a special girl, Zoe, never forget that. Keep dancing and stay lucky.'

And with that, he was gone, taking a piece of my heart with him.

London Evening News

BULLION ROBBERY MURDER CHARGE

Special report by Duncan Swift

Police last night charged a man with the murder of slain police officer Stephen Morris, who died of a blood clot caused by being shot in the leg during a bullion raid.

The death of PC Morris, who had been praised by the Prime Minister for being a hero in tackling gangsters who are hell-bent on bringing lawlessness to London, is a hammer blow to decent society. PC Morris survived the shooting, but tragically succumbed to a blood clot after surgery to remove the bullet several weeks ago.

Now Derek Brown, 18, a petty criminal from South London, has been charged with murder and will face court proceedings at the Old Bailey in due course. He had previously been arrested after attempting to flee the scene of the robbery and charged with attempted murder of the policeman. Witnesses, including the driver of the bullion van, which was delivering gold to the offices of KLM Airlines, say they saw him point the gun at PC Morris and pull the trigger. Prosecutors are expected to call for the full force of the law to be applied – meaning Brown will face the death penalty if convicted.

Detective Chief Inspector Walter Munro, head of the Flying Squad, speaking exclusively to the London Evening News, said: "We are devastated by the death of one of our fine colleagues, but are heartened by the thought that we have a man in custody already for the shooting. We hope that justice will do its job.

"In the meantime, we continue to step up our efforts to find the others responsible for this shocking and appalling robbery, in order to stamp out the gangsters in our city. We will leave no stone unturned."

Residents of Queen's Buildings, the London tenement where Brown grew up, were last night in shock over the death of the policeman and the consequences for a young man whom many knew well.

One resident, who did not wish to be named, said: "If he pulled the trigger, he as good as killed him, even if the policeman survived the shooting. He should swing for it."

Another added: "It's a dreadful tragedy, but I can't help thinking the boy could have been helped to stay on the straight and narrow more and avoided all this trouble. I blame his mother and his sister."

Chapter Fourteen

MAUD

Elephant and Castle, February 1957

You never forget your home turf.

I get a bit misty-eyed thinking about my old manor down at Queen's Buildings, especially now a few of the locals are hitting the headlines.

Life hasn't just been tough for people round that way, has it? It's been murder, apparently.

Like every good citizen, I felt outraged by what that stupid boy Derek Brown had done, but I knew he wasn't really the organ grinder. He was just the monkey. And I had my suspicions about who'd let him get hold of a gun in the first place, especially because of what Zoe had told me about Nell and Jimmy and their secretive behaviour since the robbery. They were both in it up to their necks, but Derek was facing the drop for it.

That made me feel really sad for Derek's mother Marj and his sister Em. It just didn't seem right or fair. Now, I'd never had much to do with Marj, because in my day, she was a petty little fence, poncing off other people's hard graft by selling on whatever stolen goods she could lay her grubby little hands on. And she was known for keeping more than a fair share of the profits. She came a cropper for it when word reached the ears of the Queen of Thieves, if memory serves. But that was all a long time ago, before Nell's day.

Ten long years have rolled by since I lived around these parts. I've popped back recently, just to have a mooch about and get my bearings, and it's fair to say that with recent events unfolding, the area is now ripe with possibilities.

But it wasn't easy persuading the Piccadilly Commandos to come on a trip south of the river. Getting Rose out of the West End was like prising a limpet off a rock.

'What on earth are we going there for?' she grumbled, as she traipsed after me towards the tram. 'There's only slim pickings down the Elephant and Castle, and if the Forty Thieves catch us, we'll get our heads kicked in.'

'We'll see about that,' I said, handing out hatpins and a couple of razors which I liked to keep for special occasions. 'You need to keep an open mind about these things, Rose.'

Zoe had given me a priceless piece of information last night, which was part of the reason we were going back to my old manor. Apparently, Jimmy Feeney was on the run, and he'd mentioned something about needing to lie low because of all the fuss about the robbery. Now, you didn't need to be a genius to work out that he was either shifting the gold, or keeping his head down because of bad feeling over young Derek facing a murder charge. The wind had changed direction for Nell and Jimmy Feeney – I could feel it in my bones.

I pulled on my coat and tucked an old car starting handle into my handbag, just in case. I had such happy memories of using that round the Elephant. It almost brought a tear to my eye.

The Piccadilly Commandos were little more than waifs and strays, used to working their own patch, picking pockets, so they weren't much of an army, but as we clambered on board the tram, I felt confident, like Monty and his Desert Rats going in against Rommel at El Alamein.

★

Appearances can be deceptive, so they say.

I took off my glasses and let my hair down from its bun as we crossed the river. When we stepped off the tram, there were a few amazed stares from people who recognised me, even after all these years. The shopkeeper from the other day, who was having his front window repaired after Nell's girl Ruby had chucked a stone through it, gawped at me in amazement. It was true – I'd encouraged her to do something naughty, to get all her anger out about the way her mum had lied to her about her baby brother. The postman nearly fell off his bicycle when he clapped eyes on me. It was nice to see I could still have that effect on people. And I wanted word to get around that I was back.

Rose was in a foul mood, kicking up stones as we crossed the courtyard at Queen's Buildings, with the rest of the Piccadilly Commandos shuffling along after her.

'Proper dump, this is. I don't know why you're so bothered about it.'

'Button it,' I said, tapping her lightly on the shoulder with my walking stick. 'We don't want to cause offence to the locals, do we?'

I pushed open the door to Marj's tenement block. The stairwell reeked of disinfectant. They were a very house-proud bunch over this side, and they took it in turns to sluice the stairways and scrub the steps. It made a refreshing change from the overpowering stench of urine on the stairs outside the Underworld.

I remembered Marj's door well enough; I'd had to kick it in a few times when she was hawking goods without permission from the Queen of Thieves. This time I knocked softly.

The door opened a crack, just wide enough for me to get my foot in.

Em was on the other side of it.

'What the bleeding hell are you doing here?'

I gave it a hard shove and sent her flying back down the hallway, as Rose and the others backed me up and we made our way inside.

'These are difficult times,' I said, as Em struggled to her feet, 'and I'm here to offer you my help in your hour of need.'

Patsy appeared in the doorway to the scullery. I'd only known her as a plain lump of a girl from the jam factory, with a bit of a mouth on her, but it had to be said, she'd grown into her role as a gang heavyweight. It suited her. She would definitely come in handy – if she didn't flatten me first.

'We don't need your help, fanks,' she said, moving towards me in a way that showed she meant business.

'Don't be so hasty,' I soothed. 'Let's let bygones be bygones, shall we?'

'Who is it?' A thin voice came from the scullery.

Marj peered over Patsy's shoulder. She was white as a sheet – haggard, even – and she was still in her dressing gown with her hair in rollers; it was almost lunchtime.

Her mouth rounded into an 'O' of shock at the sight of me.

'Someone we don't want round here,' scowled Patsy, rolling up her sleeves.

'Wait a minute,' I said. 'At least hear me out. I've risked a lot coming down here today, and I know that. But these are very difficult times for you, and I need to tell you a few things which might change your mind about me.'

Rose had her hatpin out, ready to defend me, and my

fingers were already twitching to use my chiv on Patsy, because I reckoned I could cut her a nice stripe before she knocked me for six.

Marj managed to find her voice.

'But I thought you'd left London, gone for good. Nobody's seen hide nor hair of you for years . . .'

'I've come back in your hour of need, Marj, to offer you any help I can give you and the rest of the girls. And these are such desperate times, aren't they?'

Marj crumpled, and started to sob.

'Oh, God, no one can help us. No one can save him.'

I took a step towards her, my arms outstretched, and she fell into my embrace for a moment.

Patsy loomed large.

'You've got five minutes,' she said, propelling me down the hallway towards Marj's kitchen table. Patsy glowered at me as she pulled out a chair for me to sit.

Then she barred the door to Rose and the others.

'Not you lot, just her.'

Marj's hands were shaking as she poured me a brew. It was nice to see she hadn't forgotten her manners. She poured one for herself and chucked in three lumps of sugar, to calm her nerves.

Her bottom lip was trembling as she whispered, 'It all got out of hand, it was all Nell and Jimmy's plan . . .'

'I'm sorry,' I said. 'You know that would never have happened in my day . . .'

Patsy guffawed with laughter. Em glared at me.

'I remember the way you treated my mum in the past. You weren't exactly sweetness and light, were you?'

'That was a long time ago,' I replied. 'I ain't exactly proud of everything I did, but I was trying to run a tight ship. It wasn't easy being Queen. I had some tough decisions to make.'

Marj was staring into the depths of her tea.

'But it seems to me that you and your family have been treated worse by Nell and Jimmy than anything I ever did to you,' I said, reaching across and taking her by the hand. 'Now the press are saying mean things about you and Em. They seem to be blaming you for it all. That's why I'm here.'

Marj let out a wail of despair and Em put her arm around her mother, protectively.

'She don't need you to remind her what kind of trouble Derek is in!'

'Jimmy has done a bunk,' I said, matter-of-factly. 'I have it on the best authority that he is on his toes. He's only thinking of himself and Nell, and how they can get away with it all. Meanwhile, he's left your son to face the consequences of that robbery and the shooting all on his own—'

'How do you know that?' Patsy cut in. 'Nell hasn't mentioned anything to us about Jimmy.'

'Oh, I bet she hasn't.' I laughed. 'She's hardly going to tell you lot anything, is she? Not now Derek's in such hot water. Jimmy has done a moonlight flit and that's the truth of the matter.'

'That bastard!' cried Marj. 'I told you, Em. We were fools to trust them at the time, and now he's getting himself out of the picture! Oh my God, my poor Derek!'

'Whatever happened to the Forty Thieves?' I said, rocking back in my chair. 'Say what you like about me, but in my day, the gang worked like clockwork and we knew our limits. We didn't run around waving guns, pretending to be bank robbers. We left all that nonsense to the blokes. We were too busy cleaning up on furs, silks and dresses, and making a bleeding fortune. I'm truly sorry for how Derek has got involved in all of this, but to my mind, there is only one person round here who is really to blame. And that is Nell.'

Marj nodded at me and wiped her eyes.

'She made him do it,' she snivelled. 'I never wanted him to get involved.'

Patsy tutted at me. 'You're just sore because Nell booted you out and took your crown! You ain't exactly been missed. It was good riddance to bad rubbish.'

'How can you forget what the gang is all about, Patsy?' I said sharply. 'You might despise me, but you've all let Nell use you to do Jimmy's gang's dirty work. Since when did the Forty Thieves dance to any man's tune? There is one person who has to take responsibility for all of this and that is the Queen of Thieves – Nell.

'Right now, what this community needs is a safe pair of hands, someone who people know they cannot mess with, otherwise your whole gang will be sunk.'

The silence was deafening. I drummed my fingers on the table. I gave it one more try.

'We've got to stop her before she does any more damage,' I said. 'We need to let people know who is really to blame for what Derek got himself involved with. Once word gets around that Jimmy's not here, men from over the East End will be coming over the water, demanding a cut . . . protection rackets, you name it. Your cosy lives will never be the same again if you don't put on a show of strength. I know I ain't perfect, but at least nobody ended up facing a murder charge on my watch.'

A clock ticked loudly on the mantelpiece.

After a few moments, Marj said, 'I'll back you.'

She turned and looked at her daughter.

'Alright,' said Em, biting her lip. 'I will, too.'

I stood up. Patsy came over to me. She was almost as tall as me and her eyes were hard, like flints.

'You'll have to earn my trust,' she said. 'But for now, you've got my backing. I think Jimmy took a liberty with Derek and he's a proper coward for doing a runner. I'll tell the other girls.'

'I'm delighted you've all seen sense,' I said, buttoning up my coat. 'And as you all know, the most important rule of this gang is there can only be one Queen. So, let's sort it out, shall we?'

Housewives were peering from their front doorsteps as the whole gang of us – the Piccadilly Commandos led by me, Em, Patsy, and Marj, who'd even brought her rolling pin – marched across to the other tenement block.

I knew the way well because I was walking up to my old flat and my own front door – the place I'd been booted out of by that little usurper Nell ten years ago, when she'd stolen my crown. I'd taken her under my wing and that was how she'd repaid me, the little Judas. Oh, I'd dreamed of this moment so many times as I was skulking about in the Underworld, pretending to be Maud, but even in my wildest fantasies, I had never imagined I'd have the backing of the Forty Thieves to take back what was rightfully mine. But life's full of surprises, ain't it?

When we got to number 32 on the third floor, I was a bit out of breath, but the excitement of it all gave me second wind, and I hammered on that door like I was trying to wake the dead.

It swung open and Ruby's cherubic little face appeared. 'Hello, Maud.'

'Who is it?' shouted Nell from the kitchen.

I put my finger to my lips to stop Ruby saying any more, but it was too late.

'It's my friend Maud,' said Ruby. 'Have you left your uniform at home because you've come to play?'

Patsy and Em shot each other a quizzical look.

'Who the hell is Maud?'

'It's my middle name,' I said, swiftly.

And as God is my witness, that is the truth.

Nell's voice echoed down the hallway.

'I'd like a word with this Maud of yours . . .'

She got two paces out of the kitchen before she stopped dead in her tracks. Nell froze, as if she'd seen a ghost.

'Alice Diamond!'

In that moment, I grabbed hold of her precious daughter, snatching her over the threshold. The little girl squealed in shock.

'Leave her be!' said Nell, moving towards me at lightning speed.

I dragged Ruby on to the tenement landing, where the rest of the gang stood behind me. Ruby struggled in my arms, but she was no match for me.

'Let my Ruby go!' shouted Nell, desperation etched on her features.

'You've got a lot to answer for, Nell Kane,' said Marj, waving her rolling pin. 'We've had enough of you!'

Suddenly, Nell regained her composure as Queen, to fight not just for herself, but for her precious daughter. She threw her head back and laughed in Marj's face.

'Don't be such a stupid cow. Do you think for one minute you'll get away with this? Are you forgetting who I am around here? My Jimmy'll cut you into little pieces. And as for you, Alice Diamond, pretending to be someone you are not so you can manipulate a little girl. You disgust me!'

'Who you *were*, around here,' said Patsy, pushing her way forward. 'You've let us all down, Nell. It's over for you. You took a liberty with Derek, and with all of us. We know Jimmy's on his toes, so he ain't here to protect you now. Me and the girls all feel the same. You should get out while you can.'

That winded her. Suddenly she didn't look like a queen. More like a boxer on the ropes when he knows he's had it.

I pulled my chiv out and held it above Ruby's head, so that she couldn't see it, but Nell could. I was back and it felt so good, after all the years of skulking in the shadows and living beneath London like some sewer rat. The blood was pumping through my veins, giving me the strength of ten men.

'You wouldn't,' said Nell. 'For God's sake!'

'Is it any different from you leaving Derek to face the drop? He's Marj's child!' I said triumphantly.

'I had nothing to do with that, and you know it,' said Nell, taking a step towards me. 'Why don't you come in and we can talk this over? I understand you've got an axe to grind with me. If it's money you want, you can have all my money. Just give me back my girl.'

She was pleading with me. It gave me a kick to have such power over her after all these years. I paused for a second to let it all sink in, relishing every moment.

But before I could make my next move, Marj lunged forward and snatched Ruby from my grasp. She picked her up as if she weighed little more than a bag of sugar, and slung her, so the girl's legs were dangling over the balcony on to the courtyard below us.

Nell screamed, a blood-curdling sound.

'It ain't just about Nell, for Chrissakes! I want Jimmy to feel pain, the same as I'm feeling it!' shouted Marj, shaking Ruby like a rag doll. 'I'll throw her over and then

Jimmy'll know how it feels to lose a child! That bastard doesn't deserve to be a father.'

'Wait!' said Nell. 'Just wait a minute!'

Marj had a wild-eyed look about her. I didn't fancy Nell's chances. Ruby's shrieks were bringing people into the courtyard now, and quite a crowd had gathered to see what the commotion was all about.

'I'll tell you something – something I have never told a living soul. And then you'll see why you have to let her go,' whispered Nell, all the colour draining from her face. 'Cut me if you like. Take everything I have, Marj, if it will make you feel better. I really don't care about any of it, or what you do to me. But she ain't Jimmy's child, as God is my witness. You won't be harming Jimmy's child – she's somebody else's.'

You could have heard a pin drop at that.

'Here, you can take my rings,' said Nell. 'We'll leave Queen's Buildings, I give you my word. Just let her live.'

She pulled off her diamond rings and threw them at Marj's feet.

I bent down and picked them up, sharpish. I let all that old flannel about her baby belonging to someone other than Jimmy wash over me. Those rings were mine to start with, you see, so she had no right to be giving those away. It was nice to get them back. I popped them in my pocket. Diamond by name, diamond by nature.

Nell turned to me.

'If you fancy yourself as Queen of Thieves, now is the time to prove it. Look at her, Alice – who do you see?'

She pointed to her daughter, who was still suspended precariously in Marj's arms.

'Look at her face. Does she look like Jimmy? Even a tiny bit?'

Nell was right. There was nothing of Jimmy in Ruby. He was so fair, with chiselled cheekbones, and she had a rounder face, with a smooth brow which framed eyes so dark and brooding, they were quite unsettling. Even when she was scared witless, there was something in her appearance which felt familiar to me – very familiar, in fact.

'Well, well. I think she might be telling the truth.' I chuckled. 'Fancy that!'

The scales fell from my eyes, and I knew then exactly whose child she was. But I wanted to make Nell say it, for everyone to hear.

The others were nudging one another and murmuring, 'Whose is she, for Gawd's sake?'

'Seems you did put it about a bit in Soho, didn't you?' I chided. 'I always suspected you were a good-for-nothing, but now it seems you were a cheap slut, too. So, you've got one chance and you'd better tell the truth, or I won't be responsible for the consequences.'

'She's Billy Sullivan's daughter,' said Nell, glowering at me. 'That makes you her aunt, Alice. If you let Marj hurt her, you're harming your own flesh and blood.'

'Oh, kids these days get up to all sorts of high jinks, balancing themselves on ledges and then falling off and hurting themselves, and ain't that the truth?' I said, chirpily. 'So, thanks for the lecture on family ties, very grateful.' I waved my stick towards her. 'But you are in no position to bargain with me.'

All those years ago, when I'd sent Nell to spy on my hated brother Billy Sullivan at his club in Soho, she'd obviously fallen for his charms. Jimmy had raised Ruby like a little cuckoo in the nest. It was soul-destroying, the kind of betrayal which no relationship could ever recover from. And therefore, more perfect than I could ever have dreamed. It's fair to say, I had taken quite a shine to Ruby from the moment I met her, because I recognised she had something about her. Perhaps blood is thicker than water, as the saying goes.

'It's all a pack of lies!' Marj screamed hysterically at Nell. 'You'll say anything to save her!'

Ruby wriggled a bit to try to push her way back over the balcony, but Marj had a tight hold under her armpits, and she was like a raging bull.

There was something fierce about Marj which I had never noticed before. The other girls had noticed it, too, in a way I didn't particularly care for. It was time to bring it to a halt before Marj got ideas above her station. I'd let it go on for long enough – probably too long, because a telltale trickle of liquid was running down Ruby's legs.

'Let her go, Marj!' I said, slamming my walking stick down on the concrete. 'I'm the boss round here – you made a promise to me. I know this is hard for you, but we ain't here to kill children, are we? You don't want to have the law on you for a murder charge as well, do you?'

Marj relented and lifted Ruby over the balcony. Then she fell into Em's arms, sobbing. All the fight had gone out of her, and she collapsed like a sack of spuds. Her show of strength had just been a flash in the pan, and thank God for that. I'd only bargained on getting rid of one pretender to my crown today.

Ruby ran over towards Nell and clung to her skirt, weeping.

'You've got ten minutes to pack some things,' I said coldly. 'The girls will help you. Then you'd better get off my manor.'

★

A huge crowd had gathered in the courtyard by the time Nell and Ruby were marched out of Queen's Buildings, with people jostling to get a good view.

Nell carried a suitcase in one hand and held tightly to Ruby with the other, her face ashen and her jaw clenched. I'd taken all her jewellery, except her favourite ruby necklace and one diamond ring that Jimmy had bought her. I left her a ten-bob note and a few shillings. That was all she had to her name when I first knew her as a slum girl all those years ago, when I took her under my wing. It seemed fitting to send her off like that, with a few coins rattling in her purse. I took all her furs, too, for good measure.

Ruby was snivelling at her side, and she had her favourite storybook and a teddy bear tucked under her arm; I let her keep those because I'm not altogether heartless, and she had raised a smile when I spent time with her as Maud.

A gang of little tearaways lobbed stones at them as they hurried off to the bus stop to start their lives afresh, a long way away from me and the Forty Thieves. It was a very fitting send-off and it's fair to say, it warmed the cockles of my heart to see the community banding together like that.

I can't say I gave a damn where Nell Kane was going to lay her head, but I'd warned her, it had better not be within a street mile of my turf.

Or next time I might not be so generous.

Chapter Fifteen

NELL

Notting Hill, April 1957

Water dripped through the ceiling and pattered into the tin pail in the corner. Mould bloomed up the sodden wallpaper above it. Ruby coughed herself awake again on the settee, so I folded my coat behind her head to make a pillow, humming her favourite nursery rhymes until she nodded off again.

I closed my eyes and leaned back in the easy chair where I spent my nights. The newspaper at the windows did little to blot out the glow of the gas lamps in the street below, where drunks were fighting. The cries of the baby upstairs could be heard through the paper-thin walls, and the creak of the neighbours on the stairs going to the shared lavvy at the end of the hallway added to the nightly symphony which made sleep impossible.

I glanced at my watch. It was three o'clock in the morning. In two hours, I'd be up to get to my cleaning job at the butcher's, swilling off the blood from the freezing marble slabs and scrubbing every surface until my hands were red raw.

Then I'd dash back home via the baker's, hoping to get a couple of day-old buns for Ruby's breakfast before I sent her off to school. Once she was safely on her way, I'd head down to Portobello Road, to a greasy spoon café run by a kindly old bloke, Mr Jacobs, to cook fry-ups all day long. His wife had not long since died and he needed someone to help him run the café and stop the local scally-wags from trying to pinch from the till when his back was turned. I'd persuaded some of the kids to play their funny skiffle music on washboards and upturned crates to entertain the customers, and now they were treating the place with more respect. But that was about the full extent of my say-so round here.

I used to be someone. Now I was lying low and strug-gling to make ends meet – the kind of person who spent their days looking over their shoulder. The last two months had passed in a blur, but one thing I can tell you is that fracas with Marj and Alice Diamond was just the start.

Derek sang like a bloody canary the day I got booted out of Queen's Buildings, and Jimmy and Albert had their mugshots splashed all over the papers as wanted men for the bullion raid. So, it was more than just my pride which took a battering. Our whole empire came crumbling down.

When I called in at Rubies, I found a notice pinned to the door saying the club's licence had been revoked by the magistrates because of suspicions it was just a front for the proceeds of crime. The locks had been changed, and I knew then I couldn't hang about in Soho. I wasn't going to give that bastard Munro the pleasure of hauling me off to the cop shop for a grilling on my Jimmy's whereabouts, so I headed off to a part of town where the cozzers hardly ever dared to venture.

Notting Hill has always had a bit of a reputation as a den of thieves and cut-throats, with narrow lanes and cobbled streets running from the slums of the Potteries, where people used to keep pigs and live alongside cesspits back in Dickens's time. Nowadays, even the big old houses had fallen into disrepair and been taken over by landlords who didn't give a shit about their tenants. The poorest and most desperate found themselves living in the kind of places rats wouldn't want to dwell. But for me, a neighbourhood where few questions were asked felt like paradise. And at least we would be safe from the clutches of Alice Diamond and the disloyal bunch who'd stabbed me in the back. I was reeling with shock at the way she'd marched back into my life to claim her crown. Where the hell had she been hiding all these years? I had so many questions, but the only thing on my mind right now was survival – keeping us safe.

Ruby had just about stopped crying when we hopped off the bus.

'Why do they hate us so much, Mummy?' she sniffed. 'I want to go home.'

I kneeled down beside her. 'We can't go back, sweetheart, not for a while. Sometimes people in this life are just evil, plain and simple. We are better off without them, and this will be an adventure, you'll see. Just like one of the princesses in your storybook.'

She didn't look convinced. A couple of tramps were grappling with each other in the pub doorway for the last swig of whisky, and snot-nosed brats were picking up fag butts from the gutter and sharing them.

'Why did Maud pretend to be my friend?'

'She's not called Maud,' I said. 'Her name is Alice and she's a wicked woman, like the witch in Sleeping Beauty. We'll never have to see her again, I promise.'

I pulled her along beside me as we made our way up Portobello Road, which was lined with barrows selling everything from vegetables and clothes to pots and pans.

It was heaving with people.

'Why did you say those things about Daddy and that other man and me to Maud?'

Her eyes searched my face. I looked away for a moment. I hadn't had time to think about what I'd say to her about Billy Sullivan being her dad. I think part of me was hoping she'd been so scared she hadn't even heard it.

'It was just a silly story I made up, to try to protect you from Marj because she was so angry and she wanted to hurt you, that's all. You can forget all about it now. Daddy is your father.'

Ruby frowned. It was a look which made me think of Billy all over again. She was the spitting image of him when she was cross, and she was growing more like him every day.

'Sometimes children have to just trust their parents to know what is best,' I added.

She didn't look convinced.

'I'm hungry,' she said, as we passed a barrow piled high with fruit.

I'd never pinched from stalls before; it was beneath me as a hoister, and it felt wrong to steal from working-class folk, but these were desperate times. I had no idea if we were going to have a roof over our heads, let alone a meal.

I picked up some apples and handed them to Ruby with a few pennies, and while the bloke was popping them in a brown paper bag, I pulled off a couple of bananas and shoved them under my coat.

I waited until we had gone around the corner before I gave them to Ruby, who gasped.

'Did you forget to pay for those?' she said, frowning at me again.

'Silly me! I'll go back later,' I lied. 'They won't mind.'

I'd never told Ruby about my work as a hoister. She was too young, too innocent. I'd been planning to tell her when she was old enough to come out shoplifting with me, once she'd left school, but part of me wanted to give her the choice to stay away from that line of work if she wanted. Now that dream lay in tatters, and it looked like thieving was going to be a way of life for us, just to survive.

A row of dilapidated white stucco houses lay before us, with crumbling plaster and peeling paint on the doors. A sign scrawled on a bit of cardboard stuck in one of the grimy ground floor windows read 'Rooms for Rent'. I made Ruby wait at the gate while I walked up the front steps, past a discarded rusty old pram and a stained mattress wilting against the hedge. I knocked on the door. A burly bloke in a string vest answered, his braces dangling from his trousers, which he could barely do up over his gut. He had a copy of the *Racing Post* in one hand and a half-eaten bacon sarnie in the other.

He looked me up and down.

'Yes, love?'

'I'm here about the room,' I said.

'Oh, it ain't here, it's over the road.' He gestured to a house over the way, which had no lights on in any of the windows. One was boarded up completely. 'Want to have a look?'

Grease was dribbling down his stubbly chin. He wiped it away with the back of his hand.

I nodded.

He caught sight of Ruby.

'Where's your husband, then?'

'He's working away,' I said. 'He'll be round from time to time, but we just need somewhere to stay for a while.'

He smirked at me, as if he had seen right through that fib. Then he pulled on his braces and produced a bunch of keys from his pocket. He jangled them as he walked down the steps and we crossed the road. He had carpet slippers on his feet, and one of them had such a big hole in it that his toe was poking through.

'I work for Mr Smeets, he owns all the houses down this way,' he said, as he put the key in the lock and pushed open the door. We were hit by a fug of damp. 'It's had electrics fitted. All mod cons. Very nice. I didn't catch your name, love?'

'Finnegan,' I shot back. 'Mrs Finnegan. And this is my daughter, Polly.'

He flicked a light switch in the hall and swore under his breath.

'Bloody bulb's gone again. The room is upstairs on the right. My arthritis is killing me, love – go on up and have a look around.'

He handed me the keys. I gripped the banister and felt it wobble. There were bare boards on the stairs, and the wallpaper was hanging in strips where the damp had made the glue come unstuck. Ruby followed close behind me, as we felt our way in the gloom.

'I'll need a couple of quid down as a deposit, in case of breakages or you doing a runner.' He chuckled to himself. 'Rent is weekly, on Fridays, Fifteen shillings, which is a bargain really, and Mr Smeets don't do credit. Clear?' he shouted up after me. 'If you don't want it, there's another family interested . . .'

I opened the door and flicked on the light. The room was dusty, dank and small, with a stove and sink on one side and a small gas-fired hot water tank above it. What furniture there was seemed to have fallen off the back of the rag-and-bone man's cart, but we were in no position to argue.

Across the hallway I heard the faint sound of a woman weeping.

'We'll take it,' I said.

Jimmy was at Brighton races placing bets with Albert when the law caught up with him the next day. I always said Albert's fondness for a flutter would be his undoing, and it turned out I was right. Not that it gave me any pleasure. When I needed Jimmy to lay down the law around the Elephant and Castle, he was twiddling his thumbs behind bars instead, with that twerp Munro gloating about it.

Jimmy's plan had been to take a private plane from the south coast and fly over to France, where they'd shipped the bullion weeks before. Albert was using his family contacts in Italy to get it shifted and converted into hard cash through the casinos down in Monte Carlo. From there, the Mafia had agreed, for a fee, to take it to Spain, where Jimmy had some crazy scheme to invest in property and clubs in a fishing village called Benidorm – not all of it, but a good chunk of the cash. Nothing I could say would make him change his mind.

'I've always fancied a holiday place in the sunshine,' he said, ignoring the dubious look on my face. 'Albert's fellas say it's a good investment in Spain. It's a way of us having a life away from the clutches of Munro if we want. Down there, no one will bother us, and we can bring money back into Britain as and when we need it.'

Now Jimmy was staring at the four drab walls of a cell in Wormwood Scrubs while he awaited trial – a trial that the press were having a field day over. Duncan Swift must have thought all his Christmases had come at once, and the papers were full of his bile.

Meanwhile, I was living on my wits with nothing to show for the years of hard graft I'd put into building up my reputation as Queen of Thieves. Years ago, I had stitched a roll of cash into Ruby's teddy bear, just for a rainy day. Well, now it was chucking it down and the money was running out. I'd already pawned my diamond ring, and you'd have thought it was little more than paste for what I got for it. That's the trouble – when you are in no position to argue, life kicks you right in the teeth.

I can't blame Derek for what he did; he thought he might get a bit of leniency by dobbing the big fish in it but, as it happens, it didn't do him any good in the long run. The murder trial finished, and the judge put on his black cap. Derek will hang by the end of the month. I think of him in the small hours of the morning, when my eyes are so scratchy from tiredness that I can't close them – willing myself to wake up back in Queen's Buildings, with him loafing about in Marj's kitchen and her nagging him to get a proper job. But he put his finger on the trigger of that gun and pulled it, changing everything.

Jimmy and Albert are facing long stretches for the robbery, despite no one other than Derek giving evidence against them. They've both pleaded not guilty. That's going to do about as much good as a chocolate fireguard, because the whole world knows they have got criminal records as long as your arm and Jimmy was the kingpin in Soho – the only one in gangland with enough clout to pull off such a brazen theft. Everyone is expecting the judge to throw the book at them because of public outrage over what happened to that poor cozzer.

No matter what the coming weeks bring, I have to keep going, and not just for Ruby.

At first, I thought I was just exhausted because I'm down on my luck. But now I know that I have a secret to tell.

The dream that Jimmy wanted most of all – to complete our family – is going to come true.

I'm having his baby.

Chapter Sixteen

ZOE

Soho, April 1957

'What d'you think of it?'

The neon sign of a dancing girl with a halo and wings glowed brightly, and a lengthy queue of punters were already waiting patiently for the grand opening of Angel's.

'It's gorgeous, Vinnie,' I breathed, hugging him. 'It's a dream come true.'

Nell and Jimmy's old club, Rubies, had been taken over by Vinnie's boss, Mr Smeets, who wanted to get a foothold in clubland. He'd bought the lease from the Italian who'd owned it since before the war and had been renting it to Nell and Jimmy. Nobody wanted to do business with them any more. The fortunes of the King of Soho and the Queen of Thieves had taken a spectacular nosedive. I wasn't exactly over the moon about it, because I still carried a candle for Jimmy, who was in prison awaiting trial for the bullion raid, but I was glad to see the back of Nell. She'd disappeared off the face of the earth, as far as anyone knew. In any case, she'd been a proper snooty cow to me, so I didn't shed any tears. I was beginning to understand the way Soho worked; people were up one minute and down the next.

I knew which way I was headed. Vinnie had promised to make me a star, and now he'd named the club after me to prove it.

A gaggle of reporters were loitering outside, and flash-bulbs went off as Diana Durbidge pulled up in her pink Rolls Royce, creating a bit of a stir.

'Darling!' she cried, clambering out and pulling me into a warm embrace. I was almost knocked sideways by the overpowering whiff of her perfume. She planted a kiss on my cheek. 'You're going to knock 'em dead tonight, Angel. Good luck to you!'

I'd never spoken more than two words to her before, but now she was treating me as if we were old friends.

'Vinnie's told me all about you, and how he has named the club in your honour! Lucky girl!'

'Thank you,' I said. 'That's very kind.'

An overweight, grubby-looking reporter barged forwards, with greasy hair flopping over his face.

'Diana! Can we get a picture?'

'Of course, sweetie! This is my new friend Angel – she's the Queen of Clubs. The club is named after her, and this is Vincent Graveney, the manager and one of my closest pals.'

The reporter licked his lips and pushed a photographer towards us.

Vinnie straightened his tie. Diana linked arms with both me and Vinnie, and I pouted into the lens, just like she did.

The reporter got his notebook out.

'Duncan Swift, *London Evening News*. Can I ask who you are, miss?'

'I'm Angel,' I replied, smiling sweetly. 'I'm just a girl from the East End who is following her dreams in the West End as a dancer.'

'Fantastic!' he said. 'It'll be in tomorrow's edition – make sure you grab a copy.'

Vinnie took me by the hand and led me through the door and down the stairs. I hadn't seen the club since the refurbishment, and it took my breath away. Everything was brand new, from the chrome bar stools to the mirrored ceiling and the purple velvet booths around the edge of the club. Tables were neatly laid out in the middle of the room, so people could get a good view of the stage, but the place was classier than before. The curtains were swags of silver cloth decorated with little cherubs, and at either side of the stage stood a huge pair of angel's wings glinting under the electric lights.

Lou was still a fixture behind the bar. He scowled at me as I strutted in on Vinnie's arm, with Diana Durbidge sashaying alongside us.

Vinnie clicked his fingers. 'Open a bottle of champagne, Lou, there's a good boy.'

Lou was old enough to be his father. It was only the need to pay his rent which stopped him from lamping Vinnie one, I could tell.

Victor was already propping up the bar with his girl-friend Sandra at his side. I didn't mind her. We were flatmates these days, and she was mad as a hatter. She and Victor liked to party, and it wasn't just drink, but some funny little pills she carried around in a silver tobacco tin. When she was on those, she went crackers. I came home one night to find her standing in the corner with a lampshade on her head to give me a fright, just for the hell of it.

I'd been staying over with Sandra at Mr Smeet's flat ever since Maud went back to her old place down at the Elephant and Castle. Vinnie had been true to his word, and he was the perfect gentleman. Even though he'd given me the key to the place, he wined and dined me and never wanted anything more than a bit of a kiss and a cuddle.

'We have all the time in the world to be together, Angel,' he'd said. 'I want to make it special, a night to remember. So, let's wait.'

Maybe it was old-fashioned, but I wasn't complaining. If anything, it made me want him more because he respected me. He gave me money to spend and told me to buy myself nice things if I felt like it.

There was no point me slumming it in that horrible air raid shelter, and since Maud had got back with her shop-lifters' gang, she was too busy steaming through Selfridges nicking stuff to bother with me. She'd got even with Nell – that was what she'd wanted – and the police had hold of Jimmy, so I suppose I wasn't important to her any more. I can't say I cared about Maud. She was useful to me at the time, because it set me on the right path in clubland, but now I had grown wings and I was ready to fly.

Lou poured us some bubbles and Vinnie raised a glass to me.

'To Angel, the Queen of Clubs!'

'To the Queen of Clubs!' chimed Diana.

That was music to my ears. I'd come so far, and this was just the start. I was young and I had so much to offer. Maybe I'd even end up in films one day, like her. The sky was the limit as far as I was concerned.

Lou turned away and started drying some glasses.

'Well, sweetheart, what do you think of the place?' said Vinnie, nuzzling my neck.

'I love it!' I said, taking a sip of my drink.

I suddenly felt a bit queasy with nerves, but I smiled broadly. My stomach was really floaty, and I began to regret the fry-up I'd had for breakfast.

'I've even got you a special outfit to wear for the first dance tonight,' he said. 'Why don't you go and try it on?'

'Good idea,' I said, dashing off across the club – not because I was dying to see what Vinnie wanted me to wear, but because I was going to throw up.

Alma was already getting ready with the other dancers by the time I got backstage. She'd worked for more club bosses than I'd had hot dinners, so having Vinnie in charge didn't bother her. She still put on the same make-up and was prepared to go through the same charade each night to keep the punters happy.

'You alright?' she said.

I caught sight of my reflection in the changing room mirror. I was pale as a ghost.

'I think I ate something funny, that's all,' I said.

She handed me a bottle of tonic water and I took a swig. It didn't help.

'Are you going to be well enough to perform? It's a full house out there.'

'Of course!' I replied.

'Well, I'd better help you put this on, then.'

She handed me a tiny silver bikini and an enormous pair of angel wings, topped off by a little halo.

We both giggled.

'If you don't like it here, you could always get a job down the road at St Paul's Cathedral,' she said, guffawing with laughter.

'Vinnie wants me to wear it.' I grimaced. 'I think it looks a bit daft, but I'd better keep him happy.'

I undressed and pulled on the silver knickers, my stomach still churning. When it came to the bra, I could barely do up the clasp because my boobs had grown so much.

'Blimey,' said Alma. 'You're going to give Diana Durbidge a run for her money tonight in that.'

She gave my waist a little pinch, squidging a good inch

180

of fat. I had always been thin as a rake until now.

'You look like you've been eating all the pies, and that ain't a good thing for a dancer, Zoe,' she said sternly.

It was true, I had been enjoying myself eating out with Vinnie at all the top restaurants. It was hard not to, having come from nothing and been raised on bread and dripping. Some of the puddings were delicious.

'I'll go on a diet,' I said, blushing.

'What's the problem here?'

It was Vinnie, standing in the doorway.

Alma drew on a ciggie.

'I was just telling Zoe that she's looking a bit broad across the beam, and she needs to lay off the treats or she won't fit into her costumes.'

Vinnie gave her a look that could kill.

'Don't you talk rubbish about my girlfriend, you old trollop.' His fists were clenched. 'And her name is Angel. Don't you forget it. Nobody calls her Zoe any more. I like the way she looks. It's womanly.'

'Alma's only trying to help—' I began.

He sneered at me. 'And that's all the thanks I get for sticking up for you, is it?'

I stood there, my mouth opening and closing like a stupid fish.

Alma eyeballed him. 'Suit yourself, dearie. I'm only telling the truth. The spotlight is no friend if you are packing extra pounds. The punters don't like it, no matter what your name is. The fact is, Angel is getting a bit porky.'

Vinnie turned puce with anger.

'I don't want to see you at the front of the stage, Alma,' he spat. 'Make sure the younger girls get a turn. This is a nightclub, not a mortuary.'

And he turned on his heel and left.

Alma looked at the floor. I could tell she was hurt by it. The other girls started whispering to one another.

'I'm sorry,' I said. 'Don't listen to him. I know you are the best dancer in here. He's just being protective of me. He just has a bit of a temper sometimes. I think it must be nerves about the big night . . .'

'It's alright ,' she said, with a shrug. 'It's a tough old game. I'm still dancing, and I've still got your back. Just don't poke my eye out with those blooming wings. And try to lay off the fry-ups, *Angel*.'

The club was packed to the rafters and after our show, all the girls mingled with the audience. Opening night had attracted a much younger crowd, more like the jazz club down the road, as well as posh people dripping with jewels. Angel's really was going to be the number one nightspot, just like Vinnie said.

I got changed into a slinky silver dress, one I'd bought specially, and it clung to my curves. I got a couple of wolf whistles as I walked across to the bar, which made me feel better about the way I looked. But the sick feeling kept coming and going, so I made a point of staying off the booze.

Vinnie was waiting for me, surrounded by a gaggle of girls who were gazing up at him and hanging on his every word. He smiled when he saw me, but there was no apology for losing his temper earlier. I tried not to let that bother me, but there was a look in his eyes which I couldn't fathom, and it made me feel as if I was walking on eggshells.

'You did well, Angel,' he said, as he pulled me into an embrace. 'Now there's a bit more work to do. Come with me.' He clicked his fingers at Lou. 'Bring us another bottle of champagne.'

Lou rolled his eyes but did as he was told.

Vinnie steered me to a table on the other side of the club, which was full of older blokes – important-looking people in suits and ties. Some of the other dancers were buzzing around them like bees dive-bombing a honeypot.

'I'd like you to meet Detective Chief Inspector Walter Munro,' he said. 'And Peter Murray, MP for Basingstoke, and this is Jeremy. He is a barrister, and a friend of Mr Smeets.'

'How lovely to make your acquaintance,' I said, in my poshest accent.

These people were the quality, the kind of folk I had spent my whole life wanting to be close to. And now it was really happening.

'Charming,' said the MP. He leaned over and whispered in my ear, 'What's a nice girl like you doing in a place like this?'

I chuckled at his lame joke and batted my eyelashes, just as Alma had taught me to do.

'Having the time of my life and hoping to meet my handsome prince, of course! And I'm spoilt for choice this evening.'

Lou stalked over and plonked the champagne on the table. Vinnie started refilling everyone's glasses, while I took a seat beside the policeman. Despite being important, his face reminded me of a mangy old dog which used to hang around the street in Limehouse, looking for scraps to eat.

'Detective Chief Inspector Munro is making sure we don't get any riff-raff in here,' said Vinnie, puffing himself up with pride. 'This is going to be a different kind of club, one which works with the police, not against it. That's what Mr Smeets wants.'

'Mr Smeets is very wise,' said Munro.

He put his hand on my thigh and gave it a squeeze. I smiled politely, but felt vomit rising in my throat, and I swallowed hard to keep it down. I didn't mind getting a bit friendly with the punters, but there was something creepy about the way he let his hand linger, his fingers stroking my leg.

'You dance so beautifully, it was quite mesmerising,' he murmured. His breath was foul, reeking of stale coffee and too many cigarettes. 'I'm looking forward to getting to know you better.'

'I'd be delighted,' I lied. 'Any friend of Vinnie's is a friend of mine.'

I glanced at Vinnie, fearing he might have steam coming out of his ears, because he was the jealous type.

But he was smiling at me, as if this was what he wanted me to do – or perhaps what he was expecting me to do.

'Mr Smeets wants you and your friends to enjoy yourselves, so perhaps we can organise that little party I was talking about?' said Vinnie, idly lighting up a smoke. 'Angel can bring some of the other dancers along, and my brother Victor's girl Sandra has some lovely friends, too. We can make a night of it.'

Detective Chief Inspector Munro's face lit up, and the MP and his lawyer mate looked pleased as Punch.

Over the other side of the club, Diana Durbidge was laughing and flirting, having the time of her life. She caught sight of me and blew me a kiss. I gave her a little wave. We might have looked like we were both starlets out on the town, but my world and hers were still miles apart.

And as Detective Chief Inspector Munro clung to my thigh as if he was about to arrest it, I was beginning to wonder just what kind of world I had got myself involved in.

The minutes dragged by as we sat around the table, with Vinnie and the blokes chatting while I simpered in appreciation at Munro's lame jokes. I tried to catch Vinnie's eye, to signal to him that I'd had enough, and I was tired, but if he noticed, he didn't seem to care. Cigars were unboxed and smoked, slowly. I perched on the edge of my seat for what felt like eternity, before I eventually piped up that I was going to the ladies to fix my make-up.

'Don't be too long, Angel,' said Vinnie. 'We'll all be going back to our place for a few more drinks, OK?'

Trying to stop Munro's wandering hands was like trying to wrestle an octopus, and I really wasn't in the mood for it with the sickness. I just needed to rest, and my bed was calling me.

I leaned over and whispered in his ear, 'Please, Vinnie, not tonight. I think I'm coming down with something. Can I just go home?'

His face set, hard, and a muscle twitched in his cheek.

'Don't let me down, Angel,' he murmured. 'I need you to be here for Munro. It's important for the business, understood?'

I nodded mutely.

By the time we got back to the flat, I was so tired I just wanted to collapse in a heap, but Vinnie sent me into the kitchen to join Sandra, who was fussing about with a decanter of whisky and glasses, while Munro and his cronies made themselves comfortable in the lounge.

'Ooh, you look done in,' she said, putting down the tray of drinks and picking up her handbag. She flicked open the clasp and pulled out a little pill box. 'One of these should do the trick.'

She offered me one of the tiny tablets, and I got myself a glass of water and swallowed it. The effect wasn't instant, but within half an hour, I had the energy to dance around the lounge with Sandra and some of her friends, giggling and laughing, while the fellas watched us. Vinnie smiled at me appreciatively, and I got a bit of a warm glow at that.

When the record came to an end, Munro stood up and adjusted his tie.

He came over to me.

'How about a little tour of the place?' he said, encircling my waist with his arms.

I blushed stupidly, turning beetroot. I didn't want to leave the party to be alone with him.

Vinnie was watching and he nodded at me.

'Be polite, Angel, show the detective chief inspector around. We've got a nice place here, it's good to show it off.'

Before I knew what was happening, Munro had taken me by the hand and was walking me towards the bedroom. He pushed the door open. I tried to hang back, laughing, making a joke of it.

'Oh, you don't want to see in there! I don't think I've even made the bed!'

But he was strong, and he pulled me into the room and shut the door, pushing me up against it. Maybe it was the pill and the drinks I'd had, or maybe it was the shock of the situation, but I found myself giggling.

'You're a girl who knows how to have fun,' he said, his hands exploring up my skirt. 'You're very special, Angel.'

'P-please,' I stammered. 'I don't think Vinnie'll like it if we—'

186

'Oh, he doesn't mind,' said Munro, leering at me, so that I could almost taste the whisky he'd just drunk and the cigar smoke he'd rolled around his mouth. 'And you *do* like it. I can tell. So don't be shy. You wear a lot less than this when you're on stage, don't you?'

His hands started tugging at the shoulders of my dress, pulling it downwards to reveal my brassière, then he pushed the hem of the dress upwards, up over my thighs, exposing my knickers.

He covered my mouth with his, so that I couldn't scream, and shoved me, arms flailing, towards the bed, using his body weight to hold me down. The pink walls; the quilted bedspread; the picture of a flamingo I thought was so sophisticated: all bore witness to what happened next.

'Oh, I like a girl with a bit of fight in her,' he sneered.

I tried to lash out, scrabbling at his face with my nails, but he simply got my hands and pinioned them at my side. Then he yanked my knickers down over my thighs.

His eyes, inky black and soulless, bored into mine.

'Come on, don't pretend not to enjoy it. You've been flirting with me all evening. This is what you really want.'

I tried to shout, to say that wasn't true – I was only doing what Vinnie had told me to do, to be nice – but the terror of it all had stolen my voice. Tears started rolling down my face.

He hurriedly unzipped his fly and I lay there, my eyes closed, knowing it was useless to protest, as he forced his way inside me. He thrust so hard, there was pain, burning pain, and then he grunted, like a pig, and it was over.

Munro rolled off me as I lay there weeping silently, my dress rucked up around my middle, my underwear around my ankles, and my dreams of a glamorous life in Soho in tatters.

'See you again, Angel,' he said, zipping up his fly and straightening his tie.

He went back out to the party, which was still in full swing.

I was too ashamed to get up and face anyone. Everyone must have known what was happening. Everyone. Especially Vinnie.

It was pitch black when I woke up, to the sound of my favourite Elvis song, 'Don't Be Cruel'. I winced in pain as I stumbled out of the bed, pulling on my silk negligé.

The lounge was littered with overflowing ashtrays and empty bottles of booze, but there was no one there. In the gloom, as my eyes adjusted, I could just about make out Vinnie's profile silhouetted by the record player.

'Vin,' I gasped. 'You scared the life out of me.'

He turned and flicked on the table lamp.

'I wanted to have a word with you, Angel. You left the party a bit early.'

My legs were weak and shaking as I approached. He only had to look at me and I felt the ground giving way. I wanted to tell him what had happened with Munro – what he'd done to me – but I didn't know where to start.

'Something bad's happened,' I began.

A look crossed Vinnie's face, like a mixture of disgust and amusement. He pulled me to him and kissed me, hard. I didn't resist him; I didn't have the strength. I was like a puppet in his arms.

'I didn't like the way you were flirting with that cozzer,' he murmured, gazing down at me. 'You looked like you were enjoying it a bit too much, leading him on. Then you just disappeared on us and went to bed, you lazy moo.'

'No, Vinnie,' I said, limply, 'you're wrong. He forced himself on me. I was only being nice because I thought you wanted me to chat to him, to help the club, like Mr Smeets said.'

'It's your word against his, Angel, and Munro is a very powerful man,' said Vinnie tightly. 'It's best for us to keep on the right side of him, not to make a fuss. So, you don't tell a living soul about this, OK? Anyway, whatever he did or didn't do is alright by me because it will help the club.'

My head was spinning. This wasn't how it was supposed to be. It was meant to be me and Vinnie, not me and Munro.

He ran a finger down my cheek. My stomach lurched. 'But, Vinnie—'

'And I didn't like the way you sided with Alma tonight, Angel,' he cut in. 'That was very silly of you. It made me look stupid.'

'I'm sorry,' I stammered. 'She was just trying to help me.'

'Well, she hasn't helped you. She's got you into trouble. You silly girl.'

'I can make it up to you.' I let my negligé fall open, and tilted my chin, to try to kiss him. 'Let me show you that it's only you that I want.'

He shook his head. 'Don't do that, Angel, you're making yourself look cheap.'

Out of nowhere, he pushed me backwards and raised his hand.

And then he hit me.

Chapter Seventeen

ALICE

Elephant and Castle, May 1957

I do so love London in the springtime.

The stores are chock-full of the latest fashions, and every self-respecting woman wants to spruce up her wardrobe. And that means it's a prime time for me and my girls, the Forty Thieves, to go shopping.

I'd been in and out of the revolving doors at Selfridges, Gamages and Marshall and Snelgrove so many times in recent weeks, I swear I was getting giddy with it. The thrill of putting my hoister's drawers back on and stuffing them full of loot had knocked ten years off me – ten years I had spent lurking in the Underworld, while Nell Kane swanned about, taking my place in West End stores.

Well, I'd given her the boot, good and proper, and nobody missed her. Perhaps her old mate Iris did, but I made it clear when I went over to her salon for a nice shampoo and set, that if she behaved herself there'd be no hard feelings. Funny how her hands were shaking when she took the rollers out of my hair, but she'll get used to having me around in time. Let's face it, she ain't exactly got a say in the matter.

Things were running like clockwork round my manor, and it was as if I'd never been away. Yes, there were a few heads to bang together, but mostly it was shopping during the day and a knees-up in the pub at night. I left Rose in charge of the Piccadilly Commandos and she was happy with that; at least she'd stopped sneaking off to twirl around the dance floor in some Carnaby Street dive. One of the commandos told me her bloke was staying away from Soho after some kind of punch up because he got more than a bloody nose. Well, it's dog eat dog in this world, but giving Rose more responsibility seems to have taken her mind off her heartbreak, at least. I always say to my girls, no fella is worth it. And ain't that the truth?

And the way things have turned out, I'm content to let Zoe, little Miss Twinkletoes, get on with it for now. She's happy hoofing it up in the clubs, making a bit of a name for herself. She even had her mug in the paper the other day, pretending her name was Angel. I never heard anything so stupid 'cause I know she's a two-faced little minx, but if it keeps her happy, I don't see the harm in it. Oh, she might high-kick her way in the limelight wearing a daft pair of wings, but the moment I want her back, she'll be dancing to my tune. You mark my words.

Anyway, it hasn't all been clear skies down at Queen's Buildings because there's been some very bad news, to do with Derek, but it wasn't exactly unexpected. I'm organising a whip-round for Marj, to send her off to Southend for a few days with Em next week, to get away from it all when the hangman's done his worst. Em's been staying home to look after her mother, whose nerves are shot to pieces, the poor cow. Nothing can save Derek from the noose, the foolish sod. It ain't often someone gets topped like that. Nell's name will be mud for all eternity round our way. It's an ill wind that blows nobody any good, so they say.

There'll be an official period of mourning and I'm planning to wear black, just like Queen Victoria did when she lost her loved ones. Perhaps not for as long as Her Majesty – it ain't my favourite colour – but you get the point. Sometimes to be a good Queen, it helps to look to history to find the best way to unite your subjects.

In fact, I'd just hoisted myself a nice blouse in black silk and a length of ribbon from Gamages to make armbands for me and the girls, as a show of solidarity for Marj's loss.

I couldn't wait to show Patsy, who was waiting for me in the Bentley in the street outside, with the engine running.

So, you can imagine my surprise when I climbed into the back to find a pair of very well-dressed Teddy boys in my motor, and no sign of Patsy.

'I hope for your sakes that your parents are six feet under?' I said, nonchalantly.

One of them was smirking beside me in the back seat, and the other was sitting at the wheel, looking like the cat that got the cream.

'And why might that be?' said the driver.

'Because by the time me and my girls have finished, even your own mother won't know you.'

It was all very well hoodlums knocking seven bells out of one another all over Soho, but when they were hijacking my car and interfering with my hoisting operation, that was taking a flaming liberty.

The one sitting next me, who was the better looking of the two, roared with laughter and stuck out his hand for me to shake it. I had to admit, he had more front than most shop windows in Oxford Street.

'I've heard such a lot about you, Alice Diamond, Queen of Thieves. And you don't disappoint. But let's be friendly, shall we? We only want to get a bit better acquainted. My name's Vinnie, and your new chauffeur here is Victor.'

I gritted my teeth and smiled, working out whether I'd be able to stripe one of them, and give the other a clump with my walking stick, before they could get the better of me.

'I don't give a shit who you are, you are both skating on very thin ice. Where's Patsy?'

'Oh, she's off having a nice cup of tea with our boss, Mr Smeets.'

'Never heard of him,' I said. 'And Patsy don't care for cups of tea with strange blokes, and especially not when she's working.' I leaned forward, my hand closing around my chiv in my pocket, ready to strike. 'You'd better not have hurt her.'

Victor chuckled and Vinnie shrugged his shoulders.

'You've got it all wrong, Alice. Our boss has a business proposition to put to you. He asked me to extend his apologies for the unconventional invite, but the Forty Thieves can be a tricky bunch to get hold of.'

Victor was already driving down High Holborn, heading west.

'Where does he live, this Mr Smeets?' I inquired.

'Notting Hill,' said Vinnie, staring straight ahead.

I'd never liked that part of town. When I was younger, it was a totter's paradise, full of rag-and-bone men and rotting heaps of manure. The houses were thrown up on the cheap and built on clay-pits, and the women toiled long hours in slum laundries while their fellas whiled away the hours playing dice games in spit and sawdust pubs.

Lately, I'd heard about shady businessmen buying up whole streets of ramshackle houses and dividing them into flats to ponce off the poor immigrants who'd sailed from all corners of the Empire to find work. They'd expected to get a warm welcome from Britannia, but what they got in Notting Hill was usually a frosty reception from the locals at best, a deathtrap of a house, an exorbitant rent, and a landlord who didn't give a damn about them.

'Quite enterprising, this Mr Smeets, is he?' I mused. 'One of the landlords out west, by any chance?'

'He's come over from South Africa and is committed to expanding his property portfolio,' said Vinnie. 'We're helping him.'

I could just imagine these two thugs making their presence felt by frightened tenants, thousands of miles from home, struggling to find a coin for the electricity meter, let alone the wages to pay a week's rent.

'Oh, I bet you are,' I said, gazing out of the window.

I'd already made my mind up about Mr Smeets and what kind of a bloke he was, living off the misery of others.

Maybe Mr Smeets wanted to put an order in for some particularly nice furs for his wife or his girlfriend. Perhaps he just wanted to throw his weight around now that Jimmy was behind bars.

Whatever the case, this tinpot landlord had made a big mistake crossing me. And I was determined that this was one meeting he'd live to regret.

We parked up in Portobello Road, in front of a clock-maker's shop. Victor opened the door for me, and Vinnie followed close behind, to stop me going anywhere other than inside the premises. They were wearing forty-guinea suits and silk ties from Bond Street, and had matching quiffs. They were quite the double act.

Inside the shop, the whole place was stuffed with antique watches. I lingered by the display cabinet while Tweedledum and Tweedledee went in to have a word with their boss. It only took a few moments to swipe a beautiful gold fob watch. I took it as payment for the hoisting I'd missed out on by being dragged over here against my will.

So, I was smiling by the time we headed through a door at the back of the shop and into a dingy office. The blinds were drawn, and the air was so thick with cigar smoke I could barely make out the figure sitting at the desk.

'Well,' I said, as I marched in and sat down opposite him, 'you've got my attention. What do you want, Mr Smeets?'

'Hello, Alice.'

He loomed out of the shadows, flicking on a desk lamp, and my blood ran cold.

His face was so unfamiliar that I might have walked past him in the street. The skin was leathery and tanned from years in the sun; his cheekbones were sharper, giving him an almost lizard-like appearance, and his hair was thinning. He was slimmer, his well-cut suit showing a frame which was more lightweight than the brute of yesteryear. There was no sign of the scar I'd given him when we last met, but I guessed that he'd spent a lot of money over the years to change the way he looked in order to evade capture. But the things he couldn't alter – his voice, his eyes – were unmistakable to me, his sister.

'Billy,' I said, rocking back in my chair. 'I'd like to say it's a pleasure, but I'd be lying.'

Vinnie put his hand on my shoulder, and I felt the barrel of a gun poking into my ribs.

'Just a precaution, Alice, given what happened the last time we came face to face.' Billy smirked.

His voice was thinner, reedier, and it bore the unmistakable traces of a South African accent.

'Where's Patsy?' I said. 'This has nothing to do with her, so you can leave her out of it.'

He laughed. 'She's off having a sightseeing tour of London with some of my other boys. She's fine, for now. So, I'll cut to the chase before they run out of things to show her. Times have changed.'

'I'm not one of your tenants that you can just bully and get your way,' I said. 'There's too many of us. It's more than just me and Patsy. The Forty Thieves has a whole network – you'll never stop us and you're a fool to try.'

'I don't want to stop you,' he said. 'It's just a business proposition. Did you really think once that stupid little prick Jimmy was out of the way, you'd just have a clear run at things, like the old days?'

'You won't last five minutes once the police find out you're back.'

'That won't be necessary. Meet Detective Chief Inspector Munro, he's with the Flying Squad.'

I turned as the door behind me opened and the rat-faced inspector strolled in – the one whose picture was always in the *London Evening News* beside that oily reporter Duncan Swift's byline. My stomach churned in disgust.

'We're happy for you to carry on in the West End,' said Billy, 'but we'll need to give you our protection, and that will cost you fifty per cent of everything.'

Munro stood at Billy's side, his arms folded.

'The days of you scampering from shop to shop, stuffing furs down your knickers and living like a queen are over,' he chipped in. 'I like things organised, and Mr Smeets and I are singing from the same hymn sheet on that—'

'Don't you mean Mr Sullivan?' I said, butting in.

'Never heard of him,' said Munro. 'But Mr Smeets here is a great friend of the police force. I was very happy to make his acquaintance.'

He picked up an old photograph in a silver frame which Billy had on the edge of his desk. I recognized it in a heartbeat. It was of me and Billy when we were kids, working together as a team around the Seven Dials in Covent Garden, before he betrayed me.

Billy smiled at me, slowly.

'You'll never be free of me, Alice.'

The pair of them reckoned they had me stitched up like a kipper.

'I'm prepared to tolerate your activities up west, and so is the detective chief inspector, but only on allotted days and times and for a share of the profits. If you don't, you and your girls will find London can be a very dangerous place. It might not happen today or tomorrow, or even next week, but there will be a string of unfortunate accidents, I can assure you.' Billy was warming to his theme.

'The same as the ones your tenants meet when they complain?'

'Oh, I can't help it if people stumble downstairs and hurt themselves, can I?' He laughed. 'I'm not a bleeding nursemaid. Anyway, at least I'm providing them with somewhere to live. You've seen the signs in shops and boarding houses, surely? London ain't exactly friendly, and it breaks my heart to say it. "No Blacks, No Gypsies, No Irish". Whatever happened to live and let live? I'm offering people a home, a place to stay, so they can find their feet. That ain't a bad thing, surely?'

'You really are a disgusting ponce,' I said flatly. 'Everyone knows you are making money out of their misery – twenty people crammed into one miserable old deathtrap of a place, with one lavvy between the lot of them, while you charge them a sky-high rent. And God help anyone who complains.'

'It's just the way things are.' He shrugged. 'If they pay up on time and behave themselves, they don't get hurt.'

Munro chortled. 'Unless they step out of line with my boys.'

They really were a proper pair of pricks. And now they were planning to tighten their grip on the West End.

'You'll have to give me a chance to put it to the girls.' I clasped my handbag on my knee. 'I am Queen, but we work as a gang, and I need to let them know the score.'

'Very sensible,' said Billy. 'I've waited such a long time to work with you like this. I dreamed of it when I was baking for years under the South African sun, digging for these . . .'

He picked up a leather pouch on his desk and tipped out some of the contents. Fistfuls of stunning white gems spilled all over his blotting pad. Munro's eyes glinted with desire.

Billy counted out a handful of diamonds and handed them to Munro, who put them in the pocket of his raincoat and left us to it.

'Why didn't you just stay in South Africa or go somewhere else?' I said, with barely disguised incredulity. 'You're rich as Croesus by the look of it.'

God only knows how many people he had trodden on to get those stones, but he could have bought a palace or a desert island and lived like a king, and still have plenty left over. Instead, he was pulling strings in Notting Hill and lurking in the shadows in Portobello Road.

'I got homesick,' he said, sweeping the rest of the diamonds back into their bag. 'You can say what you like about living abroad, but the memory of London town gets to you in the end. The heat is tiresome.' He coughed and I heard his chest wheeze.

'That sounds nasty,' I said. 'Hope you've seen a doctor.'

He didn't answer at first.

'I'm not getting any younger, Alice, and I wanted to come home, back where I belong.'

He took a sip of water from a glass in front of him. I could still feel Vinnie breathing down my neck.

'Things have moved on since I went away,' Billy went on, 'but that presented an opportunity for me to build a different kind of business empire, to get back on the ladder. I knew that idiot Jimmy would fuck it up eventually in Soho, and now that he has landed himself right in it, I want to expand my interests back into clubland. It's where I belong. There are so many opportunities there, if you know where to look and you have the finances.'

'Fascinating,' I said drily. 'But there's something else you may want to consider before you start throwing your weight around with my gang like Julius fucking Caesar.'

'I doubt that very much,' he said, puffing on the cigar which had been slowly burning in a jade ashtray at his side. 'I see reining you lot in as vermin control, basically. You are pests.'

I could tell his interest was piqued, even though he had put on his best poker face.

But I had an ace up my sleeve.

We stared at each other in silence as half a dozen grand-father clocks out in the shop struck the hour. He'd changed his appearance, but he was the same arrogant, vicious bastard – my brother, Billy Sullivan.

He coughed again, and I wondered if part of the reason for his return was because time was not on his side. People get all sentimental about returning to their turf when they haven't got long left, don't they?

When the last of the clocks had finished chiming, I said, 'You've got a daughter.'

Before he could stop himself, he blurted, 'What do you mean?'

'I mean, nine months after you went dipping your wick around Soho, there was the patter of tiny feet.'

He ran his hands through his hair.

'You'd better not be lying, Alice—'

'Blood is thicker than water, isn't it, especially when you're getting older? She's a Sullivan, I swear on my life. As to where she is . . . Well, that's for me to know and you to find out. I could say more, but the gun poking in my side is making me very forgetful.'

Billy waved his hand at Vinnie.

'It's OK. Leave us for a minute.'

He waited until Vinnie had closed the door and then he pulled out a cut-throat razor from the breast pocket of his jacket and flicked it open.

'Just in case you get any funny ideas, Alice, I haven't lost my touch.'

'I don't know what you are insinuating, but nothing could be further from my mind.' I adjusted my coat to make myself more comfortable. 'Nell had your baby after you scarpered, and she raised her as Jimmy's.'

'What's she called?'

'Ruby.'

A haunted look crossed his face, like a longing for something – or perhaps, someone.

'Nell called her Ruby?'

I remembered the necklace he'd given Nell as a present. It was so showy, typical Billy. It seemed to please him that Nell hadn't forgotten that kindness.

'Pretty little thing,' I replied. 'She's the image of you – and she's got more than a bit of my attitude about her, too.'

'Where is she?'

Now, since I'd given Nell her marching orders, I hadn't the foggiest idea of her whereabouts, but given Ruby was my meal ticket out of a tight spot, I wasn't about to let on about that.

'I'll bring her to you, all in good time,' I said. 'You'll have to let me handle it, or Nell will take fright and run. Then we can have a more sensible chat about how we can make things work for you and me, perhaps on a fairer footing. Deal?'

He broke into a smile and licked his lips, like a tiger about to devour its prey.

'Deal,' he said. 'But you are going to have to show willing in the meantime, by paying me some protection money to cover the Forty Thieves. You've got a lot to make up for.'

I rolled my eyes and opened my purse. I counted out a wad of notes, sighing as I did so. To say paying him off stuck in my craw didn't come close. I had every intention of getting that money back, come hell or high water.

'You are in no position to argue, Alice,' said Billy, as he saw my reaction. 'And don't bother trying to pull a fast one. It's easy for me and my boys to pick any one of the Forty Thieves off the streets, and next time, we won't be sightseeing.'

Chapter Eighteen

NELL

Notting Hill, June 1957

The nights were getting lighter, and every evening the street was alive with the shouts of kids playing out.

The older ones booted a tatty football up and down the road, with dustbin lids as a goalpost, while the younger kids slung ropes around the lamp posts to whirl around them, like a makeshift swing.

I peeked out of the curtains I'd made from a bolt of cloth I'd managed to pinch from one of the stalls up Portobello Road. Ruby was nowhere to be seen. I didn't like her staying out after dusk, not since Marj and Alice had threatened us. She'd wet herself at school on more than one occasion when the other kids played rough, and I didn't want her getting picked on if she got scared and had another little accident.

All I really wanted to do, after another day cooking bacon and eggs down at the café, was to put my feet up. I was nearly six months gone and my ankles were swollen, like one of the old dears I used to see shuffling up to the market around the Elephant. My hair was greasy, with dark roots showing through, and there was no way I could stretch to having it dyed my usual blonde, so I'd taken to wearing a headscarf whenever I ventured out. What a godawful sight I looked.

I clutched my belly as I made my way down the rickety staircase, and I felt the baby moving inside me. Our baby. I'd written a few letters to let Jimmy know my good news, but I didn't tell him where I was in case the authorities found out and came looking for me. I wrote lie after lie, telling him everything was fine, and me and Ruby were just living quietly until all the fuss over the robbery had died down.

I made sure I paid my rent weekly to that slob Carter, who had a pitch as a bookie on Portobello Road when he could be arsed to get out of his armchair. From what I'd gathered, he acted as the eyes and ears for the landlord, Mr Smeets. People up and down the street had a list of complaints as long as your arm about mice, rats, blowflies, dodgy electrics, leaks, broken this-and-that, meters not working, water heaters which risked third degree burns if you weren't careful. Nothing was ever mended or put right, and tenants had learned the hard way not to cross Mr Smeets.

A couple of families from round the corner organised a rent strike, and came home to find their front doors taken off their hinges and a bunch of pasty-faced thugs chucking their few belongings into the front garden. Victor and Vinnie Graveney were ready with a can of petrol and a match, and you could smell the acrid smoke for days afterwards.

I hated it with every fibre of my being, the way we were forced to live, but I wasn't in a position to do anything about it. Mrs Finnegan minded her own business, worked her fingers to the bone, and cared for her daughter Polly. She had a bun in the oven and nobody had ever seen her other half.

I wasn't unfriendly, but I couldn't let anyone get too close to us. I chatted about the weather with the old gadgy downstairs, who'd lost a leg in the Blitz and needed a bit of help with his shopping, and I always said hello to the family at the top, who had arrived from Trinidad not long before I showed up.

I hadn't managed to meet the lady across the hall from me yet. We passed like ships in the night because of the hours we both worked, but sometimes I heard her crying in the night when I couldn't sleep.

Maybe it was wrong, but I took comfort from the fact that there was someone else in the building feeling every bit as miserable as me.

Some of the lads a few doors down had parked their record player beside the open window, and music was blaring out as I went looking for Ruby.

It wasn't anything I'd ever heard before up in Soho, but I didn't mind it; it was upbeat and it made me smile. I recognised one of them as the poor sod who'd come off worse in the boxing ring against one of the Graveney twins. He tipped his hat at me as I waddled past in my housecoat.

I got to the end of the street, but there was no sight of her, so I kept walking, past the rag-and-bone man who was doing his rounds.

A bunch of boys were whooping and jeering outside the pub at the end of the next road, so I quickened my pace. I couldn't see what was going on at first, because they'd formed a circle and were a mass of greased back hair and those ridiculous, long draped jackets and drainpipe trousers.

Ruby was in the middle, dancing, kicking up her legs, while they tossed pennies at her.

'Show us your knickers, then!' shouted one

She picked up the hem of her skirt and flashed her underwear as she twirled around.

'I'll give you a sixpence to take 'em off,' said another, leering at her.

I grabbed him by the scruff of his neck, making him yelp with surprise.

'Lay a finger on her and I will break every bone in your scrawny body.'

Ruby stopped dancing. She looked at the pavement in shame.

'I just wanted to earn some pennies because we're poor.'

'Naff off, Missus!' the Teddy boy said, shaking himself free from my grasp. 'We were only having a bit of fun.' He coloured up, bright pink.

I gave him a thick ear for his trouble.

His mates started nudging one another and laughing at him.

'You're under the thumb, mate.'

That galvanised him.

'Get your hands off me, you dirty pregnant cow!' he said, shoving me, so that I stumbled back against some railings. I grabbed my belly, instinctively, to protect it.

'Mummy!' screamed Ruby.

She lashed out, kicking him in the shins.

'You little bitch!' he roared, making a grab for her, but she ran to my side, and we cowered there, while the whole gang loomed towards us. One of them pulled out a razor, grabbed hold of Ruby by one of her pigtails and sliced it clean off.

'No!' I screamed, before he could do more.

He threw her pigtail on the ground, and she started to cry, clutching the side of her head. I pushed her behind me, out of their reach. My stomach had started to cramp, and I was shaking like a leaf.

Out of nowhere, there was a sound of a whip cracking through the air.

'Sling your hook, you 'orrible lot!'

It was the rag-and-bone man, built like a brick shithouse, stinking to high heaven and with barely a tooth in his head. The commotion brought some drinkers out of the pub, and they watched, their pints still in their hands, as if we were their evening's entertainment.

The Teddy boys spat on the pavement at the rag-and-bone man's feet, but he didn't budge.

'Next one of you clowns to lay a finger on either of these ladies gets it across the face,' he said, gathering his whip, ready to strike again and this time, for real.

They looked at one another. The stand-off only lasted a few seconds. Their leader, the one who'd chopped off Ruby's plait, shrugged his shoulders.

'You ain't worth it.'

He sauntered off with his hands in his pockets, with the others following like a pack of greasy lemmings, but not before they'd all flicked the Vs at me.

I glanced down, wondering if I had actually pissed myself out of fear, for the first time in my life, just like Ruby.

But to my horror, what I saw, trickling down my legs and splashing on to the pavement, was blood.

'Is there someone indoors who can help you, love?' said the rag-and-bone man as we clip-clopped home on his cart.

'Yes,' I lied, clamping my legs together to stem the flow. 'My husband's there, he'll help. You've been so kind, thanks.'

Ruby opened her mouth to say that wasn't true and we lived alone because her dad was in the hospital; that's what I'd told her. I gave her a look which made her think twice. Our business was our business, and we didn't talk about it with strangers.

What a sight we must have looked: me doubled over, using my headscarf to mop the trickle of blood running down my leg, and Ruby with a single plait on one side of her head and her hair cropped short on the other, her eyes red from crying.

I tucked her under my arm as I limped up the stairs into the house, wincing in pain. I was scared – for her, for me and for the baby I was carrying – and for once in my life, I didn't know what to do.

As we reached our front door, I started to cry. It started as a sob, and then I sank to my knees by our front door, howling like an injured animal.

'Please get up, Mummy,' said Ruby, over and over. 'Please get up.'

But I couldn't move.

I heard the door opposite creak open and felt a pair of arms around my shoulders, warm and reassuring.

'Come on, dear, you can't lie there all night.'

I looked into her face, which was worn and tired, but her eyes were so full of kindness that it made me wail even more. She was the crying lady, the one who I heard sobbing every night, and now here I was, beating her at her own game.

'I'm Dolores,' she said, pulling me to my feet. 'Let me help you.'

Dolores busied herself cleaning me up, laying me on the sofa and tucking a blanket over my legs, while she sent Ruby to get some sugar and milk from her flat for a cup of tea.

I knew that was a ruse to give us a moment alone.

The bleeding had stopped, but I felt utterly exhausted and terrified it would happen again.

'How far along are you with the pregnancy, dear?' she asked, feeling my stomach.

'Five months, nearly six,' I said.

'Has it happened before?'

'No,' I said. 'Nothing like this.'

She pulled a fob watch from the pocket of her cardigan and took my pulse.

'I'm a nurse, and I have to tell you it would be best to go to the hospital and get checked, for the baby's sake.'

'I don't want to go,' I said.

How could I explain to her about my hatred of the authorities after what had happened with my baby Joseph being taken away when I was in prison? I was unmarried — I didn't trust doctors and the like.

She nodded, as if she understood without me having to explain.

'Is the baby moving?'

I felt it kick, right on cue.

'Yes,' I said.

'If it happens again, you must go. But for now, my best advice for you is to rest as much as you can.'

I laughed out loud.

'Don't be daft, I've got two jobs just to try to make ends meet.'

'If you don't slow down, you are risking everything,' she said matter-of-factly. 'Is it worth it?'

I propped myself up on my elbows.

'Never mind about me, I know you've got troubles of your own. I hear you crying in the night all the time.'

She sighed and turned away. 'No, you're mistaken.'

'Dolores,' I said firmly, 'I wasn't born yesterday. You're helping me, so maybe I can help you? A problem shared is a problem halved and all that.'

She took off her glasses and sat down in the chair opposite me.

'When I say I'm a nurse . . . I *was* a nurse back home, but over here all the matron wants me to do is to empty bedpans all day long. I'm the last to be served in the shops and people look through me like I don't exist just because of the colour of my skin, because I'm Black. I've spent all my savings coming over here, and I'm supposed to be sending money back to Jamaica to help my family. But I got myself into debt to rent the room and the interest on the loans keeps getting bigger. Mr Smeets sends his bully boys round to take money from me. I never know from one week to the next how much it will be. All I do know is it's never enough.' Tears welled in her eyes. 'My family pinned all their hopes on me and my job here, and I've let them down.'

'No,' I said, as Ruby came back with a cupful of sugar and a bottle of milk. 'Don't be so hard on yourself. People are treating you like shit and it ain't right. I'm sorry for all of it. You haven't let anybody down. They have let you down.'

She wrung her hands together and her voice fell to a whisper.

'The last time a couple of his henchmen turned up – good-looking boys, twins. And they said they'd smash my place up unless I have enough money to pay Mr Smeets properly. I know from some of the families down the road that they aren't making idle threats.'

'The Graveneys?'

'That's them,' she said, wiping her eyes, putting her glasses back on.

I began to wonder if Jimmy's instinct about Vinnie and Victor had been right – that they were more than just two cheeky lads trying to carve a niche for themselves, to get out of the slums. They were involved in protection rackets for this unscrupulous landlord.

'You're lucky to have your daughter here to help you, and you have a baby to think about.'

Dolores put her glasses back on and smoothed her skirt down.

I put my fingers to my throat and felt my most prized possession, my ruby necklace, the one that Billy Sullivan had given me all those years ago as a gift the night we spent in each other's arms.

Then I looked at the little girl standing before me, smiling even though her life had been turned upside down. And at Dolores, who'd travelled halfway across the world to be treated with contempt and preyed on by Mr Smeets and his thugs.

'Maybe I can do something small to help,' I said.

I'd go to the pawn shop first thing in the morning and see what I could get for the necklace. Then I could give up the morning job at the butcher's, just until the baby came, and have something left over to help Dolores with the loan.

The only Ruby I cared about was the one standing in front of me, nattering to Dolores about how Rapunzel had her hair cut off, too. I didn't give a damn about Rubies, my club, and certainly not the jewel given to me by the gangland boss Billy Sullivan.

I wasn't the superstitious type, but that necklace belonged to a different life – a time that was gone.

It was time to say goodbye to it forever.

Chapter Nineteen

Zoe

Soho, June 1957

The bruise on my cheek was fading into a hideous rainbow of colours which even thick make-up couldn't hide.

'Walked into the door again, did you?' said Sandra, as she lit up a smoke in the kitchen.

I nodded, nibbling at a piece of dry toast.

Vinnie had belted me one because I'd put too much sugar in his tea yesterday. At least, that was his excuse.

Sandra gestured to the silver tin on the table.

'Help yourself, Angel. It'll take your mind off it.'

My hands were shaking, and my head throbbed as I reached out and grabbed a couple of the small white tablets. She called them pep pills, her little helpers. In an hour, I'd be back to my old self, and I knew I wouldn't need to eat all day, which was good because no matter what I tried, I couldn't lose weight. Alma had resorted to putting me in little skirts to hide my hips.

The pills gave me energy, especially if I took another right before the performance, but the downside was I would lie awake in bed, staring at the ceiling all night. So, Sandra had some blue tablets to help me relax.

Barely a day went by without me dipping into her pill box. Life had changed a lot in the last three months, ever since Angel's opened.

And my nightmare began.

The dressing room was full of flowers, as it always was after he'd hit me. I couldn't stand the scent of them any more, and even walking past a flower seller made me feel nervous.

As well as bunches of red roses from Vinnie, there were lilies, with a card from Detective Chief Inspector Munro. I knew what that meant. Tonight, there'd be another party.

Vinnie appeared in the doorway as I was putting on my face powder.

'Do you like them, Angel?' he said.

'They're lovely, thank you,' I replied, fighting back tears.

No matter what I did, it was never good enough for Vinnie. He'd find something to find fault with and I'd pay for it later.

He ran his finger down my cheek and I winced as he touched the bruise.

'Don't cry, Angel, you'll spoil your make-up. Be sweet to Munro later, OK? Mr Smeets is very grateful for it.'

Vinnie wanted to give me away to the powerful friends of Mr Smeets, to please his boss. Try as I might, I couldn't stop caring about him or hoping that we could go back to how it was when he was so kind. I began to wonder if I'd imagined those good times, or if I was to blame for everything.

I stood up and put my arms around him, kissing him, desperately. He was like a drug I couldn't resist.

'I'm sorry for losing my temper, sweetheart,' he soothed. 'You know I don't mean it. It's just the stress of running the club.'

'I understand, Vinnie,' I said, laying my head on his shoulder. 'I'll try to do better.'

'Here,' he said, pulling a gold chain from his pocket. 'This is for you.'

It had a gold letter V on it.

'It's gorgeous,' I said.

'Now everyone will know you're mine,' he replied, with a glint in his eye as I put it on.

That was the deal for the life I was living – the life I didn't know how to escape. I had beautiful clothes and gifts from admirers in the club, but I was virtually a prisoner. Vinnie and Victor were my jailers, and Sandra was like a warder who made sure I was always fit to perform.

Back at our flat later that evening, a procession of rich and wealthy blokes mingled with me and some of the other dancers, and vacant-looking beautiful girls who were friends of Sandra's. Everyone drank and smoked until the early hours. I was dog-tired, but I knew I couldn't go to bed, not yet. For me, the show was not over. Vinnie gave me the signal.

I draped myself over Munro and whispered sweet nothings in his ear, pretending that I fancied him.

He loved that. I felt him getting hard as I sat in his lap. I gazed at him shyly and he led me into the bedroom, locking the door behind him. I let him undress me, get on top of me, take me however he wanted. I'd learned not to protest, or he'd take his belt to me. Sometimes he did that anyway.

He was a vicious bastard. He liked to handcuff me to stop me fighting back. Vinnie turned the music up in the lounge, to cover my cries.

And afterwards, when Munro and the others had left, he took off his shirt and lay beside me in the bed, smoke from his ciggie billowing upwards to the ceiling.

Then he turned and gave me a peck on the cheek.

'You're such a good girl, Angel.'

The next morning, I lay in the bath, the hot water soothing the latest bruises from Munro.

My legs and arms were stick-thin, but my belly was rounder than ever, even though my hunger pangs were gnawing away at me.

And then it happened.

I felt something move inside me. First it was like a butterfly. Then it was a kick.

I scrambled from the bath, water dripping everywhere, and pulled a towel around me.

Sandra was there in the kitchen, standing sentry as always.

'You alright, Angel?'

Her eyes were cold and hard.

'No,' I said, shaking from head to toe. 'I think I'm in trouble. I think there's something wrong . . .'

'You sick?' she said, flicking ash into a saucer.

'I think I'm pregnant.'

Vinnie drove us across town in his Daimler. A muscle twitched in his cheek, and he hadn't spoken a single word to me since Sandra told him my news.

She sat next to me in the back, applying lipstick.

I had nothing to say. I clasped my hands together, wishing I could be somewhere else – that this could be happening to someone else.

We turned into Harley Street, and Vinnie parked up outside a three-storey house with a shiny black door.

'This is it,' said Sandra. 'Let's get you sorted.'

She opened the car door.

Vinnie flicked open the newspaper and started to read. It was like I didn't exist.

'Come on!' Sandra chided. 'We haven't got all blooming day.'

My legs were shaking as I got out and I had to hold the railing to make it up the stairs. A brass nameplate by the bell said 'Dr E. Howard, Women's Clinic'.

My mind was racing. I couldn't remember when I'd last bled; I'd put it down to the excitement of being star of the show at Angel's, and all the dancing I was doing.

The thought of Munro knocking me up filled me with such revulsion. I wanted the doctor to tell me there was something else happening. Maybe I just needed an operation to fix it?

Sandra rang the bell and a woman in a clingy skirt suit answered, her hair pulled into a neat bun.

'We've come to see Dr Howard,' said Sandra.

She peered at the pair of us over her horn-rimmed spectacles. It was clear what she thought of us, because she couldn't help looking down her nose.

'Do you have an appointment?'

'We're working for Mr Smeets,' said Sandra. 'And we need to see the doctor now.'

That seemed to do the trick.

'Very well.' She strutted off down the hall, her heels clicking on the black and white tiled floor. 'Just sit here for a minute.'

She gestured to a waiting room which was filled with well-dressed women, pretending to read magazines. There was a young girl, maybe fourteen, who was clutching her mother's hand.

After a few moments the receptionist appeared.

'Dr Howard will see you now.'

She clicked off down the corridor and we followed her. Sandra pushed open an oak-panelled door and the doctor was sitting there, behind a leather-topped desk, making notes. She didn't wait to be asked to sit down. I hovered nervously at her side.

He was old, maybe fifty, with a few wisps of hair on his head, which he combed over to one side, and he had thin lips. He reminded me of the cartoon fella on the Homepride flour packet.

'Angel here has got herself in a spot of bother,' Sandra simpered. 'We need you to do the usual and help her out.'

Dr Howard took off his jacket without saying a word, went over to the sink and started washing his hands. In the corner of the room was an examination couch, with a modesty screen around it.

'Pop behind there and take your underwear off,' he said. 'There's a sheet to cover yourself with.'

I froze.

'Go on!' hissed Sandra. 'Get on with it. He's here to help you.'

I swallowed hard and then did as he asked. I lay there, waiting for him, staring at the ornate plasterwork on the ceiling.

He started by prodding around on my tummy.

'Have you ever been pregnant before?'

'No,' I said. 'I don't even know if I am.'

He raised his eyebrows.

'When did you have your last period?'

'I can't remember,' I said.

That was the truth – I honestly couldn't recall. My heart was pounding in my chest.

'Just relax,' he said, putting his hands under the sheet.

'I can't,' I snivelled.

I was scared out of my wits, and I didn't want a strange bloke touching me. I just wanted everything to be back to normal.

He was stern. 'You've done more than this to get yourself into trouble, haven't you? Don't be so silly. I just need to examine you.'

I felt his fingers, cold and probing. I gritted my teeth because I was still tender inside, from Munro, who was always rough. Then, mercifully, it was over.

'Right,' he said, going over to the sink to wash his hands again. 'Put your clothes on.'

Sandra's face was a picture of expectation as he strode back to the desk.

'Well,' she said, 'when can she come in and see you? We want it sorted as soon as possible, please.'

He shook his head.

'She's too far along. I can't do anything, not in this case.'

Sandra opened her handbag and counted out some ten-pound notes. She placed them, very deliberately, on the desk in front of the doctor.

'But I'm sure you can make an exception, as she is one of our girls. Mr Smeets would be very grateful.'

He ran his fingers through what was left of his hair.

'Impossible,' he said. 'She's about six months pregnant. The risks are too great. I don't want to be facing a coroner's inquest. I'm talking about losing more than my medical licence here – it's my liberty, or worse, if things go wrong.'

Sandra's mouth dropped open.

'But you've always been so helpful, doctor!'

'Yes,' he said, slamming his desk diary shut and standing up to show us the door. 'But you normally bring me girls in the early stages. This baby is nearly full term. Nothing is going to stop this pregnancy now – she's young and fit and healthy, although she could do with eating a bit more. I suggest you look to adoption if she doesn't want to keep it. Good day to you.'

My head was spinning, and I clung to Sandra's arm as we left the building.

'Oh, you're for it now,' she murmured. I could swear there was a look of glee on her face. 'Wait till Vinnie finds out you've well and truly got a bun in the oven, and it's nearly baked!'

That wasn't the half of it, but the silly cow had no clue.

If I was so far along with the pregnancy, the baby wasn't Munro's – it was Jimmy's.

Vinnie frogmarched me up the stairs to the flat, with Sandra trailing in our wake. She shut the door behind us as he turned to me, his eyes blazing with anger.

'Six months gone, you dirty bitch! You were up the duff all the time I was courting you! Whose is it? Who were you fucking? Was it one of the fellas from the jazz club? Who?'

I stood there, my arms covering my belly, with nothing to say for myself.

He pulled his arm back and clouted me round the head, sending me flying towards the sofa.

'You're going to have to tell me, Angel.'

'No, no, Vinnie,' I sobbed, as I lay sprawled on the carpet. 'It wasn't like that. I wasn't putting it about. It just happened once. It was a mistake. I'm sorry.'

I covered my head with my hands as blows rained down on me. He hauled me to my feet and slapped me again.

It was a beautiful mistake, with Jimmy – Jimmy, who'd never hire me out to his boss's wealthy mates to use as a whore. But I'd never tell Vinnie the truth.

'Please stop, Vinnie!' I sobbed. 'You know I only love you. It only happened once, I swear it. I don't even know his name. It was in a back alley one night. He grabbed hold of me, and I couldn't stop him.'

He looked at me with such contempt when I said that, it was like a knife cutting me.

'Oh, I love you, Vinnie!' he mocked. 'But you couldn't keep your knickers on, or your legs shut, could you? Now, whose is it?'

He made a fist.

'She ain't going to tell you,' Sandra drawled. 'You'll have to take her up the hospital if you carry on, Vinnie, and that ain't going to help us, is it? Mr Smeets don't like fuss.'

He relented, thrusting his hands into his pockets and pacing the room.

'You're no good to us now,' he said, 'not in this state. The party's over for you here, Angel.'

He kicked me like a dog, and I whimpered.

'Pack your things, I've got another job for you,' he spat. 'Nobody wants to see a pregnant mare performing in a nightclub.'

I gathered my dresses, my beautiful shimmering outfits, my favourite heels, and my satin and silk nightwear and stuffed them in a case, while Sandra watched me, idly blowing smoke rings. I slipped Jimmy's ring inside a make-up bag when she wasn't looking. I unpinned the newspaper cutting from the club's opening night from its place on the mirror. It had me and Vinnie, smiling together, with Diana Durbidge, under the headline QUEEN OF CLUBS, and I was so proud of it.

'You daft cow,' murmured Sandra. 'You had it all. You should have treated Vinnie with more respect. Don't you know which side your bread is buttered?'

'You don't understand, it wasn't like that,' I said,

struggling to close my suitcase. 'Someone took advantage of me.'

That was such a bare-faced lie and it stuck in my throat to tell it, but I was fighting for my survival, and I knew it.

'It was my first time. I didn't know you could get pregnant the first time. What's going to happen to me?'

Her face softened. 'I know it's tough, but we've got it good here with Vinnie and Victor, trust me. The only thing you've got to focus on now is the work that Vinnie wants you to do. Do what you are told, and it will all sort out, and he might forgive you after you've had the baby. Come on, he's waiting.'

I nodded. I had no choice but to follow her. I was six months gone with nowhere else to go, and no matter what Vinnie did, I couldn't get rid of the feeling that I wanted to be near him. I wanted him to put his arms around me, to hold me close, and for us to dance together and dine in beautiful restaurants. I loved it when he looked so proud of me, when I performed in Angel's.

Now all I saw in his eyes was a look of disgust.

He didn't speak a word to me as we drove through the backstreets, up to King's Cross and behind the station, to a warren of terraces, blackened by years of filth.

I clambered out, suitcase in hand, as he knocked on the door. A woman answered, her hair in curlers and a ciggie dangling from her lip. She greeted him like an old friend.

'Oh, hello, love!'

Music was playing on a radio in the scullery out the back, but it couldn't disguise the sound of a man grunting and a woman's high-pitched gasp in the front room. I knew those noises only too well, because Sandra had taught me how to fake it to keep Munro happy. The whole place smelled of damp with a faint whiff of disinfectant.

There was a row of gentlemen's coats and hats hanging from pegs in the hall, rather like a railway station café. Vinnie opened a tea caddy on the hallway table and helped himself to a fistful of notes.

'Is this a new girl?' said the woman, looking me up and down.

'She's up the duff, Betty, six months gone,' said Vinnie, scowling. 'She can help you with the maid duties until it's time.'

Betty's face set like concrete. 'You shouldn't have kept that little secret, should you? Silly girl.'

'I didn't have a clue about it,' I protested. 'Honest.'

Vinnie shook his head and turned on his heel to go.

Betty locked the door behind him and popped the key in her pinny.

'Well, you've made your bed, love,' she said, climbing the stairs. 'And now you are going to have to lie in it.'

Chapter Twenty

ALICE

The Old Bailey, London, September 1957

Lady Justice glinted in the sunshine, her golden sword held high above the city in one hand, and her scales weighing the evidence in the other.

She was a magnificent sight, but I ain't ashamed to admit that the court gave me the jitters. So, it was Maud, rather than me, who turned up to witness the final day of Jimmy's trial for the robbery of the century. He'd been found guilty of the bullion raid, but today was the fun part – sentencing.

I fastened my ribbons tightly under my chin and pulled my bonnet close around my face in case any of the cozzers prowling nearby recognised me as I walked up the steps and into the building. But I needn't have worried. There was safety in numbers because half of London had turned out for a ringside seat. Say what you like about times changing, but you can always rely on a Londoner to enjoy the spectacle of a criminal down on his luck.

We crowded into Court Number One, with its impressive domed roof and oak benches. God, it brought back memories, but for once, I wasn't standing in the dock.

This time it was Jimmy Feeney and his accomplice, Albert Rossi, standing there, both suited and booted in their best bib and tucker. They looked like a pair of Savile

Row tailor's dummies. I'd probably credit the dummies with more intelligence, because what crook worth his salt pulls off that kind of a heist and then gets caught laying bets at Brighton races? I'd been tickled pink reading about that bit of the evidence in the paper, because the prosecution had had a field day. He'd made them look like a right pair of prats.

Now, before you start to judge me too harshly, there was another reason for me entering the hallowed halls of the Old Bailey. Weeks had rolled by, and I still hadn't seen hide nor hair of Nell and Ruby. On the one hand, it showed I had been very efficient in sweeping her off my manor. On the other, it was landing me in it with my brother Billy, and I was running out of excuses as to the whereabouts of his daughter. I'd had just about enough of having to toe the line, to avoid further complications for me and the Forty Thieves.

I was Queen, but in name only, and that situation was highly unsatisfactory after everything I'd been through to get my crown back. I'd managed to fool the girls that we should only go shopping twice a week to avoid me drawing attention to myself, after such a long absence from the West End stores. I pretended to be a little bit rusty with my hoisting, perish the thought.

Paying their wages was another matter, and I had to think creatively because half my profits were going straight into the coffers of Billy Sullivan. Luckily, Nell had a ready supply of cash stored at the flat, but I'd got to the stage where I was pawning her jewellery. Well, when I say I was pawning her jewellery – Maud was. I found she got a better price over in Hatton Garden, on account of her being a woman of faith, and the jewellers seemed to be a bit more generous to her, especially with her hard luck stories. Plus, the last thing I wanted was word getting back to the Elephant and Castle that the Queen of Thieves was putting things in hock.

As much as I wanted to see Jimmy put behind bars, I needed a chance to have a quiet word in Nell's ear, so that I could keep my part of the bargain with Billy.

Call it instinct, but I had a feeling she'd be unable to resist coming to court, just to catch a glimpse of her fella. Every gangster expected his woman to be there in court when he was sent down.

And I wanted to be there, right by her side, when she turned up.

After all, we were family, weren't we?

We were packed in like sardines in the public gallery, as the court clerk intoned 'All rise!'

The judge walked in, dressed in his scarlet robes. Oh, I could tell just by looking at him that he was a proper hang 'em and flog 'em type, and poor Derek could attest to the former, God rest his soul. We were just sitting down when a heavily pregnant woman waddled in, her hair covered by a headscarf. She glanced around, desperately trying to find somewhere she could park her considerable bulk. An usher took pity and found her a seat by making a couple of blokes squish closer together on the end of our row.

Jimmy glanced at her. It was only a momentary flicker of recognition, but she smiled to herself, and his shoulders relaxed a bit. It was only when I looked more closely that I realised the pregnant woman was Nell. She'd lost all the sheen that she used to have – the one she got from being queen bee. Her face was haggard, with worry lines etched deep – the kind you get when you don't know how you're going to pay the rent and you've got a baby on the way and your other half is in the nick. My heart would have gone out to anybody else in those circumstances, but not her. She only had herself to blame for her predicament.

The judge banged his gavel and silence fell over the courtroom.

'James Feeney and Albert Rossi,' he began, glaring at them like they were shit on his shoe, 'you have both been found guilty of a violent and carefully planned robbery – a robbery for which you have shown not one shred of remorse. It is a robbery in which a police officer tragically lost his life.

'Yet, despite the evidence of your accomplice Derek Brown and that of the men you attacked in the pursuit of your goals, you continue to deny your involvement. You have refused to co-operate with the police in tracing the missing gold. You continue to protest your innocence, in the face of a guilty verdict reached by a jury.

'The idea that the perpetrators of this heinous crime were not you, James Feeney, the self-styled King of Soho, and your deputy Albert Rossi, is beyond credibility, and an insult to the memory of the police officer who died as a result of your evil plan. Derek Brown has already paid the ultimate price for that, as the law requires.'

A murmur went round the public gallery at that.

'But your roles will not go unpunished,' the judge went on. 'Society will not stand for such an outrage, and you will feel the full force of the law, as far as I am able to apply it in this case.'

The whole room was holding its breath. Jimmy stared back at the judge and Albert looked down at his shoes. He always was such a dapper chap, I wondered how he'd cope in a prison uniform.

'Therefore,' said the judge, 'I sentence you both to twenty-five years in prison, to be served as a whole tariff. Take them away, officers.'

The court erupted with people jeering at the pair of them and shouting 'Murderers!' and 'You should hang!', sending the clerk into a frenzy of 'Silence in court! Silence in court!'

Nell gasped audibly and then covered her mouth with her hands to stop herself crying out. She lowered her head and I could see tears coursing down her cheeks, her shoulders shaking with grief as she stared at the floor. She was fighting to keep it all in, not to give herself away as someone who knew and loved Jimmy Feeney, but I was watching her like a hawk. She glanced up, staring straight ahead, with such a broken look on her face. It was like a light had gone out in her world.

The police officers cuffed the pair of them and the last thing we saw was the top of Jimmy's head as he went down the stairs to the cells below.

Nell was carried forward on the tidal wave of people leaving the court. I had to elbow a few of them out of the way to reach her, but the fact I was wearing my Salvation Army uniform helped clear the path for me, which was a mercy. I waited until she'd opened the door of the Old Bailey before I made my move.

'The sword of justice has fallen on the guilty and now it's up to us to pick up the pieces,' I whispered, as I walked down the steps beside her.

She turned to face me, as if she'd been scalded, seeing straight through my disguise.

There was no question of her running away, not in her condition.

'Get away from me, you old bitch!' she hissed.

'Don't be like that,' I soothed. 'What happened to Jimmy ain't my fault and you know it.' I pointed to her bulging stomach. 'When's that due?'

'Mind your own business,' she said, covering her bump protectively. 'You've got what you wanted. Just leave me and my family alone.'

'Oh, Nell,' I sighed, slipping my arm through hers, 'I can't do that. You *are* my family, whether you like it or not. It's a fact of life, like death and taxes, and we are going to have to face up to it. Together.'

She tried to shake me off, but I clung to her like a limpet.

'Get off me!' she shouted.

'May I be of assistance, ladies?' said a gentleman in a raincoat.

A couple of police officers had started to walk towards us, to see what the fuss was all about.

'I'm just helping this unmarried mother-to-be,' I said to the gent. 'It's the Lord's work, I am sure you'll understand.'

I gave him a knowing glance, brandishing my copy of the *War Cry*. He nodded and went on his way.

Nell clocked the cozzers and the funny looks we were getting, and stopped struggling.

'That's better,' I said. 'Don't draw attention to yourself. Let's go and talk about it all over a nice cup of tea.'

She glared at me, as if that would be as welcome as swallowing razor blades.

'I'll treat you,' I said.

I had worked up quite an appetite by the time we got to the Lyons' Corner House down on the Strand. Nell appeared to have lost hers, despite eating for two.

The place was full to bursting, but a Nippy in her black -and-white uniform showed us to a corner table.

227

'We'll have the full afternoon tea, with cakes and scones,' I said, beaming.

Oh, I loved tea houses, with their gleaming stainless steel tea urns and hot counter, tempting cakes and cosy nooks – mainly because whichever Gladys was serving was usually too dozy to notice when half the cutlery or china went walkabout into my handbag.

'You'll never get me out of your life, Nell,' I said matter-of-factly, as a plate of scones arrived, dripping with butter.

I helped myself to one; it was just the ticket after a day in court. Nell turned her head away and gazed across the restaurant. I pushed one towards her.

'Go on, eat, you must be starving.'

She picked it up, her fingers trembling, and took a bite, chewing slowly.

'That's better,' I said. 'A woman who is expecting needs to keep her strength up. Think of the baby.'

'Just cut it out,' she spat. 'Whatever it is you want from me, let's get it over with. I've got to get home for Ruby.'

'Well, that's exactly why I'm here,' I said.

A look of sheer terror crossed her face.

'You are not coming within a street mile of my daughter.'

'She's my niece,' I said softly. 'I don't want to hurt her, or you. I've done a lot of thinking these past months. Now that justice is done and Jimmy's behind bars, I think many of the Forty Thieves, myself included, might come to the conclusion that you've been punished enough.'

She couldn't hold back; the floodgates opened, and it all came tumbling out. That's always the way with pregnant women – they do get over-emotional if you know how to push the right buttons.

'You have no idea what I've been through,' she said, shaking. 'I nearly lost the baby.'

She fought back tears. Most people would have found it all quite moving, but it seemed to give me more of an appetite, and I devoured another scone as she was blubbing. The Nippy arrived with the teapot just in time, because I had developed a bit of a thirst. Nell looked like she could use a brew, too, and she was going on a bit, frankly, so it would be an excuse to shut her up.

'I'm sorry to hear all that, Nell,' I said, pouring us both a reviving cuppa. 'Is the little one alright now?'

'Yes,' she said curtly. 'Not that it's any of your business.'

I sighed.

'You're not the only one with troubles,' I said. 'I've had a bit of news of my own to consider – the kind of news that makes you think a lot about family.'

I had more ham about me than the local butcher.

I could tell she was intrigued, although she stared into the depths of her teacup, to avoid looking at me.

'Doctors say my nerves are shot to pieces and I might not have long left.'

Nell guffawed with laughter and her eyes flashed with anger.

'Oh, that's priceless, Alice. You must think I was born yesterday.'

I gripped her by the wrist.

'I ain't joking. It's the kind of nerve trouble that gets worse with age, and you are the only family I've got left. I was thinking about passing on my inheritance, and who might be suitable—'

'We don't want your money,' said Nell, wincing slightly because I did have quite a firm grip.

I dug my nails in to make my point.

'Are you seriously going to turn your back on my charity? Think about the baby, Nell – and what about

Ruby? What kind of a life are you living? What kind of a mother are you? Jimmy ain't going to rescue you – he's inside for the next twenty-five years. That's a long, slow decline into the gutter, from where I'm sitting. Ruby is going to bear the brunt of it. Maybe you won't even be able to look after the baby, and they'll take it away from you, just like they did with Joseph.'

At that, she started to sob. I let go of her and produced a handkerchief – one I'd stolen from Gamages the other day. It was quite beautiful; silk with polka dots. I made a mental note to ask for it back when she was finished with it.

I opened my purse and handed her a few fivers.

'Here,' I said. 'This is just goodwill, to help you until the baby comes.'

She couldn't look me in the eye, but she snatched that money as if it were her only lifeline.

'That's better, very sensible,' I said, smoothly. 'Now, I ain't saying this can happen overnight, Nell, because I would have to work things out with the girls, and Marj will always be a sticking point, but perhaps there's a way to get you back into Queen's Buildings, and back in my gang.'

'*Your* gang?' She almost spat her tea out.

'It was mine before you got your grubby little hands on it,' I shot back. 'But that's all water under the bridge now, is what I'm saying. At least it will be if you will let me be an aunt to little Ruby.'

'What kind of an aunt could you ever be?' she scoffed. 'I wouldn't let you look after a pet rabbit! You dressed up in that ridiculous outfit to win her trust. You snatched her from her own home and terrified her and lied through your teeth. She knows you're a wicked woman, Alice. That's one thing I have made sure of.'

I signalled for the Nippy to bring us the bill.

'And that, dear Nell, is why you are going to tell her it was all a silly game and nothing more. Stop being so bloody selfish and think about your children. It will pay you to keep your friends close and your enemies closer. You can't run away from this, Nell. I can have you followed home and find out where you live this afternoon. You ain't exactly inconspicuous.'

She looked like the back end of a bus. In fact, I was planning to do exactly that, just in case, because I liked to get a good return for my money. I wasn't a bleeding charity.

'I have spies all over London,' I added. 'I'm sure the police would be very interested to know your where-abouts . . .'

All the colour drained from her face. She knew when she was beaten.

'Alright. You can see her, but it can't be too often. She's already been through enough upheaval, and it's affected her badly.'

'Bring her to Kensington Gardens by the boating lake tomorrow afternoon at three and we can take it from there,' I said. 'Then we can all be one big happy family.'

Chapter Twenty-One

NELL

Notting Hill, September 1957

I felt sick to the pit of my stomach for what I was about to do, but gazing at Ruby as she dozed on the sofa, I knew I didn't have any choice.

Alice Diamond had found a way to get back into my life. The money in my purse meant we would be able to eat and pay the bills for the coming month, without having to worry. I could even afford to get some things for the baby, because so far, I didn't have a stitch put by.

I'd been planning to go and nick some things from one of the shops, but with the exhaustion at the end of every day in the café and looking after Ruby, I just hadn't the energy to go hoisting.

Dolores was an absolute godsend, like having a guardian angel by my side, ever since that day when she'd found me collapsed in the hallway. I'd helped her out with some cash to keep Mr Smeets at bay by pawning my necklace, and we'd become firm friends. That was worth more than any gem to me, and to Ruby, who loved making us both a cup of tea while we put our feet up for a natter.

But with every week that passed, there was some new outrage from Mr Smeets and his boys. The family upstairs didn't pay the rent on time, so he cut off the electricity to the whole building. In the end, they did a moonlight flit and Victor Graveney went looking for them, with an iron bar to make his point. I couldn't help wondering who would be next.

I didn't trust Alice as far as I could throw her, but she was offering me a way out of the nightmare. It wasn't a case of swallowing my pride to let her help – life had beaten that out of me. I was drowning here in this deathtrap of a house, and as a mother, I had to do whatever it took to make sure my kids would survive, even if it meant making a pact with the Devil.

The leaves were turning the most beautiful shades of gold as I strolled with Ruby through the park in the autumn sunshine. Kids were messing about on bicycles and running the gauntlet of the park warden as we wandered towards the boating lake.

'I want to tell you who we are meeting today, Ruby,' I began, 'because I need you to be on your best behaviour.'

'Are we going to see Daddy?' Her face lit up.

She had no clue about Jimmy being sent down. I'd kept it all from her, just telling her he was still very poorly in hospital, and we couldn't visit yet.

'No,' I said, swallowing hard because the thought of her wanting to see Jimmy gave me a lump in my throat. 'Daddy's not well enough to see us yet. It's the lady you met before, when we lived in Queen's Buildings. You knew her as Maud.'

'The one who was really called Alice and was the wicked witch?' she said, giving me a puzzled look. 'I didn't like her, she scared me.'

'Oh, but it was all a misunderstanding. The nasty woman who really wanted to hurt you was Marj. Alice isn't wicked – she's a nice enough person if you give her a chance. I was wrong about her.' A shiver ran down my spine as I said it. 'In fact, she's your auntie, and I want you to be polite to her. Can you do that for me, sweetheart?'

Ruby shrugged.

We sat down on a bench, because I was out of breath and the baby was kicking me right in the ribs. We'd only been there about five minutes when I spotted Alice, wandering along with a bunch of balloons and a massive bag of sweets.

Ruby clung to me.

'It's alright,' I whispered. 'I'll be right here. Go on, darling.'

She stood up and pulled her socks up, then she skipped towards Alice, who held out a balloon for her and offered her a sweetie.

I watched as the pair of them walked around the boating lake, with Ruby keeping her distance from Alice at first, but by the time they'd reached the other side, she had taken Alice by the hand and the two of them were laughing. A man on the park bench on the other side of the lake stopped reading his newspaper and gazed at them as they passed by. Alice pulled some bread from her pocket, and they fed the ducks near him.

To onlookers, it would have seemed like they were a family. There was something about Ruby which echoed Alice, even though I hated to admit it: the sturdiness of her features, the thick, wavy hair, and her spark and the way she laughed. I hadn't seen her smile much lately, let alone laugh, but Alice had her chuckling.

I'd let her down so badly as a mother. They say a child is a good in itself, no matter who the parents are. And Ruby was living proof of that.

She was grinning from ear to ear as Alice brought her back to me.

'Same time again next week?' said Alice eagerly.

She handed me an envelope with more cash in it and I nodded. I couldn't refuse her, and we both knew it.

Alice presented Ruby with the balloons and the rest of the sweets.

'What do you say?' I prompted.

'Thank you, Auntie Alice,' chimed Ruby, running off to chase some pigeons.

Perhaps it was the shock of allowing Alice to befriend my daughter, but when I got home, the sickness got worse. I was doubled over the sink, chucking my guts up, when Dolores came in to check on me.

She felt my stomach, which had gone rigid. I was panting and in pain.

'This baby's getting ready to come,' she said. 'I'll pack you some things for the hospital.'

'No!' I said. 'I don't want to have the baby there.'

'Don't be silly. You've already had bleeding. You need to go to hospital, it's the safest place for you and the baby. We'll get you a taxi and I can look after Ruby.'

I knew what she was saying made sense, but I was so terrified, I hugged Ruby tightly as I was leaving, fearing it may be the last time I ever saw her.

'Be a brave girl, and remember Mummy will always love you.'

'Will you bring me a baby brother, Mummy?' she asked, her dark eyes full of longing.

'Yes,' I said, patting my tummy. 'I promise.'

The squeak of the matron's shoes on the linoleum floor brought back memories of my time in the infirmary at Holloway when I had my first baby, Joseph. I wanted to be anywhere but here, but there was no way out. The hands of the clock on the wall opposite me seemed to be racing by, but with each hour the pains got worse and there was still no sign of the baby arriving.

I clutched the bed rails, screaming in agony, sweat pouring from me.

'Oh, Jesus, Mary and Joseph, make it stop!'

'Come on now, don't make such a fuss,' Matron scolded. 'Women have been giving birth since the beginning of time and they didn't scream the place down, did they? Let's see how you are getting on.'

She pulled back the sheets.

A puddle of red was pooling between my legs, and I caught the worried look on her face. She dashed over and rang the ward bell for assistance, and before I knew what was going on, I was being wheeled through the double doors and down the corridor.

'What's happening?' I panted. 'Where are you taking me?'

'We need to get this baby out now,' she said, stroking my hair as we raced through the hospital. 'Baby will be fine. Don't fret. You've just got complications.'

I was wheeled into a room filled with bright lights.

A doctor wearing a surgical gown placed a mask over my face.

'Just relax, Mrs Finnegan, breathe deeply.'

And then the room faded to black.

When I came round, Matron was smiling at me, but I was so groggy, I could barely focus. I tried to sit up, but a searing pain in my belly made me cry out.

'Take your time, Mrs Finnegan,' she said, propping me up on some pillows. 'Baby was delivered by Caesarean section, and you are going to feel very sore. No sudden moves or you will split the stitches.'

She placed a little handbell by the side of my bed and then presented me with a bundle.

'It's a boy,' she said. 'A beautiful baby boy.'

His eyes were tightly shut, but the moment I saw him, I fell in love. The agony in my abdomen no longer mattered.

I stroked his tiny fingers and kissed his perfect face.

'My baby,' I said.

'Well done,' said Matron. 'You've been very brave indeed, Mrs Finnegan, and what a lovely child you have there. What will you call him?'

'James,' I replied, looking at him in wonder.

He was the image of Jimmy, with the same chin and his lovely blond hair.

Matron smiled to herself and then pulled back the curtains, which were closed around the bed next to me.

A young woman was lying on her side in a hospital nightgown, her red hair tumbling over her pillow. Her arms were stick-thin, and covered in bruises and what looked like burn marks. What's more, she was snoring like a train.

Matron yanked the sheets back.

'Wake up! Your baby needs feeding! This is no time for you to be sleeping. This is a maternity ward, not a holiday camp! You've got a job to do, and that job is to be a good mother to the baby that the good Lord has seen fit to provide.'

Matron stomped off down the ward.

It only took me a split second to recognise the young woman, as she grumbled herself awake and rubbed sleep out of her eyes. The baby at the foot of her bed began to cry.

It was Zoe.

'What are you staring at?'

She sat bolt upright and glared at me, the corners of her mouth curling with contempt.

'I didn't expect to see you here, Zoe,' was all I could manage.

She shrugged. Her baby was screaming its head off.

'I could say the same about you.' She smirked, with such an insolent look. 'I would have thought you were a bit old to be a mother.'

If I'd had the energy, I'd have jumped out of the bed and slapped her, good and proper. The cheeky cow.

Matron marched back up to Zoe's bedside with a baby bottle full of milk and lifted the infant out of his cot.

'Will you please feed your baby?' she said sternly. 'You are disturbing the other mothers on this ward.'

'No,' said Zoe, lying back down. 'I'm tired and I want some sleep.'

'You are a disgrace,' said Matron. 'Unmarried and uncaring!'

The baby was so close to my bedside now. I peered at it, curious to catch a glimpse. A wave of shock went through me.

'I'll help,' I said, wanting to get a closer look. 'I know this girl. She used to work for me. I don't mind feeding the baby while she gets some rest.'

'She doesn't deserve any help,' clucked Matron, who practically had steam coming out of her ears. 'In all my days, I have never known a girl so ungrateful.'

'Honestly,' I said, 'it's no bother. I can feed him. My baby is still asleep. I'll ring the bell when I'm done.'

My heart was pounding, ten to the dozen.

Matron took my sleeping baby and I held Zoe's child in my arms. He gulped the milk hungrily and clasped at my fingers while she turned her back on me, to face the wall. I gazed at his tiny, perfect face. The blond hair and his chin were so like my baby's. The resemblance was undeniable.

My stomach flipped and I wanted to cry out. The room started to spin. This innocent little scrap, this tiny baby, had just broken my heart in two.

Zoe rolled over.

'I suppose you think you're so much better than me, don't you, Nell? You've always looked down your nose at me, haven't you? And now you're a bloody saint for helping me, but you don't know the half of it. You're lying through your teeth about being married – *Mrs Finnegan*, my arse! Everything about your life with Jimmy was a lie, and that's a fact!'

She had such a twisted look on her face, full of pleasure at the pain she was about to cause me. But gazing at her baby boy, who was now dozing happily in my arms, I already knew the truth; tears were rolling down my cheeks.

'That's right,' she laughed hatefully. 'You can see it, can't you? You're nothing special to him and you never were! He loved me and he wanted me. He's your precious Jimmy's child.'

The rest of the afternoon passed in a blur. Zoe pulled the bedclothes over her head and slept on, ignoring the baby every time he cried. I lived for the injections of morphia they gave me to take away the pain in my stomach, but also to relieve the agony she'd brought into my life.

It didn't matter how or why he'd done it. The fact was, he had. Jimmy had slept with Zoe, gone behind my back, knocked her up. And all the while, we were planning another child. I should have realised it at the time from the way he was behaving around her – the way she flirted with him. But I felt so secure in our relationship because he was always begging me to marry him and treated me like his queen, that it never crossed my mind to suspect anything serious was going on.

Now the anger for what he had done was burning inside me; yet here I was, nine months later, holding our baby, our son, the image of our baby Joseph who was so cruelly taken from us.

Our new baby, James, was a son he'd only get to know over brief prison visits, under the watchful eyes of a screw. That was if I even wanted to introduce him to our child after the way he'd cheated on me. And yet, in the back of my mind, I knew that I'd been living a lie for the past ten years with Ruby, so who was I to judge him? I ached to feel Jimmy's arms around me and to hear his voice, and then we could just have at least half a chance to work this all out. The whole world seemed to have turned upside down and all I had were memories of how things used to be. Whatever we'd both done, we could face the future together, couldn't we? Neither of us were perfect, but perhaps we were perfect for each other.

When baby James cried, I rang the bell, and the midwife would bring him to me to feed, and then she'd bustle off to change him. Then, Zoe's baby was carefully lifted from his cot at her bedside and taken off for a bottle. She didn't look at him or hold him or even acknowledge his presence, the poor little mite.

At teatime, Matron came round to see Zoe again, shaking her awake.

'If you aren't going to care for your child, there are plenty of families who will offer him a loving home. Have you considered adoption?'

She shrugged.

'I don't care what happens to him,' she said, eyeing me coolly. 'His father is a lying shit who promised me the earth, just to have his way with me. And being pregnant has brought me nothing but trouble. I don't have time to care for a baby.'

'Very well,' said Matron. 'I will have someone from the adoption agency come and talk to you about it tomorrow, and you can sign some papers.'

'Good,' she said. 'I've a career as a dancer to think about. Once this is all sorted, life can go back to how it always was.'

She scratched at the scabs on her arm. What a sight she looked, with her cheekbones protruding and her skin so sallow. All the sparkle had gone from her. I couldn't imagine anyone paying money to see her dance in that state. I was boiling with rage for what she'd done with Jimmy, but somehow, I found a space in my heart to pity her.

'Whoever is treating you like this, you don't have to go back to him,' I said. 'And you should think twice about giving the baby away, Zoe. You might live to regret it.'

'You know nothing about my life!' she shot back. 'You're in no position to preach to me. You've lost your club, and you're just a nobody whose husband's in the nick and can't even keep it in his trousers. Anyway, aren't you going to ask me about his affair with me? It must be driving you insane, thinking about the two of us!'

'No,' I said. 'There's nothing I need to know. Jimmy made his mistake and it's for him to explain it to me, in his own time.'

That made her see red.

'I wasn't a mistake! He wanted to marry me, and he gave me a ring – see?'

She produced a ring from her brassière and stuck it on her finger. It was a gold band studded with small emeralds.

'Whatever he may have told you, Jimmy loved me, and he still does,' I said quietly. 'The only person he ever wanted to marry was me. He's going to be very pleased to hear all about our son. I doubt he ever gives you a second thought, Zoe.'

That took the wind out of her sails.

'I don't care about Jimmy,' she said. 'Because I've got Vinnie and he's in charge in Soho now.'

'Is he the one who's been hurting you?'

I wouldn't put anything past that bully boy and his twin brother. She was a shadow of the bright, sparky girl who had got herself a job in Rubies and stolen the show. The change in her was truly shocking.

She put her arms around herself and hugged her knees.

'I haven't the faintest idea what you are talking about,' she said, looking straight through me. 'Everything is going to go back to normal now the baby's come, and I'm going to be star of the show again at Angel's. Vinnie even named the club after me. He loves me. You'll see.'

She leaned over and yanked the curtain closed between our beds. It was a relief not to have to look at her, to be honest.

'Suit yourself,' I said. 'But a leopard doesn't change its spots, Zoe.'

She tried to hide it, but I could hear she was crying to herself, very quietly.

That night, baby James sicked up half his feed and wouldn't settle, so I held him in my arms until I nodded off. One of the midwives on night duty popped him back in his cot at the foot of my bed so that I could rest, but I lay there, listening to him whimpering, staring at the ceiling.

In the early hours, when all around were sleeping, every-thing became eerily still. It took every ounce of my strength to swing my legs round to get out of the bed, wincing in pain as I did so. The light was on in the corridor outside, but the ward was plunged into darkness. I felt my way to the end of the bed and found the cot, my fingers creeping across the blanket, just to check on him.

But instead of a warm baby, sleeping soundly, I felt a cold body, his fingers almost rigid. I put my hand over my mouth to stifle a scream. Then, I picked him up and held him to me, but there was no breath and no heartbeat.

My baby was dead.

I have lived that moment over and over, willing it to be different, but it always turns out the same: me standing at the end of my hospital bed, clutching the body of my newborn son. I don't know how long I stood there, rocking him to and fro in the dark, as Zoe's baby slept soundly, perfectly, in the cot which was so easily within my reach.

Life was not fair. She didn't deserve that beautiful healthy baby, just like Matron had said. The thought that her child, Jimmy's son, was going to be raised by another family, just like my firstborn, Joseph, was too much.

I laid my baby down on the bed, so softly and gently, and then I scooped up her baby and kissed him. He was such a warm little bundle, wriggling a little in his sleep as I laid him in the cot at my bedside. Zoe didn't stir; she was out for the count.

Then I picked up my darling James, cold and grey, and tucked him into the cot at the foot of her bed. I kissed his forehead and tenderly stroked his cheek.

'Mummy loves you, always.'

Life was so uncertain, but I could offer Zoe's baby my constant love – a mother's love, which was so much more than she could ever give. There was no space to feel angry with Jimmy for what he'd done – not if I was going to go through with this. I promised then that I would cherish him as my own child, because somehow, life had given me a second chance at motherhood.

And I was fully prepared to take it.

The scream of the tea lady when she passed the cot by Zoe's bed and saw the grey face of my dead infant will live with me forever.

Mothers all over the ward were wailing in disbelief, and Matron came running like the clappers. She pulled back the covers and felt for a pulse. When she found none, she placed a blanket over the little one's body and wheeled the cot from the ward.

Zoe barely reacted, and it was then that I knew I had done the right thing. She just lay flat on her back, listless as ever.

'Don't you care?' said a woman opposite, who was nursing twins. 'Your baby has died in the night! Can't you find it in yourself to shed a single tear, for the love of all that is holy? If you'd cared a little more, he might have lived!'

'Mind your own business,' said Zoe, staring at her blankly.

'I'm sorry for your loss, Zoe,' I said, clasping the baby in my arms a little tighter. He began to cry. 'There, there, James,' I said. 'Don't fret. Mummy's here.'

There was no flicker of recognition from Zoe at the sound of her own son's crying.

She looked at me, dead-eyed. 'I didn't want the baby

– he was more trouble than he was worth. You wouldn't understand. I just want Vinnie back, that's all.'

The woman across the way muttered, 'Shame on you!'

By lunchtime, Zoe had hauled herself out of bed and was packing her few things in a tatty suitcase.

The last I saw of her, she was wobbling her way down the ward in a pair of patent leather high heels – a Blitz of a girl, with long red hair hanging in rats' tails. She wore a too-thin coat over a summer dress, her bare legs blotched with bruises.

As the ward doors swung shut, I could have sworn I heard Matron say, 'Good riddance to bad rubbish.'

When she had gone, I asked Matron for a pen and some notepaper, and I wrote to Jimmy, to tell him all about his new baby son.

Dearest Jim,

I'm writing this from the hospital, to say you are the proud father of the most beautiful baby boy.

He's gorgeous and so strong. He looks the spitting image of you. He's got a good pair of lungs on him, but we are both doing just fine. I will write you more when I can, but for now, we send you all our love and the biggest cuddle.

· A big kiss from Ruby, too.

Yours forever, Nell xxx

The same afternoon, at visiting time, Dolores popped into the ward, with Ruby skipping excitedly at her side. She gave me a beautiful box of chocolates, which we opened and shared, to celebrate the birth.

Ruby was the happiest I have ever seen her, peering

into the cot and fussing over the baby.

'Oh, he's so big and healthy,' said Dolores. 'What a sweet child!'

She picked him up and handed him to Ruby, for a cuddle.

'Meet your brother, baby James,' I said, beaming with pride.

Chapter Twenty-Two

ANGEL

King's Cross, October 1957

All the fellas know me as Angel, and I work hard to please them because that's what Vinnie wants.

He's promised, once I've paid him back for all the trouble I've put him through, that I'll be welcome in the club, and I can come back to live in the flat in Soho.

Sometimes I lose count of the number of clients I see. Betty hammers on the door when the time is up, bringing me a reviving cuppa which is always scalding hot. Some days it feels like four or five blokes an hour. I don't see their faces when we're doing it, or think about them at all, really. I blot it all out and dream about me and Vinnie instead – how it will be when we are finally able to be together.

They like it when I talk dirty to them, on account of my posh accent. It reminds them of their wives, who won't do the things I will.

On breaks, I go out in the backyard for a ciggie with the others, girls from all over the place. We do have a laugh. Some of them pretend to be French or Belgian, calling themselves Fifi, because the blokes love that and pay extra. Sometimes, when they talk to me it's clear they come from Newcastle or Liverpool, and that sets me off giggling.

I know I'm different from them, because I'm only here

working off a debt for something that was my own stupid fault. I'm not a brass or a tom, or whatever it is the local urchins call them when they throw stones at our front door.

Sometimes Sandra pops round, just to check on us all, and she tells me, 'You'd never had it so bleeding good, Angel, and you screwed up, didn't you? Just work hard and you can make it right.'

She brings me pills to keep me calm or give me energy, and heavier stuff for the others. I've tried it once or twice, the needle, and it made me forget everything, which wasn't what I wanted. I wanted to remember me and Vinnie and where I was headed.

But the morphine was useful to trade with the others for ciggies or a nice bit of underwear or make-up. Sandra liked to keep a close eye on her little chemical helpers, but she wasn't so bright. I hid my stash in a bag under a loose wooden floorboard in the corner of my room, and she never had a clue.

Vinnie had to hire other girls to fill in for me when I was in the family way, and that was a right nuisance – it cost him a small fortune. I don't think he's so very angry with me, not so much these days, especially now the baby is no longer here to trouble us.

'It's better off dead,' he said, as he sat beside me in the scullery when I got back from hospital. 'That sprog was getting in the way of your career.'

'I never wanted it anyway,' I replied, laying my head on his shoulder, just for a moment. 'I wish none of it had ever happened.'

The way he looked at me then was just like it used to be. And that gave me hope; hope for us and for the future.

I twisted the gold chain he'd given me around my fingers, feeling the letter *V*, which had quite sharp edges.

'I still wear it, Vinnie,' I whispered.

''Course you do!' He chuckled, planting a kiss on my cheek. 'You're my girl, ain't you?'

I poured him another brew from Betty's teapot, but he pushed it away and stood up, glancing at his gold wristwatch.

'I've got to go, Angel, I've a bit of business to be getting on with.'

'I'll see you next week?'

He was already halfway down the hallway.

He shouted over his shoulder, 'Perhaps, Angel!'

He called himself Mr Smith, but I'm not sure if that was his real name. He wore a bowler hat and a pinstripe suit and worked in the city as an insurance man or an accountant or something. Friday was his usual day to pay me a visit. Mr Smith lived at the end of the Metropolitan line and his wife didn't understand him.

When we were done, he straightened his tie and said he needed to rush because he was going to be late for the train and where did the time go?

Betty had already taken his cash; no one got past her door without emptying their wallet first. She looked soft, with her plump little face and her motherly hips, but she was hard as nails when she needed to be. Few of the girls ever stepped out of line, but if they did, she made a note of it.

Vinnie or Victor would sort it when they turned up. God knows, I learned that the hard way. I bore the scars from those early days; the cigarette burns to teach me a lesson. Vinnie apologised afterwards, sending me flowers to make up for it because I think he felt bad about hurting me to get his point across. I was his special girl – he always said so.

So, Mr Smith dashed off to catch his train, leaving his newspaper behind, and by the time I realised, he was long gone.

I wasn't one to keep up with the news, but when Betty stuck her head round the door with a cup of tea, I had a quick look, just to pass the time.

That was when I felt my world spinning out of control.

There, splashed all over the front page, was Vinnie with Diana Durbidge.

They were engaged.

My mouth fell open as I gazed at the picture of them, so beautiful together. She was laughing with her head thrown back, the way she always did, her silver satin dress accentuating every curve. She had a fox fur slung around her bare shoulders, with a huge diamond ring nestling on the third finger of her left hand. Vinnie stood beside her, gazing down adoringly.

THE KING AND QUEEN OF CLUBS!

Soho celebrated the surprise engagement of two of its brightest stars last night, with a huge party at the top nightspot, Angel's.

Champagne flowed as a host of glamorous faces joined in the party after nightclub owner and entrepreneur Vincent Graveney popped the question and presented the stunning actress Diana Durbidge with an enormous diamond ring.

"I'm so in love, I am the luckiest girl in London,' said Miss Durbidge, 23, who has a string of box office hits to her name. 'Vincent is such a gentleman, and although we have known each other for a while, we have grown very close over this past year. I am delighted I'm going to be his wife."

Mr Graveney, 21, said: "I feel the best years for Diana and myself are yet to come. London is our home town but the world is our oyster. I'm so proud of her. She's so beautiful and talented. I've never met a woman who could hold a candle to Diana Durbidge."

A big wedding is planned for the summer, with film stars and dignitaries expected to fly in from all over the world.

Meanwhile, Mr Graveney confided he is planning to whisk his fiancée away on a trip across the Channel to Paris, the most romantic city in the world.

I'm sure readers of the London News will wish them the very best in their married life together. And bon voyage!

I locked the door.

Outside in the street, kids were playing kick the can, and it ricocheted from wall to lamp post and back with a clatter.

I glanced around my room, with its faded yellow wallpaper and blown plaster, worn red velvet chair, and mirror spotted with black where the damp had got in.

I hardly recognised the haggard face staring back at me: her sallow skin, her red hair thinning at the roots, and two high-coloured patches of rouge on her cheeks. Her mouth was a crimson gash and her lashes were caked in mascara, clinging like spiders to eyes that had seen too much in too few years.

I wasn't born to be poor.

I was born to dance.

I'd been the Queen of Clubs, but now Vinnie didn't want me.

I'd been at the top in Soho, and now I was on the scrapheap in King's Cross.

The floorboard creaked a little as I lifted it and carefully laid the contents of my bag out on the bedspread, unwrapping the silk scarf to reveal my full syringes.

Vinnie had lied to me. He was never going to let me out of here. He had his sights set on bigger things: Diana Durbidge, beautiful, talented and rich.

He had taken everything from me. My dreams, my dignity and even my name. What on earth had I done?

I picked up the syringe and tied the silk scarf tightly around my arm, tapping to make the vein bulge, just as Sandra had taught me. Just one scratch, then everything would feel better again.

I stuck the needle into my arm and felt the liquid, so cold as it entered my bloodstream. I needed more. Quickly, I fumbled for the second syringe and plunged that in, emptying it. The rush sent me tumbling back onto the pillow.

My eyelids were so heavy, and blood was roaring in my ears.

Someone was hammering on the bedroom door, but the knocking was muffled and growing more distant.

A girl was walking towards me with her red hair in filthy ribbons. She was wearing a too-short skirt and a woollen cardigan, lovingly knitted by someone who cared, someone far away in Devon, where the grass was green. And she was smiling at me. Her complexion was so fresh, like peaches and cream.

Someone called her name.

'Zoe!'

My eyes rolled back in my head and the room faded to black; I was floating, warm and peaceful, oblivious to the fleas and the damp and the smell of sex.

The girl beckoned for me to follow.

'Be careful . . .' I murmured.

There was a whole world out there, full of wealthy people – people who took advantage of girls like her. She could get herself into trouble and then she'd be for it! But she wasn't listening. She was young and brave, with a pound in her pocket that she'd pinched from her mother's tea caddy, and she wandered through an arcade off Piccadilly, where the posh folk liked to go.

'Keep up, slowcoach!' she said.

For a moment I was struggling and out of breath.

'Wait!' I whispered. 'Wait for me.'

Then I spied her standing in front of a beautiful shop, filled with the finest things that money could buy.

The door swung open.

I stepped inside.

London Evening News

NEWS IN BRIEF

The naked body of a woman was found slumped in a doorway in King's Cross last night. It is believed the woman, of no fixed abode, had been working as a prostitute and died of a drug overdose. Police say there are no suspicious circumstances. The coroner has been informed.

Chapter Twenty-Three

ALICE

Notting Hill, October 1957

'I want to meet my daughter!' Billy banged his fist impatiently on the desk in front of him. 'Bring her to me!'

'It ain't that simple,' I said, sitting down opposite him. 'You've seen her at the park. I've stood within a few feet of you while we fed the ducks and you've had a good look at her, haven't you?'

'It's not enough. I want Ruby to know me, and to get to know her!' He coughed and grabbed for a glass of water.

'And you shall. I just need a bit of time to arrange it—'

'You've had enough time!' he barked. 'Bring her to me here tomorrow.'

'She'll talk,' I said. 'She'll tell her mother and then everything will be ruined. Nell will go to ground, and you'll never see Ruby again.'

'No,' he said, his eyes boring into mine. 'No, that won't happen because you'll suffer for it if she does, I can promise you that.'

He spun his chair around, so he had his back to me.

'I want to see Nell, too,' he said, lowering his voice. 'It's time for us to meet again, Alice. I don't care how you do it, but she needs to know I'm still alive.'

He spun back around. His face was etched with pain, almost hollow with longing, but only for a split second.

'You've never got over her, have you?'

'She's given me a beautiful child, a daughter,' he said, recovering his composure. 'An heir. I need to see them both. And I'm not going to take no for an answer. They are my family, whether they like it or not. You've got twenty-four hours.'

Now, the funny thing was, I'd known for a little while that Nell and Ruby were living right under Billy's nose, but he was none the wiser.

She was shacked up in one of his deathtrap houses only a few streets away, along with the other poor sods who'd run out of decent places to stay. The day I met her at the Old Bailey, I'd had David the magician follow her home. She wasn't exactly difficult to spot, in her condition.

He'd been keeping an eye on things ever since, and apparently, she had a job in a greasy spoon down Portobello Road. She'd made quite the impression there, making friends with the owner and encouraging him to let some of the local kids play their skiffle music to the customers, with the washboards they'd nicked from their mothers and upturned crates from the market. The place had become quite popular. It was amazing how Nell had the ability to make the best of the situation.

She'd made friends with a woman in her building, and David had seen all three of them walking to the shops together. When Nell went into hospital to have the baby, the same woman took Ruby to and from school. But one of the Graveney twins – Victor, probably – was also keeping an eye on that woman, and she'd paid him some cash, quite a wodge of it. It sounded like moneylending, which was just the sort of low-down stuff that Billy liked to trap people into, with never-ending and exorbitant payments to clear the loan.

Right now, Nell was back home from the hospital with her baby, but she'd been resting up for a few days. I thought it was time to pay her a visit.

And what could be nicer than turning up with a brand-new pram – a Silver Cross, like the ones those posh nannies use down in Holland Park? In fact, it was exactly one of those prams, because I swiped it when the nannies left the babies out in the front garden for fresh air. Don't get me wrong, I didn't liberate the pram with the baby in it. I just popped the sprog in with its friend in the pram next door before I wandered off, whistling to myself.

Then, I wheeled my way through the backstreets of Notting Hill until I got to Nell's. David hadn't quite done it justice when he'd described it to me; it really was in a dreadful state – a tumbledown wreck of a place.

I knocked on the door and Nell answered, with a babe in arms.

'Surprise!' I said, as she recoiled down the hallway. 'Ain't you pleased to see me?' I invited myself in, hauling the pram up over the threshold and into the kind of tenement I'd known in my childhood. The best you could say was the woodworm kept the cockroaches and the mice company.

'Can't you leave us in peace, Alice?' she said, shushing the baby as he started to cry.

'That's a bit churlish,' I replied huffily. 'I've only gone and got you a lovely pram and that's all the welcome I get!'

She didn't bother even looking at the pram I'd hoisted for her. Instead, she turned on her heel and started to slowly climb the stairs. I followed, pulling a bottle of sherry from my carpet bag.

'Let's raise a toast and wet the baby's head, and then we can go out for a lovely stroll.'

She didn't have the strength to argue with me, I could see. She had dark circles under her eyes and was shuffling slightly.

'Difficult birth, was it?' I inquired.

'You could say that,' she replied. 'But it was worth it.'

I glanced around the room. Even the poorest factory girls in Queen's Buildings could do better than this. The baby was making do with a drawer for a cot, and there was no bed for Ruby, other than a tatty old sofa. A row of freshly washed nappies was drying in front of a meagre fire in the grate, and baby clothes were soaking in the sink.

Nell looked as if she hadn't slept in days.

'Well, let's have a look,' I said, peering at the little bundle in her arms. 'Boy or girl?'

'It's a boy. Baby James,' she said, brightening.

She laid him carefully into the drawer on the kitchen table and tucked him in. He was the image of Jimmy, it had to be said, with the same chin and a smattering of blond hair. She had every right to be proud of him, even if his father was in the nick with no chance of remission.

'I expect Jimmy's over the moon about it, ain't he?'

'The papers said he's in Wandsworth,' she said, stroking the baby's cheek tenderly. 'I wrote and told him the good news. I'm just waiting to hear back. We haven't been able to be in touch in ages.'

She was lost in her own thoughts, gazing at her son.

I picked up a couple of chipped teacups from the draining board, sloshed some sherry in both and handed her one.

'Can't we do this another time?' she murmured, sinking into her battered old armchair.

'No,' I said briskly, raising my cup in her direction. 'As it happens, we can't. To baby James!'

She took the teeniest sip.

I fished out my purse and pressed a ten-pound note into her hand.

'That's for the baby, it's to bring it luck.'

She tucked it into the pocket of her pinny, without a word of thanks.

'Now, get your coat on,' I said. 'We need to pick up Ruby from school. There's something I want to show you down Portobello Road.'

I tried not to take offence at Nell's lack of enthusiasm for having me around, but there was one person who was pleased as Punch to see me: Ruby.

She ran towards me through the school gates with her arms outstretched, and it melted my heart to see her breaking into a huge smile.

'Auntie Alice!'

I pulled out a paper bag full of her favourite sweets – sherbet lemons – and she popped one in her mouth.

'Have you seen my baby brother?' she asked proudly. 'Ain't he smashing?'

'He certainly is!' I said. 'And I even bought him a lovely new pram so you can help talk him out for walks.'

She slipped her hand in mine and started chatting about her lessons.

Nell kept her lip buttoned as we sauntered along towards Portobello Road. She was sensible enough to keep up the pretence that she was happy to have me around, but I could see she was twitchy, like a caged animal, trying to work out how to escape.

The market traders were in full flow, selling their wares with shouts of 'three for ten shillings' and then dropping their prices to keep the punters interested. We were carried along up Portobello Road on a sea of people in moth-eaten winter coats and felt hats that had seen better days, past stalls selling everything from talking dollies and flannelette sheets to necklaces that would turn green once the gold plate had worn off.

Victor was loitering outside the antique clock-repairer's shop, smoking, with a scrawny blonde on his arm, laughing at whatever pathetic jokes he was making.

He smirked at me and put his beefy arm across the doorway to stop us going in.

'We're closed, Alice.'

'Mr Smeets is expecting us,' I said. 'So I think you'll find the shop is open. Unless you want to explain to him that you turned us away?'

Victor pushed open the door and went inside to check with his boss. A look of panic swept across Nell's face.

'What the bleeding hell are we coming to see that bloke for?' she whispered. 'I ain't going in there to meet Mr Smeets!'

She started to turn the pram around, to walk off in the other direction, so I grabbed hold of her firmly, linking my arm through hers.

'It will be fine,' I said. 'I'll explain everything once we're inside.'

'I don't want to get involved with him. He's a flaming monster!' she said angrily. 'You might have got yourself tangled up with him, Alice, but there's no need to drag me and my kids into this, is there? It's bad enough having to pay him rent every week. Surely I can send Ruby home with the baby, at the very least?'

She was desperate, but there was no way I was going to let Ruby go anywhere.

Victor reappeared, just in the nick of time, because Nell was hopping around as if she was walking on hot coals.

'Mr Smeets says it's fine to come in.' He shrugged. 'He don't like people hanging around outside the shop unless they've got business with him. You'd better go inside. You're making the place look untidy.'

He was one of those blokes who just relished every moment of being in charge.

'Thanks,' I said, through gritted teeth. I really was itching to give him a proper clump.

I propelled Nell and the pram through the doorway, while I kept a tight hold of Ruby.

A watchmaker was quietly working on a grandfather clock in the corner, with its guts spread out on a cloth on the floor beside him. The only sound was the ticking of dozens of other timepieces, and even with the office door shut, the air was thick with the smell of cigar smoke.

I knocked on the door and pushed it open before Billy had time to speak, shoving Nell and the pram in first, and bringing up the rear with Ruby.

He had the blinds drawn, as ever, and it was hard to make him out in the haze. He stood up and came around to the front of his desk, gazing at the little girl. Nell stood rooted to the spot in absolute terror because of Mr Smeets's reputation, but I watched her fear change to disbelief as she realised who he really was.

'Hello, sweetheart,' he said, kneeling down so that his eyes were level with Ruby's. 'I'm your Uncle Billy.'

Nell sprang forward, like a tigress protecting her cub, and put herself between Ruby and Billy.

'Get away from my daughter,' she said, with barely suppressed rage. 'We don't want anything to do with you.'

Billy stood up, brushing the creases from his trousers, and put his finger very gently under her chin, tilting it so that she had to look up at him.

'What have you done to your face?' she said, horrified.

'Oh, Nell,' he said. 'I had to make so many changes. It was quite painful at times, and I know I've got you to thank for some of what I went through. You played your part in my downfall. So, what you want now is irrelevant, can't you see that? I just want to be in Ruby's life. We have a blood tie, and I want to honour that.'

He held her in his gaze for a second, like a hunter about to slay a fawn. His eyes were fathomless, liquid with a mixture of the desire he obviously still had for Nell and the power he had over her. I swear all the clocks stopped ticking.

'You have no right,' Nell said weakly, her hands beginning to shake. 'She's mine and Jimmy's daughter. You should have stayed wherever it is you've been hiding all these years. You're going to have the cozzers on you when they find out you're back.'

He laughed.

'I don't think we want to get into that in front of Ruby, do we? We have so much to catch up on, but perhaps now is neither the time nor the place.'

His lips were curling at the corners, in a self-satisfied smile.

'Is he really my uncle?' Ruby whispered to me.

'Yes,' I said. 'He's family.'

Billy strode around to the other side of the desk and opened a drawer. He pulled out a green velvet bag and carefully lifted something from it. It was Nell's favourite ruby necklace.

She gasped as he held it up.

'I found this in one of my pawnbroker's,' he said. 'I wanted to give it back to you, as a sign of my goodwill. I know you've always loved this necklace. We both know why it's so special. And the fact you had to pawn it shows me just how low you've sunk, haven't you? It's quite pathetic.'

Nell didn't answer. She was blushing beetroot with humiliation and shame.

She stood there, rigid with fear, as he placed it around her neck, very gently, and did up the clasp, moving her hair out of the way and brushing against her collarbone. Tears welled in her eyes.

He leaned in and murmured, 'Don't fight me, because if you do, you're going to lose everything and everyone you love.'

Nell turned to me, anger seeping from every pore.

'Call yourself the Queen of Thieves?' she said. 'You've sold me and my family down the river to feather your own nest. You make me sick.'

Ruby started to cry and tugged at Nell's sleeve.

'Please don't be cross with Auntie Alice, Mummy, she's my friend.'

Nell pulled her daughter close. 'I'm sorry, sweetheart. It's grown-up stuff, things you shouldn't have to listen to. Don't be scared.'

'You're a very sensible girl, Ruby,' said Billy, beaming with paternal pride. 'Now, I'll leave you two ladies to resolve your differences however you see fit, but I've told you how it's going to be from my point of view. Come and see me in a couple of days when Ruby's at school, and we can come to an arrangement we are all happy with.'

It sounded like a pleasant enough invite, but we both knew that Billy was giving an order.

And Nell was in no position to refuse him.

She barely said a single word to me as we walked home. The silly little fool was so bound up in her own thoughts, she failed to notice that clown Victor following us a few paces behind. Billy had got his claws into her, and there was no way he was going to let her do a bunk, so now his henchman knew where she was dossing.

Now, I know seeing Billy Sullivan in the flesh after all these years had come as a shock to Nell, but I couldn't help feeling offended by her talking as if I was pimping her out to my brother.

It was just uncalled for. A man had a right to see his child, didn't he? Even if he was Billy Sullivan.

It made me realise there was something more I needed to do, to nudge her in the right direction in terms of Ruby's future. The bond between Nell and Jimmy had been stretched by his stay in prison, and now it was time to break it. It was for her own good.

I've never been one to put pen to paper; it reminds me too much of cozzers taking statements. But that evening, I wrote a long letter to Jimmy in Wandsworth nick, enclosing an old photograph of me and Billy Sullivan as nippers, back in the days before the Great War, when we were inseparable.

I'd swiped that from Billy's office when he was distracted by his family reunion.

I was sure Jimmy would spot the family resemblance between us two and Ruby.

In fact, I was counting on it.

Chapter Twenty-Four

NELL

Notting Hill, October 1957

I walked home from Portobello Road in a complete daze, with Ruby skipping along at my side and Alice looking smug, like the cat that got the cream.

Billy Sullivan was back from the dead and now he wanted to control my entire life. He was the monster making money from people's misery, masquerading as Mr Smeets, trapping his tenants in poverty. And now he had come to claim his daughter.

In that moment, I considered ending it all to escape from him, but gazing down at baby James and Ruby, I knew I had to keep going, for their sakes.

Alice was humming to herself, as if her horse had just come in at the races. I was almost eaten up with the desire to tear a strip off her, to scratch her eyes out after what she'd done not only to me, but to my family. But I had to put Ruby first. She didn't want to hear me raising my voice again; it terrified her, and she'd had enough argy-bargy in recent weeks to last a lifetime.

So, I waited until Ruby was heading up the stairs to our flat before I turned to Alice and whispered my disgust.

'Even by your standards, that was below the belt,' I said. 'I will never forgive you for what you've done. You'd better watch your back.'

'Oh, you're a fine one to talk about betrayal,' she whispered back. 'You've made a bleeding career of it, and now you can't stand a taste of your own medicine, ain't that right? And look at how you're living! Billy has plenty of cash and he will take care of you. Don't bite the hand that feeds you, that's my advice.'

I parked the pram up in the hallway and carefully picked baby James out and held him close. He was sleeping soundly.

'This is Billy Sullivan's empire, so take a good look,' I said to Alice, as we climbed the rickety staircase, with its peeling wallpaper and rising damp. 'A putrid heap of a house built on human misery. Remember that, Alice. You might think you're getting what you want out of him now, that you're safe from his evil ways, but it's fool's gold. You mark my words.'

I didn't invite her in to the flat, and she had enough sense to leave me in peace. I'm ashamed to admit it now, but I needed a drink. My nerves were shot to pieces.

Ruby was settled on the sofa reading her book of fairy tales, and James was still dozing in the drawer on the table.

'I just need to pop out and get some eggs and bread for your tea, alright, sweet?' I said to her, grabbing my purse.

She looked up at me, her eyes so like Billy's, but hers were full of love, it almost broke my heart.

'I liked meeting my new uncle, Mummy,' she said. 'Please don't be cross with Auntie Alice any more.'

'Of course I'm not cross any more,' I lied, kissing her forehead. 'Now, you be a good girl and keep an eye on the baby. I won't be long.'

I popped a blanket over her legs.

The light was fading, and the electricity was still cut off. I had a few candles in jam jars, which I lit and put well out of Ruby's reach, on the shelf and on top of a cupboard where I kept some of our things. I lit a small fire in the grate with the last of the coal, prodding around in it with the poker to try to bring it to life and give out a smidgen of warmth.

Then, I pulled on my coat and headscarf and headed out, back down the deathtrap of a staircase – which was now plunged into darkness – and out into the street, where rubbish was blowing about. I thrust my hands deep into my coat pockets, hurrying to the pub round the corner. The evening was already well underway, with hoots of laughter and snatches of song, but when I walked in, the whole place fell silent. It wasn't exactly what you'd call a friendly local.

I glared at everyone, summoning my last ounce of strength from my days as Queen of Thieves, and it must have done something because blokes went back to their pints and a murmur of conversation started up.

The landlady loomed behind the bar, her sleeves rolled up, looking like she could give it out when the mood took her.

'What you having?' she said, eyeing me with suspicion. 'You ain't from round here, are you?'

I fumbled for a few coins in my purse.

'Port and lemon, please. I live in one of Mr Smeets's houses up the road.'

Her face softened.

She poured me a large one. 'You poor cow. I suppose you'll be needing this, then.'

As I glugged it down, a funny-looking bloke wearing a battered army greatcoat came in, with a cat at his heels. I watched as he pulled cards from his sleeves and then made them disappear into thin air, to a smattering of applause.

He passed around his hat and then sat counting out his coins, as the cat purred loudly.

The landlady refilled my glass, more out of pity than anything else, because I was a few pence short.

'Had a bad day?' she said.

'You could say that,' I replied, managing a hollow laugh.

This time, I sipped at the drink, reliving the hideous moment Billy came back into my life, as if I were trying to remember a dream. He still had a kind of power over me, even after all these years, which was mesmerising, but it wasn't love. I was appalled by him – terrified, even – and knowing how he made his money revolted me.

Alice was right when she said he'd care for Ruby – but at what cost? Billy could do whatever he wanted; he was the boss of gangland now, even if he was hiding in the shadows and pulling strings like some hideous puppet-master.

I fought the urge to vomit at what my life would be with him in control. I'd never escape, I'd never be safe, and he would take his revenge on me, slowly, terribly, at the time of his choosing and in a way which brought him the most pleasure. I was sure of it.

My mind was racing. I wanted to run, to get us out of Notting Hill, but I didn't have a clue where to go, and besides, I had hardly any money. Yes, there was the ruby necklace, but if I pawned it anywhere local, Billy would find out and there'd be hell to pay.

I still had some cash tucked away inside Ruby's teddy bear. It might only be enough for a train ticket out of London, but at least it was a start. As I stared into the bottom of my empty glass, I knew that I owed it to myself, Ruby and baby James to try to get away.

I'd return to the flat and pack what little we had.

We were leaving at first light.

★

A gang of those grotty Teddy boys were slinging punches at one another as I scurried home. I crossed the street to avoid them, but it didn't stop one of them yelling 'Slag!' at the top of his voice when he caught sight of me.

My mind was made up. We were getting out of this neighbourhood and out of the city, forever. I didn't care where we ended up, but we needed to be anywhere but here in Notting Hill.

The front door creaked loudly as I shoved it open, and then I stopped dead in my tracks.

There were raised voices coming from upstairs; a man was shouting and a woman pleading. Then, seconds later as I was clinging to the wobbly banister, trying to make my way up the stairs as quickly as I could, there was the most almighty crash and a little girl screamed.

I recognised the sound straight away. It was Ruby.

Fumbling my way in the gloom, I followed Ruby's high-pitched shrieks of terror. The door to Dolores' flat was hanging off its hinges and the room was only half-lit by a couple of oil lamps on the kitchen table. A chair was overturned and there was broken crockery all over the place. Ruby was standing in the middle of the room, with a poker in her hand. It was covered in blood. Dolores was sobbing in a heap on the floor, with the body of a dark-suited man on top of her. His skull was smashed in, and blood was oozing out from a deep gouge, seeping over the back of his jacket and puddling on the bare floorboards.

'It's alright, sweetheart,' I gasped, running to Ruby, easing the poker from her fingers. She stood there, dazed.

'Oh God,' Dolores groaned. 'Help me!'

I hauled the man off her. His tongue was lolling and blood frothed at his mouth, but his eyes were closed and he wasn't breathing. He was already dead. I recognised him in an instant. It was Victor Graveney.

'He was hurting Dolores,' Ruby sobbed, her whole body shaking in terror. 'He was hurting her, so I made him stop.'

Dolores pulled her knees in and hugged them tightly, rocking herself back and forth. Her dress was torn where Victor had tried to force himself on her, and she was covered in his blood.

'He kept saying I had to find another way to pay him,' she said, over and over.

The sound of a baby crying came from my flat. I knew in that instant what I had to do.

I helped my friend to her feet and put my hands on her shoulders to calm her.

'We have very little time, Dolores. I need you to change into something else and pack what things you have. I am going to take care of this, but you must swear to me now, that you will never speak a word of it to anyone.'

'We'll hang if they catch us!'

'No,' I said. 'We won't, because they are not going to catch us, Dolores. Trust me.'

I led Ruby by the hand to our door and we went inside.

'I need you to help Mummy to make this right,' I said. 'You must forget everything you saw and everything you did.'

'Is he hurt badly?' she whimpered. 'Please can we call a doctor to make him better?'

'No, sweetheart,' I said, pulling her to me, feeling the beat of her terrified heart racing against my chest. 'We can't. He was a very wicked man, and you must never be ashamed of what you did because you saved Dolores. But you can never tell anyone. It must be our special secret. Do you promise?'

'I promise,' she said, tears rolling down her cheeks.

'Now, I need you to go and pack your teddy and your books and your clothes, and put some things in for Mummy and baby James, too, OK?'

I tore down the makeshift curtains from our window and dashed back into Dolores' flat.

'Help me wrap him up in this,' I said.

He was such a lump of a man, it wasn't going to be easy to shift him. Dolores stood rooted to the spot, while I put my hand inside his jacket pocket to remove his wallet.

'What on earth are you doing?' she said. 'Robbing him?'

'We can't make it easy for the cozzers to identify him,' I said. 'I need to get rid of anything too personal.'

I was talking ten to the dozen, trying to suppress the panic rising in my chest. 'You were never in this flat this evening. You were babysitting the kids for me, alright? Then, maybe he could have been a burglar.'

I pulled out his wallet, opening it to reveal several crisp pound notes. I handed them to Dolores.

'I think these belong to you.'

Then I threw the empty wallet into the fire, where it caught light.

I slipped my hand inside the other breast pocket of his jacket and pulled out a brown envelope, bulging with photographs and negatives.

Before I knew what I was doing, I'd opened it and looked inside.

'Oh, Zoe!' I murmured as I gazed in disbelief. 'What on earth have you got mixed up in?'

Her agony was clear to see in the stark black and white images, as she was raped, beaten and degraded at the hands

271

of that bastard Munro who, from the look on his face, was delirious with twisted pleasure. It was more of Munro than I ever wanted to see in this life, or the next, to be frank.

Other photographs showed a different girl, wearing skimpy black leather outfits as she performed an eye-watering array of sexual gymnastics which made me wonder if she was, in fact, double-jointed. Some of the blokes looked familiar from the newspaper – perhaps they were MPs, I couldn't quite remember – but there they were, snapped in their birthday suits, having the time of their posh lives at an orgy.

There was one man who turned up time and time again in that bundle of pictures, and for the life of me I couldn't work out why I knew him. Whoever he was, I couldn't help wondering whether Billy had been involved in some kind of twisted blackmail plot, using hidden cameras, so that whatever vile treatment was meted out by these powerful fellas to Zoe and girls like her could be used by him in the future.

I stuffed the envelope down my bra, keeping those images safe for the time being.

'Come on, Dolores,' I said. 'It's now or never.'

We wound the cloth around Victor's body and dragged it over to the fireplace, leaving a hideous trail of crimson in its wake. I grabbed the canister of oil that Dolores kept for her lamps, and spread it all over Victor's body and across the floor and up her curtains. Then I took what was left and sloshed it onto the sofa and armchair in my flat.

Ruby was waiting at the doorway, clutching our suitcase. Dolores managed to throw some things into a carpet bag while I went to get the baby. I picked him up. He was so sweet and innocent, I swore then nothing was going to break up my family. Not even a murder.

Like a woman possessed, I seized two lit candles from the top of the cupboard and dropped them onto the sofa and easy chair, which went up with a *whoosh*. The furniture was already well alight when I closed the door on it.

'Go downstairs and wake Mr Reed,' I said to Dolores. 'Tell him you can smell burning and we need to get out.'

With the baby safely tucked under my arm, I took a last look at the bloodstained scene before me in Dolores' flat. There was no more time to waste. I smashed one oil lamp on her sofa and another on the body of Victor Graveney, which was soon ablaze, like it was Guy Fawkes Night.

He was a vicious bastard, part of Billy Sullivan's evil empire.

And now he could burn in Hell, for all I cared.

'Fire!'

People streamed out of their houses as flames licked out of the windows and Mr Smeets's slum tenement blazed like a tinderbox. We stood outside in the street, silently watching it burn, with sparks flying and a huge pall of black smoke spiralling skywards.

It took a while for the fire brigade to arrive, but when they tried to quell the flames, they were beaten back by the ferocity of the heat.

'Is there anyone inside?' said a fireman, his face covered in soot from his failed attempt to get up the stairs.

'No,' I said. 'We all managed to escape. It was a death-trap. We were all using candles to light the place because the landlord had cut the electricity off. I think one of them must have got knocked over by accident, but I can't be sure of it.'

Ruby squeezed my hand and looked at her feet.

He shook his head. 'I've seen it all before, love. It can so easily end in tragedy. You are all very lucky to be alive.'

The wail of a police siren could be heard in the distance. My heartbeat quickened as it drew closer.

A family from a few doors down brought us out some tea and blankets, throwing them around our shoulders.

Rumours rippled among the growing crowd.

'Smeets did it on purpose to punish his tenants . . .'

'Come and stay with us for the night. You can't stand out here freezing with that baby,' said a woman in a pair of carpet slippers and a dressing gown, with her hair in rollers, peering into the pram.

A voice came from over my shoulder. It was Carter, who'd hauled himself out of bed to see what the commotion was all about. He was standing on his front doorstep, slack-jawed with disbelief.

'I think you'll have lost your deposit for damage, Mrs Finnegan,' he spluttered. 'Mr Smeets will want to talk to you all about this!'

'Well, you know where Mr Smeets can shove it,' I murmured under my breath, as old Mr Reed, Ruby, Dolores, me and baby James were shepherded to safety into the houses a few doors down.

Dawn broke, cold and grey over the street, where the unmistakable stench of burning hung in the air.

I had dozed in an armchair on and off for most of the night, my mind whirring with thoughts, and now I had a plan. There was no time to lose.

Dolores was rubbing sleep out of her eyes in the chair opposite me while Ruby was still snoozing on the sofa. I couldn't bear to think of her being tainted as a killer; she was an innocent child. I was prepared to do whatever it

274

took to protect her.

'I've got to get to work,' said Dolores, buttoning up her cardigan and fixing her hair. 'The matron will dock my pay if I'm late.'

'Can't you tell her your house burned down?' I said. 'Surely that's a good enough excuse?'

'I don't think she'd believe that, and if she did, she wouldn't care,' said Dolores, with a wry smile.

'What an old battleaxe she is.' I laughed, to try to lift her mood.

She put on her glasses and looked at me, frowning.

'Where will we go, Nell?'

'I've got some ideas,' I replied. 'I just need to sort something out. The neighbours say we can stay with them here as long as we need and they won't tell Smeets. But I promise I will have something better sorted by the end of the day.'

'What if the police start asking questions . . .?' Her voice trailed off. 'I've never been in trouble with the police before.'

'Dolores, I swear to you now, if it comes to it, I will take all the blame and say I did it. But in return, you must promise me that you will never tell a living soul that it was Ruby. She's just a child, an innocent little girl, who was trying to save you. We must just stick to our story, alright? If they find a body, we will suggest it was a burglar and we knew nothing about it. He must have knocked over an oil lamp.'

Dolores clasped my hand, gazing down at Ruby.

'I'm so scared, Nell. Mr Smeets will never let me go, even if one of his thugs is dead. He'll find out and he'll kill us all.'

She started to weep. I put my arms around her.

'You're in shock, Dolores, but I promise you, Mr Smeets will not be able to hurt you – or any of us.'

I pulled the brown envelope from my blouse.

'Because of these,' I added.

I leafed through, selecting a handful of the photos – some of the most disgusting ones with Munro, and few with the other blokes. A paper was folded on the table by my side, with the crossword half done. I ripped a page out and carefully wrapped it around the pictures, and a bunch of the negatives, too.

'I need you to hide these under the till at the café,' I said. 'Do yourself a favour, and don't look at them.'

I fished around in my handbag for the café's front door key.

'It's important that we just carry on as normal,' I said, in my most reassuring tone. 'As far as anybody knows, we've just escaped with our lives and we're looking to find somewhere new to stay, that's all. You can tell Mr Jacobs at the café I'm just hunting for a new place for us, and I'll be around later, OK?'

'Alright,' said Dolores, buttoning her coat. She looked absolutely terrified, like she was already on her way to the gallows.

'Please, Dolores,' I said. 'Just hold your nerve and we will get through this.'

For the first time in my life, I was looking forward to visiting the police station.

Once I'd got Ruby off to school, I whistled my way through Bayswater to Paddington Green, wheeling the pram with James sleeping like an angel. The pictures were almost burning a hole in my bra. I thought of Zoe . . . What she'd been through believing that Vinnie Graveney loved her and was going to make her a star – the poor foolish cow. The sad reality of her situation as a plaything for Munro was there captured on film, frozen in time. I had a pretty good idea who had set the whole thing up, too.

I'd pushed all thoughts of her from my mind since I left the hospital. James was my baby, and I would never tell anyone otherwise, because it was the best thing for him. But the photographs brought a fresh wave of pity for this deluded, pathetic girl from the slums, who'd stumbled her way into clubland and ended up way out of her depth.

And now Munro was going to pay for what he'd done.

I heaved the pram up the steps and through the wooden double doors into the cop shop. The desk sergeant had a moustache like the bristles of a broom and a face like a wet weekend.

'You can't bring that in here!' he tutted at the sight of my pram.

'It's a baby, not a wild animal,' I scoffed. 'My name's Nell Kane. Do yourself a favour – go and tell Detective Chief Inspector Munro I've come to see him. I'll leave the baby here. Just make sure no one nicks him, OK?'

A few minutes later, Munro's shiny leather shoes squeaked on the polished wooden floorboards as he came barrelling down the corridor towards me.

'Miss Kane,' he said chummily. 'I've been hoping to catch up with you. What a pleasant surprise.'

'Can we talk in private?' I said, smiling sweetly.

That took some effort, because the images of him starkers, having it off with Zoe in an unspeakable manner, were seared in my memory.

He steered me into an interview room – the one where I'd spent a very unpleasant night months ago, before my whole world had unravelled. I felt his hands wandering down my back and across my backside, and it took every ounce of my strength not to turn around and slap his stupid face. Instead, I laughed.

'Ooh, someone's going to get their fingers burned if they keep doing that.'

He looked at me with utter contempt.

'I doubt that very much.'

I pulled out a chair and he sat down opposite me.

Then slowly – very slowly – I pulled the envelope from my blouse.

'Is this part of a new cabaret act?' he said drily.

I put my finger to my lips for a moment and gave him a theatrical wink.

Then I started laying the photos out in front of him, one by one, watching his expression change from bemusement, to horror, and then disbelief.

'Gotcha!' I said.

The temperature in the room dropped several degrees.

'And before you get any funny ideas about seizing these and locking me up, there are plenty more where they came from. Looks like you've been had, Detective Chief Inspector Munro.'

'What do you want to make this all go away?' he said hoarsely, his lips barely moving.

'I want enough money to start over somewhere abroad. Spain's nice, I hear. And I want aeroplane tickets for me and my two kids, one-way, and better conditions in jail for Jimmy, as part of the bargain. I'll meet you at London Airport tomorrow afternoon, and the minute I know I'm getting on the plane, I'll hand over the photos. Deal?'

He nodded, but it was painful to him, like I was sticking pins in his eyes.

It was at that point that I realised who the mystery

bloke in the photos was – the one I'd been racking my brains about. Maybe it was laying the pictures out on the table which gave me a whole new perspective. It was His Honour Judge Jackson, the beak who'd put Jimmy and Albert behind bars. The dirty devil.

'And you can ask His Honour here to stump up a couple of thousand as well,' I added. 'He's been a very naughty boy indeed, hasn't he? A friend of mine will come into the station to pick up the cash tomorrow in return for photographs he'd rather his wife didn't see.'

London Evening News

BODY FOUND IN NOTTING HILL HOUSE FIRE

By Duncan Swift

The badly charred body of a man was found amid the ruins of a house which was gutted by fire in Notting Hill last night.

Residents watched in horror as flames ripped through the building some time after 10.00 p.m. A number of people who lived there are believed to have escaped unhurt, and no one has yet been reported missing.

Police are appealing for information about the identity of the man.

The property is owned by landlord William Smeets, who has renovated a number of old houses in the area in recent months and let them to families, some of whom have arrived from all corners of the Empire to find work in London.

"It's obviously a very tragic incident," he told the London Evening News in an exclusive interview from his offices in Portobello Road. "My tenants are good people and I do my best to provide high-quality accommodation to suit their needs, but accidents do happen, with the best will in the world. I will be offering the police my full assistance to find the identity of the man who perished."

Fire Chief Simon Jarvis, who attended the scene, said: "It seems a candle or oil lamp may have been the source of the blaze. We are lucky not to have more casualties."

London Evening News

Special report by Duncan Swift

Prison chiefs acted swiftly to quell a riot in Wandsworth Jail last night, led by a notorious former gangland boss.

Robber Jimmy Feeney, known as "Jimmy the Razor" for his brutal attacks on rivals, led an uprising in which five warders and dozens of inmates were injured.

Sources said the violence erupted after Feeney, who is serving a twenty-five-year sentence for a bullion raid in which a police officer died, started smashing up his cell after receiving a letter "of a personal nature".

A stand-off ensued as prisoners joined his protest and barricaded themselves in the recreation room, armed with snooker cues, chair legs, and anything else they could use as weapons.

"He read something about his family which upset him, and he just went crazy," said a police source. "He was yelling his head off and was totally out of control. He snapped someone's arm like it was a twig and went rampaging through the prison. It took five police officers to hold him down."

Other criminals, sensing an opportunity to do harm, joined in the fray.

Eventually, after the prison governor called in reinforcements, the offenders were captured, but not without a fierce fight.

Feeney is expected to appear in court soon charged with offences related to the riot, which will add years to his already lengthy sentence. He is expected to be transferred to Broadmoor high-security psychiatric hospital for assessment.

Chapter Twenty-Five

NELL

Notting Hill, October 1957

The best laid plans often go completely tits-up, don't they? Or so they say in gangland.

When I called in to the café to pick up the packet of photos that Dolores had hidden there earlier in the day, it was gone.

I gave a couple of thick ears out to the skiffle boys in case they'd pinched the photos, and were getting secret kicks looking at mucky stuff, but they swore blind they'd done nothing wrong. The only thing one of them recalled was seeing a bloke in an army greatcoat with a cat hanging around the café. I knew who they meant – he was the same fella who'd been doing tricks for cash in the pub the night of the fire. Quite what he'd want with them was anyone's guess.

I had no option but to give Dolores the negatives of the judge, so that she could get the money from Munro. She didn't want to come to Spain, but at least this way she'd have more than enough for her to buy her own house, away from the likes of Mr Smeets, and start a better life. Nothing could ever make up for what she'd been through, but it felt right to do what I could to help.

We hugged each other tightly at the school gates as I collected Ruby. I knew then that I was saying goodbye for a long time, possibly forever, to the woman who'd been a friend to me when I was at my lowest. I doubted I'd ever find someone as kind as her again.

'Are you sure I can't persuade you to come with me?'

'No,' she said firmly. 'London is my home.'

We took one last walk together down towards Holland Park, to hail a cab to take us to London Airport. There we were: a baby and an excited schoolgirl and me, carrying one battered suitcase, fleeing the city I'd been born and raised in, waving goodbye to Dolores, as we headed off towards an uncertain future.

But I'd have flown to the moon if it meant raising my family free from the clutches of Billy Sullivan.

Planes were coming into land as we drew up at the airport, with lots of well-dressed people hurrying off on their trips abroad.

I stood out like a sore thumb with my tatty clothes, my family and the pram, but I didn't care. I waited patiently outside the terminal for Munro to show up, watching the minutes tick by, with Ruby scuffing up her heels on the pavement in boredom.

A Bentley gleamed in the last rays of evening sun as it pulled up beside me. Patsy was behind the wheel, looking boot-faced. It's no word of a lie to say the sight of her almost gave me a heart attack. But what followed was worse.

Alice Diamond stepped out, swathed in one of her finest furs, and that vermin Detective Chief Inspector Walter Munro followed after, grinning.

'Look, Mummy!' chirped Ruby. 'Auntie Alice has come to wave us off!'

'What in the name of God are you doing here?' I said, as she sidled up to me and Ruby skipped over to give her a big hug.

'Me and Walter have been having a bit of a chinwag,' she said, 'and we've come up with a proposition for you.'

'Whatever it is, the answer's no,' I said, my knuckles turning white as I gripped the pram tightly to steady myself. 'I'm in no mood to bargain with you – or him. The last time I checked, Detective Chief Inspector, I held all the cards. Remember? I'm in no mood to mess about. I've got a plane to catch.'

Munro reached inside his jacket and pulled out an envelope stuffed with cash, as well as airline tickets and a passport in my name.

'These are for you,' he said. 'I've kept my word.'

I glanced at them. There was only one ticket for me, and nothing for Ruby or baby James.

'The baby will go with you, no problem,' he said. 'But your daughter must stay.'

'You must be out of your mind,' I said. 'I'm not leaving her here.'

Alice hugged Ruby tightly.

'Would you like to stay with Auntie Alice for a special treat?'

My little girl glanced up at me, uncertain of how to react. She was fond of her aunt – I could see that in her eyes – but that was nothing compared to the love she had for me, her mother.

Munro seized his moment and launched his attack.

'I've got a witness who'll swear he saw Victor Graveney going into your building shortly before the fire,' he said, 'and funnily enough, he didn't come out alive. That's before we get on to the old bloke downstairs, who says he heard a lot of shouting between a man and a woman before the fire started.'

'You're going to have to do better than that, Munro,'

I said, pulling out the envelope with the compromising pictures and the negatives of him assaulting Zoe. 'I never set eyes on Victor Graveney in my building, and the old bloke from downstairs is getting on a bit. You are really skating on thin ice, aren't you? So, I suggest you just sort out the ticket for Ruby and we'll be on our way, and you can have these.'

'It's not that simple, Nell,' he said. 'What was left of Victor was badly burned, but it couldn't hide the fact that he had a massive hole in the back of his head. I'd hate to be anywhere near Vinnie Graveney when he finds that out, wouldn't you?'

'You can't prove anything,' I said coldly.

'Vinnie won't see it that way,' he replied.

Ruby bit her lip and stared at the floor.

'Do you know something about that, sweetheart?' said Alice gently.

Ruby shook her head defiantly.

'She's a child! What on earth would she know about anything? Just leave her out of it, for Chrissakes!' I spat.

Munro cut in, 'But supposing you are arrested on suspicion of his murder. Do you think for a minute the authorities will let you keep either of your children? They'd be taken into care, straight away, put into a children's home or up for adoption. And that's before we get on to the lovely lady who popped in to collect something from me earlier today. How long do you think she'd last in prison?'

'You twisted bastard,' I said. 'And the idea of you and Alice being in partnership together is just ridiculous!'

'I'd say it's magical, actually,' said Alice, patting Ruby on the head.

'And what about Billy? Does he know any of this?'

'Nell, what he don't know can't hurt him, can it?' she replied smugly.

'Jimmy will find a way to get even with the pair of you, just you wait,' I said, anger burning up inside of me.

Alice pulled a newspaper from her carpet bag and waved it under my nose.

'You obviously haven't been keeping up with events, Nell, and I can understand that because you've been busy blackmailing Detective Chief Inspector Munro. But if you take a look, you'll see Jimmy's been carted off to Broadmoor for causing a riot.'

I reeled backwards as if I'd been shot.

'What are you talking about?'

'It says here he got a letter with some personal information which upset him.' Alice's eyes glinted with malice. 'Can you think what that might have been?'

'You evil witch,' I said, realising exactly what she'd done and knowing that I couldn't talk about it in front of Ruby.

'Families can be so complicated, can't they?' She smirked. 'So, you're being offered a choice, and we don't have long because, like you said, you've got a plane to catch. Either you get out now, away from Billy and all this mess, and I promise I will look after Ruby as if she was my own. Or you stay here and face the music. Detective Chief Inspector Munro may lose his job, and probably his missus, if you can find a way to get those pictures out, but you will lose a whole lot more, I promise.'

Ruby ran to me and started crying hysterically, clinging to my skirt.

'Please, Mummy, don't leave me!'

It was a terrible choice – a choice a mother should never have to make – but I was trapped, and they knew it.

I handed the envelope full of photographs to Munro.

Then I prised Ruby's fingers away, one by one, kissing her face, promising her I'd return. But I knew I was lying.

'I'll come home soon. It's just a little holiday,' I said, my knees almost giving way.

She started to scream, and Munro picked her up, struggling, and plonked her in the back of the car, where she hammered on the window, tears streaming down her face.

With my heart breaking, I turned my back and started to push the pram away from my own flesh and blood, towards the airline staff with their starched uniforms and immaculate make-up, to escape to my new life in Spain.

The plane jolted me back in my seat, screeching down the runway as it lifted high into the air. Baby James snuggled into my lap. We were flying, free, soaring upwards.

Jimmy and me thought we ruled the city. Perhaps we did for a while, but when all the trappings and the glamour were stripped away, I discovered too late that what really mattered was our family.

Fate, meanwhile, had other ideas.

Outside the window, the sun sank low over London and the sky burned orange and then the deepest blood-red. It was the most beautiful and terrible sight, and I clutched the baby tighter, weeping for everything I'd stolen and everything that life had taken from me.

Somewhere down in the hell of gangland, the Devil had made a pact with Alice Diamond, and he was sitting there, staring at his cloven feet, wondering how on earth she'd managed to get the better of him once again.

EPILOGUE

ALICE

Elephant and Castle, 1960

Family . . . honestly!

You can't live with 'em and you can't kill 'em, and ain't that the truth?

But it never ceases to amaze me how the love of a child can heal wounds between relatives and give them a reason to get along together.

Maybe it's the time of life we're at, but Billy and me both value Ruby more than any jewel he's robbed or anything I've ever hoisted. She's a sweet kid who'll never really understand why her mum walked out on her. I've put a few ideas in her head about the new baby being more important in Nell's eyes, just to ease the pain a little.

But, even when she wakes up screaming from one of her nightmares, she knows she's got her Auntie Alice and her Uncle Billy, who will always stand by her, because blood is thicker than water.

Billy dotes on Ruby. She's got him wrapped around her little finger, which is just how I like it. She's going to inherit his fortune when he goes, and that cough of his ain't getting any better, so who knows when that might be? The antique clocks in his shop tick their way through the minutes as he runs his businesses, wields his power and makes his money in the most disgusting manner. I hear them chime the hour, and one day, I know his time will be up.

Meanwhile, me and Detective Chief Inspector Munro – or Walter, as I like to call him – get along just fine. The Forty Thieves go about their business just as they always did, and Munro has a nice sideline in protection rackets for some of the porn shops which seem to have sprung up all over the place, thanks to Vinnie Graveney's little venture which he's running behind Billy's back. Vinnie's never got over the disappearance of his twin Victor, and that oily hack Duncan Swift has run story after story appealing for information in the *London Evening News*, but to no avail. The police tolerate the porn shops, but Walter does make him pay through the nose for the privilege.

I don't know what Soho is coming to these days, but the cash comes in handy to pay Billy, who thinks he's getting a cut from my gang, perish the thought.

Sometimes kids on my manor might tease Ruby that her dad Jimmy the Razor has gone nuts in jail and her mum's dumped her. But that don't last long, because I send the girls round to put their windows in.

The latest thing is, she's got a few silly notions about wanting to learn to dance, but I told her I knew a beautiful girl with red hair once, who was a proper Miss Twinkletoes and she danced and danced until she dropped down dead. Or so the story goes.

Instead, I've started teaching her a trick called 'going shopping'.

We do have some great games up in Queen's Buildings.

Because I'm her Auntie Alice.

And Ruby is my princess.

Author Note

Finishing *Queen of Clubs*, the second book in the *Queen* series, about the exploits of Alice Diamond, Nell Kane and the Forty Thieves, has fulfilled a dream that I would one day bring the bustling world of 1950s London to life as fiction.

I hope you have enjoyed reading the book as much as I have loved exploring this era, which practically fizzes with energy.I felt very at home writing about the 1950s because my mum was a teenager in London at this time. When I was growing up, she told me all about how she used to enjoy starching her petticoats and going off to sip coffee in the trendy *2is Cafe* in Soho, where much of the book is set. Her first Saturday job was in one of the dress shops up near Oxford Street where Alice and her gang plied their thieving trade. But the world my mum knew was quite innocent, full of the thrill of new music such as rock and roll and skiffle, or exploits such as simply taking the tram or the bus "up West" from the family's rented flat above a dairy in Acton. But I have dug deeper into the murkier side of clubland and its backstreets because that is the world which some of the Forty Thieves inhabited. Soho in the 1950s was not an easy place to be a woman.

I also researched the terrible abuses suffered by those who were forced to live in the post-war slums of Notting Hill, under rogue landlords epitomised in the book by Mr Smeets. In real life, one such notorious landlord was Peter Rachman whose henchmen terrified and beat up any tenants bold enough to complain about the appalling condition of their rented accomodation and destroyed property to terrify them into silence.

Gambling was still illegal and spielers and backstreet dives where people could play cards and dice were all the rage up in Soho, alongside drinking dens and nightclubs, where those who could afford it enjoyed the post-war boom in increasingly daring nightclub acts. Disaffected young men quiffed their hair and wore crepe soled shoes, turning to violence for thrills, as Teddy Boys. They caused outrage among the older generation who had fought for freedom in the war. The end of rationing brought huge changes to dress styles with yards of material available more cheaply than before, which many girls made up into swishy skirts to go dancing in. Kids just wanted to have fun, to throw off all the restrictions and rules they'd endured as youngsters during those long war years.

They were questioning authority in a way which would have been unthinkable before and they had a drive and determination to succeed which gave them an edge, rather like Zoe in *Queen of Clubs*.

London was still being rebuilt after the Blitz, although business was booming. Bombsites were everywhere but jobs were plentiful and people had money to spend on fun and frivolity. For Alice and her gang that meant people had a bit more disposable income to buy the luxury items they had stolen. The Forty Thieves entered an extremely busy time, as furs were still a huge status symbol for women. Even my Nan, a housewife, proudly sported a mink stole when she went out for a night with my Grandad, although hers was bought and paid for rather than pinched.

On the cusp of the 1960s, cheek by jowl in this world of impending social change, the hacks of Fleet Street plied their trade in search of a headline. They drank alongside the policemen from the newly-formed Flying Squad in watering holes all over Soho, at the same time as they cosied up to gangland bosses such as the legendary Billy Hill, who flaunted his notoriety for daring robberies which the law could never quite pin on him. The ganglang Chaps of Soho, who had carved their path to power with razor blades in the 1930s and 1940s, were still very much a force to be reckoned with although the a pair of young upstart twins from the East End, the Krays, were beginning to make their presence felt.

In some ways, the 1950s was just the warm up for the huge social changes of the decade which followed, because the lives of the majority of working class people still reflected the housing and social conditions that they and their parents had lived with during the Second World War. But there is such a great juxtaposition of old and new, that the 1950s have an energy which I find compelling as a writer.

I hope I have recreated some of that here in the pages of this book and that you have enjoyed the ride. Stick with me. There's more to come.

And I always love to hear from you, my readers. Please join me for all my latest book news on my Facebook page @BeezyMarshauthor, connect with me on Instagram and Twitter @beezymarsh, or check out my website https://www.beezy-marsh.com

Acknowledgements

I would like to thank my editor Rhea Kurien for her insight and encouragement which really made writing this book a joy and also to Sanah Ahmed at the team at Orion Dash and Orion for providing great editorial support and such an eye-catching cover to encapsulate the 1950s.

My agent Giles Milburn, of Madeleine Milburn Literary Agency, is a great help for a writer of historical fiction because he shares my enthusiasm and fascination for how the Forty Thieves lived and worked. I am also grateful to Emma Dawson and all the team for their support.

My greatest thanks go to my family and my friends who once again have put up with me obsessing over my latest creation and characters for the past year or so. Reuben and my boys, Idris and Bryn, have probably heard more Cockney swear words than I'd care to mention. Sally, Clare, Tania, Lisa, Jules, Heather, Lou and the coven girls thank you for so many fun times while I was writing.

Thanks also to my mum-in-law, dress historian Professor Lou Taylor for her invaluable insights on the clothing and fashions of the 1950s.

Now I can't wait to dive into the 1920s to bring you the next instalment, *Queen of Diamonds*!

If you loved *Queen of Clubs*, don't miss the gritty, thrilling and unputdownable first book in the series . . .

Gangland was a man's world – but the women knew different

London, 1946.

Alice Diamond, the Queen of the Forty Thieves, rules over her gang of hoisters with a bejewelled fist. Nell is a slum girl from Waterloo, hiding a secret pregnancy and facing a desperately uncertain future.

Sensing an opportunity to exploit Nell's vulnerabilities, Alice takes her under her wing and, before long, Nell is experiencing the secret world of hoisting, with all the dangers – and glamorous trappings – that comes with this underworld existence.

Alice has a longstanding feud with Billy Sullivan's all-male gang in Soho, and thinks Nell could be a useful weapon in her vendetta. But Nell has a secret agenda of her own and is not to be underestimated. And the more she is exploited by both Alice and Billy, the more her hunger for revenge grows. As she embraces the seedy underbelly of London, will she prevail in carving out her own path to power and riches ...

... and crown herself the Queen of Thieves?